Under the
White Gaze

UNDER THE

WHITE GAZE

Solving
the Problem
of Race and
Representation
in Canadian
Journalism

CHRISTOPHER
CHEUNG

PURICH
BOOKS

Printed in Canada on FSC-certified ancient-forest-free paper (100% post-consumer recycled) that is processed chlorine- and acid-free.

UBC Press is a Benetech Global Certified Accessible™ publisher. The epub version of this book meets stringent accessibility standards, ensuring it is available to people with diverse needs.

LIBRARY AND ARCHIVES CANADA CATALOGUING IN PUBLICATION

Title: Under the white gaze : solving the problem of race and representation in
     Canadian journalism / Christopher Cheung.
Names: Cheung, Christopher, author.
Description: Includes bibliographical references and index.
Identifiers: Canadiana (print) 20240365844 | Canadiana (ebook) 20240365887 | ISBN
     9780774881111 (softcover) | ISBN 9780774881135 (EPUB) | ISBN 9780774881128 (PDF)
Subjects: LCSH: Minorities – Press coverage – Canada. | LCSH: Race – Press coverage
     – Canada. | LCSH: Journalism – Social aspects – Canada.
Classification: LCC PN4914.M53 C3 2024 | DDC 070.4/493058—dc23

UBC Press gratefully acknowledges the financial support for our publishing program of the Government of Canada, the Canada Council for the Arts, and the British Columbia Arts Council.

UBC Press is situated on the traditional, ancestral, and unceded territory of the xʷməθkʷəy̓əm (Musqueam) people. This land has always been a place of learning for the xʷməθkʷəy̓əm, who have passed on their culture, history, and traditions for millennia, from one generation to the next.

Printed and bound in Canada by Friesens

Set in Dante MT Pro and Anton by Lara Minja, Lime Design
Copy editor: A.G.A. Wilmot
Proofreader: Carmen Tiampo
Indexer: Judy Dunlop
Cover designer: Lara Minja, Lime Design

Purich Books, an imprint of UBC Press
The University of British Columbia

www.purichbooks.ca

If you've ever felt left out or misrepresented by journalism, this book is for you.

CONTENTS

Gazing Behind

I have a hard time finding the Canada that I know in the news.

Growing up, my teachers taught us that we lived in a multicultural country, but they really didn't need to because I could see that for myself. Every class I attended from kindergarten on was a miniature United Nations. Our daily attendance was an international roll call: Alam, Cheung, Nardi, Pabla, Raeisi, Tabora, Zhang.

All of Vancouver is diverse, but my neighbourhood of Oakridge was at a special crossroads of class and culture, straddling the posh west side and the blue-collar east side. I was born to a family from Hong Kong, and my classmates had roots from all over: China, India, Iran, Japan, Korea, Taiwan, the Philippines, Vietnam. We might've been considered "minorities," but we were the majority.

Differences were everywhere. At recess, we shared a global selection of snacks from tangy fruit leather to paper-thin roasted seaweed. When the school bell rang, parents and grandparents showed up to tell my friends to put on their coats in languages from Punjabi to Tagalog. The Cantonese church my family attended, in a building purchased from Mennonites, was just up the hill from a

Sikh gurdwara, where the city's Vaisakhi parade starts every year. On the walls of living rooms in nearby homes were crosses and crocheted Bible verses, but also shrines and portraits of ancestors. Under these same roofs were families of every size and class. I'd visit friends who lived in mansions with their melancholy mothers, supported by fathers who did business overseas, and those who lived humbler lives, spending their evenings at the family restaurant serving hot bowls of phở.

My sense of a shared community only grew as I got older. Every time I walked the streets, took the bus, or visited another neighbourhood, I came to understand more and more how the city I lived in was made up of people of different identities – which is why the local news frustrated me when people of colour were too often missing, misrepresented, and marginalized.

Their lives revealed insights about society, everything from the cultural transformation of communities to the strength of our social safety nets. But were these stories being told?

Nope.

Was it because journalists were unfamiliar with the places in which we lived? Was it because they didn't speak our many languages? Was it because their lives were so very different from our own?

In time, I began to wonder which was worse: turning on the news and finding people of colour and their experiences absent from the places in which they live, or seeing that journalists were recycling the same stories about people of colour over and over again.

For all Canada's boasting about multiculturalism, its journalism was suffering from obvious omissions and problematic portrayals of people of colour. Numbers shouldn't be the only thing that dictate who is worth covering, but they do tell us how we're falling behind. Currently, people of colour make up 27 percent of Canada's overall population[1] and more than half of the population in urban centres like Toronto and Vancouver, but this growing percentage is not reflected in the makeup of the country's newsrooms or in the coverage they put out.[2]

If you're white, the news is giving you a redacted portrait of who you share your community with.

If you're a person of colour like me, this mismatch between what you experience as reality and what you see on the news feels extra personal when the people you're familiar with, the places you frequent, the cultures you belong to, and the issues you care about are represented inaccurately. That is, if they're in the news at all.

This glaring absence is why I entered the industry: to see if I could help fix the problem of representation. I didn't set out to do this in a big way, leading boycotts or protests demanding that newsrooms commit to inclusive hiring practices or quotas of representation in stories. I simply wanted to see more reporting on the Canada that I knew.

In the summer of 2014, I sent my résumé to every newsroom in the city in hopes of getting some experience. After many rejections, the editor of the *Vancouver Courier* took the time to invite me in for an interview. After a brief chat, he asked, "When do you want to start?"

The paper was housed in a building on a slope in the shadow of the Granville Bridge. It was half underground, and the friendly journalists who worked there put together the semi-weekly broadsheets in a cozy, bunker-like newsroom with carpets and sagging leather couches. I couldn't have asked for a friendlier place to be introduced to the industry.

I had previously thought that every journalist carried a media pass like a magic amulet, one with the power to compel people to answer their questions. It turned out, however, that movies and TV shows got this part wrong. All you do is show up.

With politeness and persistence, I returned to the neighbourhood I grew up in and asked people I'd always been curious about if they would mind sharing their stories. I sat down with the first sweet maker to set up shop in Punjabi Market as he showed off a colourful case filled with confections made from nuts, dairy, and flours. On the other side of 49th Avenue, I visited the cobbler who'd immigrated from China and worked in a pulp mill on Vancouver Island before turning to footwear, repairing everything from juttis to hockey skates on behalf of a nearby store owned by the family of NHL player Frederick "Cyclone" Taylor. And a few blocks down from the cobbler, at the family-run Au Petit Café, I chatted with the son who told me the story of his escape as an eight-year-old from Vietnam to Vancouver, in between taking rapid orders for bánh mì on his Bluetooth earpiece.

I was captivated by their stories. I wanted to do the same for my community as the *New Yorker* did with its Talk of the Town, publishing slice-of-life reportage. To me, American writer Gay Talese, a pioneer of 1960s literary non-fiction, dubbed the New Journalism, described the job best. Good reporters, he said, were masters at the "art of hanging out."[3]

But hanging out goes both ways. For interviewees used to the public spotlight or those familiar with the media landscape, no problem. But those who don't consume English news media, because they're too busy or because there's a language barrier, can be wary of journalists like me parachuting into their lives to ask personal questions and snap photos on behalf of outlets they've never heard of, not fully understanding what they're lending their names, faces, and responses to.

It was veggies, of all things, that taught me just how hard this can be. My grandparents lived in a house across the street from my family, where my grandfather kept a vegetable garden. Every year, we'd feast on the chayotes, green beans, and winter melons he lovingly tended to each morning. There were dozens of gardens like his in our neighbourhood, taking over not only backyards but also front and side yards with overwhelming vines, leaves, and flowers. Many of the gardeners were Cantonese like us, such as Mr. Chow with his wax gourds and Mrs. Chang with her bitter melons. Others were immigrants from different parts of the world who started growing their favourite crops on Vancouver soil, like Mr. Stubos from Greece, with his giant tomatoes and sour cherries. Social scientists have called this a corporeal, culinary citizenship: by growing crops they're familiar with, people feel a deep sense of rootedness in their new homes as they re-establish food cultures they've been separated from.[4]

While living in other parts of the city, I met people with similar stories, like Auntie Mee Mee with her goji berries and Mrs. Fung with her Sze Yap bitter greens, which were missing from even the largest of our local Chinese supermarkets. On summer evenings, there wasn't a street or alley without lush gardens and some senior tending to them with a grandchild in tow. From these gardens grew community, because each was too bountiful for a single family. I watched my grandfather and others chat over garden fences, sharing their harvests and their heirloom seeds with one another.

Imagine my surprise, then, when I opened up the *Sun,* our daily paper, and read about how Vancouver is catching up with other North American cities, joining in on an urban farming "renaissance."[5] Renaissance? These yards have been feeding Vancouverites since before I was born. Curious about what this renaissance might entail, I read on.

The story, one of many on this subject, celebrated gardens on forgotten properties being tended to by hip young urbanites looking to consummate a green lifestyle, with help from local government. It was farming by way of the Brooklyn playbook, which had gone viral, not the made-in-Vancouver approach that I saw in the yards around me. One such urban farmer, interviewed by *Montecristo* magazine in an article titled "Vancouver's Urban

Farms: A Growing Reality," said that most homeowners' lawns are about decoration for "leisure value or visual appeal."[6] He boasted about his "resistance," "challenging" the idea of what a yard could be if it were farmed. He and others went on to talk about "reconnecting" people with food systems and their neighbours in this grand effort.

More green is good, sure, but these stories missed something. These new Vancouver farmers and the journalists reporting on them hadn't checked their own city to see if what they were doing was actually new, something Google Street View could have told them. If this was, as they called it, a "resistance," then my grandfather and thousands of urban farmers like him were the original overthrowers of the status quo, one melon at a time.

Frustrated by this mismatch between journalistic perception and reality, I was determined to set the record straight with a story of my own. My *Courier* editor enthusiastically approved my pitch. I asked friends if they had gardener grandparents, and I wandered immigrant neighbourhoods of the city's east side with all the flattery I could muster. They were happy and easy to chat with. My Cantonese helped as it was the only language that many spoke fluently; however, it was hard to convince them to talk on the record once I revealed that I was a reporter.

I wanted them to spill the beans on their beans, but they answered me with similar degrees of detachment:

"This is nothing special. Everyone does this."

"I'm not an expert. You should ask an expert."

"Why would anyone find this interesting?"

As a reporter, I did not encounter such rejection when speaking with potential interviewees who were white, but I would run into these responses again and again from people of colour, on stories of every topic. Was it self-consciousness? Was it anxiety about exposure on a public platform they weren't familiar with? Whatever the reason, their deference to others, the downplaying of their own experiences – or their disinterest in sharing – spoke to the marginalization in news media that bothered me so much.

When I started journalism school at the University of British Columbia, one of the first things our instructors asked us was a seemingly simple yet epistemological question: "What is news?" One definition was information that is new. But with that came a follow-up question: New to who?

We were taught to craft stories with a target audience in mind, but who was that exactly? We talked about reading levels, wanting to ensure that an average high schooler would be able to comprehend our coverage. We talked about writing to the laity, people lacking inside knowledge of a particular field of study who would need a journalist to do some explaining. We talked about class, as stories interesting to readers of a magazine replete with Rolex ads would likely differ from what's of interest to readers of a commuter daily with a free booklet of buy-one-get-one coupons for burger combos.

Typically, the target audience is imagined as the average Canadian. I wrote many stories before I realized that this so-called average Canadian that I was writing to, this so-called mainstream audience, had a clear racial and ethnocultural identity, and that identity ...

... was white.

Other journalists were doing this targeting, and somehow, I picked it up too. It didn't matter that I strived to get more people of colour represented in media coverage. I had thought that simply making us visible was a win, but I hadn't thought about *how* we were being portrayed.

I began to notice patterns in my stories. Cheer on this [insert identity here] person who did this remarkable thing! Cry about this migrant's trials and tribulations! Celebrate this ancient cultural practice, which comes with a lot of symbolism and cool costumes! Aside from these narratives, there were also patterns in the way that I overemphasized identity and difference. These realizations led me to a problem that was hard to understand, hard to confront, and hard to fix.

Behind the stories that I wrote to help with representation, I noticed a white gaze.

I took on the white gaze in everything from my language choices to my story frames. I treated white Canadians of European descent as the default viewpoint. They were the baseline. They were the "us" and everyone else was the "other." When writing about non-Western cultures, I'd go to great lengths to explain them to a white audience, reporting on them with an air of discovery and distance, padding my stories with little encyclopaedia entries.

Let's take a brief pause here and acknowledge the complicated feelings that can arise when we talk about whiteness. I saw this allergy from a young age, with adults like my parents being aghast whenever I used the word "white." They feared it was racist because it drew attention to another person's race, therefore highlighting differences that could divide. The mere mention of the words "white" and "whiteness" can make some people angry, avoidant, defensive, disarmed, and offended. Sociologist Robin DiAngelo talks about the desire for "colour blindness" in her book *White Fragility*. She believes the civil rights movement had the side effect of leading people to adopt a sense of avoidance: "Pretend that we don't see race, and racism will end."[7] I saw this allergy in my readers, too. Whenever I mentioned whiteness in my stories, white-identifying readers would take personal offence. Frances Henry and Carol Tator, two of Canada's leading scholars on race, have some words for them: "It's important to emphasize that when we speak of Whiteness, we are not critiquing White people as individuals, but rather see Whiteness as an invisible social process by which power and privilege is exercised in a society divided by colour, as well as other social markers."[8]

When we hear reports about how Canadian journalism is "overwhelmingly white," what exactly does that mean?[9] In 2023, the Canadian Association of Journalists' newsroom diversity survey found that 75.5 percent of journalists in the country are white.[10] That might sound pretty close to the percentage of white people in the country, but the survey notes that journalists of colour are clustered in a handful of large, national newsrooms. In small, whiter communities outside of cosmopolitan cities, journalists of colour interviewed by *J-Source* shared their experiences with the "revolving door" of newsrooms, due to challenges of "low pay, high demands, racism and isolation."[11] There are, however, two depressing categories where there is a high degree of racial representation: part-time work and internship roles.

As for who's in charge, white journalists make up an even higher percentage of newsroom leaders. They are the ones who decide who gets hired, which stories about people of colour are important, and how such stories get packaged for audiences. Lived experience matters when it comes to identifying, researching, and producing stories. Newsrooms will continue to overlook, or struggle to report on, stories that represent a growing share of their prospective audience if they do not have journalists from different backgrounds in decision-making roles who can bring these stories forward.

This also affects mentorship. While I had great role models that taught me skills like how to find unique stories and how to make the most out of interviews, they were all white. I had no racialized mentors to teach me how to navigate the industry as a rare person of colour. Diversity can be a "second job," wrote Vann R. Newkirk II in the *Columbia Journalism Review,*[12] with unspoken labour such as being the default diversity advocate in newsrooms or having to check in with other racialized journalists after working on traumatic stories that concern identity.

I happened to enter the industry around a time of increasing conversations about race and representation in media, spurred on by Idle No More in 2012 and Black Lives Matter a year later. I saw news outlets respond to these movements with pledges to diversify their staff and their coverage. "We believe what makes us different, makes a difference. And as a team, the diversity of our backgrounds, interests and experiences is what enriches our work, and our workplaces," read one from the *Toronto Star*.[13] I couldn't help but feel hopeful when I saw movement like this from legacy outlets, who seemed to recognize the white dominance of their own newsrooms and the industry at large and were taking action.

While I have no doubt such commitments were written with good intentions, I couldn't help but look at this another way: diversity was hot! Editors responded enthusiastically to stories I pitched that touched on race, ethnicity, and culture, and as a journalist of colour, I had the face and lived experience to sell them. But it was also a lot of pressure. You could call it a diversity reckoning, but it was also a diversity rush, with white editors on the hunt for journalists to help diversify their newsrooms and coverage. Editors from publications across the country must've seen my headshot and byline, because they started coming to me with pitches. One of them said they enjoyed my pieces on "Asian personalities" and asked if I could do more. I didn't want to be tokenized and pigeonholed, but I also didn't want to pass up opportunities to bring representation that was lacking into noteworthy publications.

You can see the danger in newsrooms treating diversity like a missing ingredient, making hires or commissioning pieces from journalists of colour, because this puts such work into a silo. I've seen newsrooms rely on journalists of colour for the "diversity beat," sparing white journalists from having to think about diversity, let alone focus on it as if their very jobs depended on their coverage of it.

But we need to include *all* journalists in the work of diversifying journalism, because there is room for diversity in all areas of reporting. To truly diversify, newsrooms need to change the very recipe of how they do journalism, not just sprinkle a few stories here and there for diversity's sake. That requires interrogating the gaze from which news is reported. That means confronting the whiteness of newsrooms and how journalists do their work.

I have to admit that the thought of this made me uncomfortable. I too treated diversity like a missing ingredient until I realized that we could have a person of colour on every front page in the country and still fall behind on representation if those stories are told from a white point of view.

Representation in journalism is about more than just journalists covering under-represented groups and going, "Look, they exist!" It's important to ask what kinds of stories are being told about people of colour. How are they portrayed? Whose voices and perspectives are privileged? Whose are left out? Who decides which stories deserve coverage? What is the lived experience of the journalist telling a story and how does that inform or take away from the coverage? Is the story of interest to the people of colour being written about?

Just as we can't talk about reconciliation without talking about colonization, we can't talk about diversity in journalism without talking about whiteness. It's easy for newsrooms to say that they want to diversify, but what exactly are they diversifying from? If diversity is one side of the coin, whiteness is the other. If coverage or a particular perspective is lacking, newsrooms need to admit whose perspectives they have too much of. If journalists of colour are marginalized, newsrooms need to admit who holds the power. It's easy for newsrooms to talk about a happy-sounding thing like diversity, but it's harder for them to swallow the existence of a negative-sounding thing like racial inequality. Any newsroom that wants to diversify but refuses to confront the dominance of whiteness in the workplace and in their reporting will fail.

If you're picturing Canadian newsrooms like those depicted in popular cinema, from the classic *All the President's Men* to the Oscar-winning *Spotlight* to the whimsical *The French Dispatch,* you're missing something. These cinematic newsrooms are portrayed with reverence, full of scrappy reporters and wise editors serving as society's watchdogs.[14] Certainly, all newsrooms have their heroes on the hunt for scoops. But the reality is that these are complicated workplaces with inherent power dynamics. You can't picture the modern Canadian newsroom without racial challenges and a struggle to represent the diverse communities they serve.

In recent years, many have been speaking up about the "forever battle of a journalist of colour,"[15] putting up with unequal treatment and white managers' views of what constitutes diversity. "Canadian media is designed so that journalists of color give up," wrote Soraya Roberts in a *Longreads* essay titled "The Great White Nope."[16] "Politically, socially, economically – in every way – Canada misrepresents itself. What results is an entirely misinformed public but, more than that, a public represented by an industry that cloaks itself in white and believes that saying nothing will make it invisible."

Non-representation is a form of "oppression," added Shree Paradkar, the *Toronto Star*'s first internal ombud.[17] And oppression happens when newsroom leaders allow "one dominant group – whites – to play gatekeeper to all the stories, generation after generation."

Meaningful discussions about diversity can be overshadowed at a time when journalism itself is facing existential questions about its own survival in an increasingly demanding and ever-changing media landscape, with shifting delivery systems and precarious funding models. Mass layoffs at legacy media outlets and the emergence of new digital products are the norms in the industry, and journalists can get caught up in the daily grind of churning out content to compete for eyeballs rather than contemplating the craft. "Feeding the beast," we sometimes call it.

The shakeups came fast and furious even as I was working on this book. I handed in the first draft mid-2023, tacking on more bad news with each subsequent version. Meta started blocking users from sharing news on Facebook and Instagram, not wanting to negotiate with publishers to license their content in response to Bill c-18.[18] The CBC announced that it would be cutting ten percent of its workforce, amounting to 600 positions and 200 unfilled positions.[19] Then came Bell's announcement to sell off stations, cancel newscasts, and cut nine percent of its workforce, a loss of 4,800 jobs.[20] Black Press, publisher of 150 community newspapers, filed for creditor protection and announced its sale.[21] Vice Media, the digital upstart that gained a following for its edgy content, said it would stop publishing on its site entirely.[22]

Grim as all this is, I argue there are other existential questions. If it's the job of journalists to seek out and report the truth, how can they do so without asking who they are *not* serving? Or how the lived experiences of those in the newsroom shape which truths are reported? If they don't ask these questions, their audiences lose out, receiving an incomplete picture of current events and the society in which they live.

It's now been a decade since I became a journalist. That's not very long, but considering how many people of colour have left the industry with fewer years than that, it's a milestone. Diversity has been a big part of my career so far, whether that's through my own work, mentorship, class visits, public events, or being interviewed in turn. In the world of entertainment, if you win an Emmy, a Grammy, an Oscar, and a Tony Award, it's a grand slam known as an EGOT. In my work as a journalist, I've won awards with "diversity," "inclusion," and "ethnic media" in their name, some named after late journalists who were white. I've joked about winning the racialized reporter's EGOT, which is nice I suppose, but it makes me wonder how many years it'll be before we can stop reminding journalists about representation because it will simply be accepted as common practice. Because I've managed to stick around in the industry, the requests for speaking engagements and pieces of writing are far more than I can handle. On panels and with publications I've freelanced for, I've looked at the names beside me and it's obvious that I was selected to be either the only person of colour or the missing yellow crayon among a carefully chosen rainbow.

I'm still learning. But I know things now that I wish I'd known when I was starting out. That's where this book comes in: to help you spot the white gaze in journalism, from local broadcasts to chewy features to the bite-sized nuggets of news that pop up on your social media feeds.

I hope journalists will find it useful, whether you're just starting out or are already years into your career. There are many journalists who report on race but have never read any scholarship on the subject and its intersections. However, just reading the scholarship won't do either, as many social scientists who study media either left journalism long ago or have never done journalism. This book attempts to bring different perspectives on news media together: sociology, geography, feminist and critical race theory, and more, alongside the world of practising journalists – from reporting stories to newsroom life to industry insights. I hope the lessons in this book challenge how you approach race and representation as they did for me.

Regardless of how you identify, your help is needed. When John Miller was the deputy managing editor of the *Toronto Star* in the early 1990s, he remembered riding a streetcar downtown and thinking to himself, "My God. The city has changed." In an interview with the *Review of Journalism,* he said that he barely saw the reality of the diverse city that he covered because he worked in an office during the day and drove back home at night. "I was as guilty when I was at the newspaper of being blind to this as they are," said Miller of editors reluctant to address diversity in their newsrooms.[23] These conversations were overdue then and are just as important now.

If you're not a journalist, my hope is that this book helps you be more conscious about your own media diet where race, ethnicity, and culture are concerned. It's like being conscious about the food you're eating on a daily basis: asking where it comes from, who made it, what was put in it, and what you might be taking in.

Before we continue, what would you consider to be problematic journalism on race? Perhaps articles from Canadian newspapers in the nineteenth century that called Indigenous peoples "degraded" and "savages"?[24] Or articles like the *Victoria Daily Times* in 1922 calling for a ban on immigration from Asia to "Save B.C. for White Race"?[25] If it's explicit examples like these, you're not going to find very many in mainstream news media today. Instead, there are stories aplenty that promote assimilation, make judgments about cultural inferiority, and use race as an explanation for people's behaviour. The racism and stereotypes contained within these stories can be hard to detect, like hearing a racial comment at a party that makes you uncomfortable but you're not sure why. Is the speaker parroting racial stereotypes that have become normalized? Or are they dog-whistling to racists? Whatever the case, this book will help you catch the stories that are inaccurate and harmful, and explain how the reporting could've been done better.

I first wrote about the white gaze in Canadian journalism in a series of essays for the *Tyee,* an online news magazine in BC. There was a small group of readers who took the time to tell me that I was being terribly racist for investigating race. They didn't seem to understand that doing so isn't meant to be an attack on white journalists, nor is it a call for white journalists to be banned from writing about cultures they don't have a personal connection to. *All* journalists, even journalists of colour like me, are susceptible to taking on a white gaze. Investigating the white gaze in journalism simply means investigating how journalists are doing work that touches on race. And in Canada, as we'll see in the chapters that follow, that white gaze has the tendency to delete, dehumanize, and even demonize racialized communities.

Chapter 1 begins by challenging the idea that journalists should take on the "view from nowhere" when attempting to be objective. When reporting on under-represented groups, it's crucial for journalists to be conscious of the standpoint from which they're reporting and of the audience they're reporting to. As journalist Pacinthe Mattar powerfully stated, "Objectivity is a privilege afforded to white journalists."[26] This chapter also examines what a "gaze" is and why journalists need to watch out for its ability to shape their work.

Chapters 2 and 3 unpack tropes that journalists have come to rely on when reporting on racialized communities in Canada. We've all read stories about sad refugees and criminals of colour, but even seemingly positive tropes like "model minorities" and cultural celebrations can prove to be misleading or harmful if not handled with care.

Chapter 4 shows the importance of intersectionality. Journalists, knowingly or not, often rely on race as an explanation for people's behaviour. This ignores the role of other dimensions like class, gender, sexuality, religion, and more. Journalists who consider these intersections introduce much-needed nuance to the stories they are reporting.

Chapter 5 examines how racialized places are commonly covered as interesting sites to explore, un-Canadian problem-ridden anomalies, or are wiped off the map altogether. Foodies out there will recognize, in this chapter, the special destination known as the "hidden gem," a popular showcase for newsrooms who want to offer up exclusive expertise through a taste of culture.

Chapter 6 tackles criticisms journalists receive when they report on race, from "There are more important issues to report on!" to "We are all part of the human race!" Journalists come across efforts like this to shut them down on the daily, especially via social media channels. This chapter will counter those increasingly widespread arguments that reporting on race is offensive or unnecessary.

Chapter 7 looks at how the language of diversity is evolving faster than style guides can adapt. In determining the right words for stories on race, language, and cultures, this chapter highlights the importance of specificity, the harms of othering language, and cases in which too much colour can hurt coverage.

Journalists are storytellers telling a collective story. "The sum total of all the individual news articles, op-eds, and analyses is a meta-narrative – the overarching story we're telling and being told about ourselves and our society," wrote journalist Ashton Lattimore in *Poynter*.[27] Without representation, we don't have a clear picture of who we are.

When examining my own reporting for the white gaze, as well as that of other journalists, I did have moments of self-doubt about whether I was looking for something that did not exist. I felt affirmed when I learned that I was not alone, that most media scholars are in consensus that there is a pattern of racism in Canadian journalism, and that in general, journalists produce a negative view of people of colour.[28] I include many of their insights in this book.

Regarding the white gaze, we have Toni Morrison and other Black American writers to thank for popularizing the term. They used it to talk about literature, but it's a helpful tool that we can use to analyze the representation of racialized experiences in journalism. Most of the discussion on the white gaze comes from the US.

This book will examine how the white gaze manifests differently in Canada, especially with respect to how we view multiculturalism.

Regarding Indigenous representation in Canadian journalism, that is not the primary focus of this book; however, I do reference Mark Cronlund Anderson and Carmen L. Robertson's *Seeing Red: A History of Natives in Canadian Newspapers*, which explores the century and a half of colonial misrepresentations of Indigenous peoples and how these misrepresentations persist today. Another key text is Duncan McCue's *Decolonizing Journalism*, a practical reporter's guide and an inspiration for this book. While Indigenous peoples are othered in different ways when compared to other non-white groups, learning how they are portrayed in news media offers insight into how the country's colonial roots have shaped its conception of national identity, and how the white gaze uniquely manifests in a place like Canada.

Regarding what news media will be sampled, the vast majority of this book's analysis will be using recent examples of English-language journalism in Canada. This book is not concerned with the coverage of international issues from a Western perspective in Canadian news outlets, but rather how people of colour are represented in a country with a history and a continuing legacy of European colonialism. French-language journalism is not explored. The book does, however, include some discussion on the role of what's been called "ethnic media," "minority media," and "multicultural media," and their representations of people of colour. In my opinion, these monikers are terrible labels, but that's further evidence of the white gaze at work for you, positioning such news outlets as the media of the other. "Diasporic media" is perhaps the least othering of these terms.

Regarding Vancouver, my home city and its surrounding communities will pop up a lot as it's where I work as a journalist. Vancouver serves as an example of how even in one of Canada's largest and most racially and ethnoculturally diverse urban centres, where racialized people make up 55 percent of the population, journalism can nonetheless fall behind on representation.[29] As other Canadian communities diversify, Vancouver holds many universal lessons about representative journalism. While many ethnocultural groups are discussed in this book, you'll notice greater detail when it comes to Chinese Canadian experiences as they are the ones I'm most attuned to, due to my own identity. I believe these examples show how one of Canada's oldest diasporas can still face misrepresentation today.

Journalism is continually evolving, as is how newsrooms champion representation. Rather than supplying you with a black-and-white list of what is considered good representation and bad representation, may this book serve as a guide on how stories are constructed and how othering portrayals of people of colour can be banished and replaced by authentic representation. For newsrooms worried about their audiences shrinking, there is evidence that representative journalism can help audiences grow.[30] I hope you will be encouraged to seek out, share, and support news outlets working to reflect the range of experiences in their communities.

I know race isn't an easy topic to talk about. But as the Canadian Press puts it, the job of journalists is to provide "concise and accurate reporting that explains all of Canada to all Canadians."[31] I was aware from a young age that diversity is a part of our society. What's the point of doing journalism if it's not reflective and representative of where we live and who we are?

1

Of Gaps and Gazes

During my first years as a journalist, I was excited by every small victory I experienced when I wrote about people of colour. I felt a thrill when including sources surnamed Kim and Kaur among the ranks of Western names. I felt honoured to be able to interview and interpret on behalf of people who only spoke Cantonese, knowing that many immigrants rarely get a chance to share their experiences with English-language media. I felt delight when I got to sprinkle in details that would normalize cultural differences – that someone did tai chi or had a meeting over bubble tea versus more common references about going to the gym or a date over drinks.

There were big victories too, like when my stories made the front page. I'd stop in front of every newspaper bin I passed to take in the moment. One of the features I was most proud of was on the immigrant gardeners of Vancouver's east side. I had convinced enough of them to be interviewed, and a gardener I'd approached out of the blue even agreed to pose for the cover, wearing his slippers, sunglasses, and straw hat as he showed off his beautiful cucumbers and fuzzy gourds.[1]

There was always something surreal in seeing a person of colour on the cover, looking back at the reader with a sense of importance. I wasn't oblivious to the fact that my own non-Western last name stuck out too. Getting these markers of difference into the news – names and narratives printed in ink, racialized faces and places rendered in bold Ben Day dots on the page – was satisfying and affirming.

Among my early stories were inspirational ones about model minority immigrants who sacrificed themselves by working 365 days a year. I wrote stories about "ethnic" food as if they were exotic finds rather than the everyday eats of people from the cultures they belonged to. These were news frames I was familiar with, and I parroted them. My editors were happy. My readers were happy. My sources were happy. By getting more people of colour in the pages, I thought I was challenging the dominance of whiteness in journalism.

I could not see the spectre that had made its home on my shoulder. Somehow, I had allowed the imagined white audience to shape my stories. I became an unknowing tour guide, choosing language and topics in service of that audience, excluding those I sought to represent. Sometimes, I erased details that they would not be familiar with. Other times, I over-explained for their benefit. As a result, the lives of people of colour were surveyed from a distance, instead of having their stories told as directly as possible. Rather than present their experiences fully, they were presented under a white gaze.

How did this happen?

Introducing the White Gaze

"There was always this voice that was not talking to me."[2]

American author Toni Morrison, known for her revelatory novels about Black life, once said this about reading writing that was "talking to somebody else over my shoulder." Morrison could detect when a work about Black experiences was not directed toward a Black audience, such as being filled with long explanations of experiences that would be unnecessary for someone in the know. "I can feel that voice when it's being addressed outside rather than within, and that gave it a kind of awkwardness," she said.

As a Chinese Canadian journalist, I related to Morrison. If I was writing to an audience of readers who understood my background, I wouldn't have to explain things like family dynamics or dining etiquette. But if I was writing to an audience of readers who didn't, I would have to pause every so often to supply context.

It's a burden, especially when we're hyper-aware that white audiences have preconceived notions about the groups that we belong to. We know that whenever a certain topic comes up in a story – for Morrison, it might be Black poverty; for Chinese Canadian me, it might be stories about work ethic – they will bring to it the stereotypes they already have in mind.

How to resist the white gaze? While Morrison and her contemporary Black American writers were the first to explore this notion in the world of fiction, it's a struggle shared by Canadian journalists writing about a multicultural country stuck in an ethnocentric way of seeing.

The concept of "the gaze" comes from twentieth-century French thinkers in the fields of critical theory, sociology, and psychoanalysis, from Jean-Paul Sartre to Michel Foucault.[3] They called it *le regard*: the act of seeing and being seen. There's a power imbalance between the subject doing the gazing and the subject that is gazed upon. To gaze is to look with intent. And in this process, the subject projects meaning onto the object. As a result, the object is framed by the limits of the subject's positionality and perception.

These ideas were picked up by Frantz Fanon, a political philosopher and psychiatrist born in Martinique, then a French colony. In 1952, Fanon published his first book, *Black Skin, White Masks,* which examined how Black identity is constructed and produced via his insights being Afro-Caribbean Francophone.[4] "I wanted quite simply to be a man among men," he wrote. But "the white gaze, the only valid one, is ... dissecting me. I am *fixed*." The gaze of white subjects made him "responsible" for their assumptions about his body, his race, and his ancestors: "cannibalism, backwardness, fetishism, racial stigmas, slave traders." To be under the white gaze is to be "sealed into that crushing objecthood."[5]

Over the years, the concept of the gaze has made its way into many different fields.[6] There's the gaze of the state, used in security studies.[7] There's the tourist gaze, examining travel and how places are produced for consumption.[8]

One of the more famous gazes is the "male gaze," first identified by English art critic John Berger and popularized by British film theorist Laura Mulvey in the early 1970s,[9] used to analyze depictions of women in art. Under the male gaze, women are all too often presented and represented for the sexual pleasure of cisgender heterosexual men. And it hasn't gone away – you can catch the persistence of the male gaze in plenty of recent movies and TV shows. Some visual examples are gratuitous female nudity or slow pans over women's bodies. In Marvel films, there is a male gaze behind the appearance of the superhero Black Widow, played by Scarlett Johansson. There are many close-up shots that linger on Black Widow's butt while she is wearing tights.

Beyond visuals, the gaze is about how a subject defines the object in relation to itself. In *Iron Man 2*, Tony Stark, Iron Man himself, flips through photos of Black Widow, including one of her in lingerie, and says, "I want one." Johansson eventually spoke out against how her character was introduced. "The character is so sexualised, you know?" she told the *Guardian*. "[She is] really talked about like she's a piece of something, like a possession or a thing or whatever

– like a piece of ass, really."[10] That's the power of the gaze in action, affecting characterization.

For journalists, being unaware of the white gaze's power to objectify people of colour can lead to inaccurate and harmful depictions. "Legacy news organizations in this country were created by white people, for white people," Anishinaabe journalist and author Waubgeshig Rice once wrote.[11] "White people are traditionally the central characters in Canadian journalism, and every experience is measured against that."

Missing, Misrepresented, Marginalized

Surely more racialized people in the news would equal more representation, right? And fewer white people in the news would make coverage less white?

If only it were that easy. This is part of the trickiness of the white gaze. It can sneak into stories that don't have a single white character at all. It can sneak into stories written by journalists of colour. It can sneak into stories in spite of the fact that the journalists behind them have good intentions about representation. And sometimes, misleading stories that possess the white gaze might even do a bit of good in the world, causing some audience members to have positive feelings toward an underrepresented racialized group. Representation can be so lacking that audiences welcome it, even if it's imperfect.

So how can the white gaze be detected in a work of journalism? Especially in cases where people of colour are among those happy with the coverage?

As all those big thinkers of the past concluded, the gaze is all about power. So rather than look at the subject matter or the characters present in a story, you'll want to look at how the journalist behind the story comes to define everyone and everything that isn't white.

American writer Hannah Miao offers a definition that captures the seemingly contradictory ways that the white gaze can manifest: "It's being watched from a lens of otherness that is sometimes violently obvious, and sometimes so subtle that you find yourself wondering whether you made it up entirely. It is fetishization and repulsion, appropriation and persecution, misrepresentation and erasure, all at once."[12]

I've mentioned my frustration when people of colour are missing, misrepresented, and marginalized in Canadian journalism. I believe these three problems are at the core of how the white gaze affects how people of colour are depicted.

To be missing is an obvious problem: when people of colour, their cultures, the places they frequent, and the issues they care about that affect their lives are all absent from coverage. When journalists with a white gaze look for news to cover, they simply don't see these racial and ethnocultural groups. There's a big gap, and audiences are left without a sense that people of colour exist or that they are important.

To be misrepresented means that people of colour are undeniably present in coverage, but that their presence is skewed. Journalists with a white gaze rely on racial stereotypes that range from the negative to the seemingly positive, demonizing certain groups while fetishizing others. Audiences are left with distorted depictions of various people groups.

To be marginalized means that people of colour are present in coverage, but their presence is minimized or sidelined. They might be relegated to a sidekick role, accompanying a white protagonist. They might be talked about, but not heard from. The focus of such stories is, in the words of Augie Fleras, about "how others are baffled by them and (re)act accordingly,"[13] and not actual stories about people of colour. Think about those stories with visuals of people of colour from far away, captured with a telephoto lens as if they're wild animals in a nature documentary. Audiences are distanced from these people, as if they're unknowable actors or the backdrop to more important stories.

"The View from Nowhere"

One of the longstanding pillars of journalism is objectivity. In other words, journalists have attempted to avoid possessing any gaze in the delivery of their journalism for years. What better climate for the white gaze to pass undetected.

In American journalism, objectivity began to emerge in the nineteenth century – a pivot from the partisan newspapers of the day – before being fully articulated as an ideal and ethic of the profession in the early twentieth century.[14] Journalists are taught to be vigilant for anything that might contaminate the neutrality of their work. From the CBC's Journalistic Standards and Practices: "We do not promote any particular point of view on matters of public debate."[15]

Journalists report facts. Journalists report all sides of an issue. Journalists report without inserting their own opinions. But is it really possible for journalists to adopt a "view from nowhere"? Media scholars like Jay Rosen use this term to describe that non-position of a position adopted by journalists when collecting reliable information and sharing their findings. Rosen says that American journalists have developed "almost a lust" for the view from nowhere and treat it as the authoritative way to do reporting.[16] The term comes from a book of the same name by philosopher Thomas Nagel, referring to humans' ability to "transcend our particular viewpoint and develop an expanded consciousness that takes in the world more fully."[17]

Nagel's description of the view from nowhere sounds noble for a profession that serves as society's watchdogs. But can journalists really remove themselves from their work? Can journalists really produce balanced journalism that takes all sides into account?

As early as 1972, there were critics of journalistic objectivity.[18] Some called the idea of neutrality-as-objectivity a myth, as it's nearly impossible to present the news without some subjectivity.[19] Media scholar Meenakshi Gigi Durham says that there is inherent bias in reporting that stems from "the social location of the reporter, the news organization, and conventional journalistic practices."[20] Rather than being able to offer true objectivity to their audiences, journalists go about picking sources from multiple sides of an issue as part of a "strategic ritual," to give themselves the appearance of credibility.[21] No one can accuse journalists of failing to be objective if they've given everyone a chance to speak, right?

In his book *Losing the News*, American journalist Alex S. Jones makes the case against that kind of "he-said/she-said reporting, which just pits one voice against another."[22] This isn't to say that journalists should chuck objectivity out the window. Instead, authentic objectivity is about being an "honest broker ... not trying to create the illusion of fairness by letting advocates pretend in your journalism that there is a debate about the facts when the weight of truth is clear," says Jones. News outlets will generally call out false claims and use facts to contextualize such topics as human-caused climate change, the COVID-19 pandemic, and beliefs about voter fraud during the 2020 US presidential election, rather than give equal space to the views of big oil or anti-maskers for the appearance of balance.

Journalists Bill Kovach and Tom Rosenstiel point out that while journalists cannot be objective, their methods can be, comparing it to scientific inquiry based on evidence and results.[23] And like scientists, journalists should be scrutinizing their own biases or conflicts of interest as they do their facts and sources. Media ethicist Stephen Ward invites journalists to have a look at their own "cultural baggage." Self-consciousness, he argues, is an important part of objectivity.

For you journalists out there, it might be strange to hear that you must look inward before going out to do the day-to-day work of reporting. Journalists should not allow the belief that they can be impartial to prevent themselves from examining the positionality and power dynamics behind their own practice. To report on under-represented groups that are frequently othered and marginalized, it's important to be aware of how your own experiences of class, race, culture, gender, and more – not to mention the weight of the news outlets being represented – can affect your journalism. If you don't acknowledge that you do practise the profession with a "view from somewhere," you'll never be able to detect the white gaze that inevitably finds its way into your work.[24] Perhaps there's someone in your newsroom who's better suited to covering a story; or at the least, offer suggestions toward how to report the story in ways you did not consider.

The Global Reporting Centre, based out of the University of British Columbia, published the *Empowerment Journalism Guide*. The guide includes a checklist of three questions for journalists to consider before embarking on a story, all of which I believe are important to ask before jumping to cover people who are very different from you and who your audiences might consider to be the other.

Why are *you* telling this story?
Who is the story for?
Why tell *this* story?[25]

When caught in the daily grind, journalists can sometimes forget what a responsibility it is to be representing the under-represented and the misrepresented to a mass audience. As American philosopher Linda Martin Alcoff tells us, speaking for and speaking about others is an "act of representing the other's needs, goals, situation, and in fact, *who they are.*"[26]

"Objectivity Is a Privilege Afforded to White Journalists"

In a 2020 *Walrus* piece, Canadian journalist Pacinthe Mattar highlighted a double standard that exists in newsrooms. "Under the banner of diversity, racialized people are told to bring ourselves and our perspectives. But, if we bring too much of them, we get held back," she wrote.

The provocative title of the piece, "Objectivity Is a Privilege Afforded to White Journalists," points to a problem experienced by journalists of colour in newsrooms. White colleagues might accuse them of intentional or unintentional bias when covering a story related to their actual or perceived identity, as if journalists of colour are uniquely vulnerable to dropping professional ethics and standards by reporting on people who share a similar trait.

In 2017, Desmond Cole, a Black journalist, decided to leave the *Toronto Star* after an editor said that it was inappropriate[27] for him as a columnist to be protesting carding and racial profiling by the police, a move that was criticized as a "double standard"[28] considering that many *Star* columnists have activist streaks.

The 2020 resurgence of Black Lives Matter, in the wake of the murder of George Floyd, continued that conversation[29] on objectivity in the journalism industry in a big way after reporters were seemingly barred from covering the protests by their bosses for being Black.[30] It's an offensive notion that suggests journalist of colour are unprofessional, working to promote an ideological racial agenda, do not have the ability to control their emotions, and cannot be trusted to report on people or groups they share some marker of identity with. Again, this higher burden of proof of so-called objectivity is not commonly expected of white journalists.

The ultimate result of this double standard being applied to journalists of colour? Editorial dehumanization of one's peers, according to Canadian journalist Matthew Amha. "To work as a Black journalist in Canada today is to report on the murder of children who might as well have been you as if they were strangers," he argued in an essay for *The Maple* titled "The Objectivity Trap." "It's to dispassionately report on the kind of disasters that forced your parents across an ocean in search of new life, and weaponize conventional wisdom to buttress stories of neighbourhood and sectarian violence with stereotype, myth and stigma."

Journalists of colour who don't write dispassionately face accusations of practising "advocacy journalism" or, like in Cole's case, unprofessional activism. These days, there are even accusations of journalism as a whole being biased and partisan, called "woke media" for reporting on anything to do with race, gender, inclusivity, and inequality. While the word "woke" has been used in Black American circles for almost a century,[31] to describe an awareness of social inequality, it only entered everyday usage in the 2010s, with conservative commentators and politicians coming to view wokeness as a bogeyman. Wokeness has been blamed for everything from the "cancelling" of white people when they do racist things that they used to be able to get away with, to the destruction of Canada as institutions confront the dark truths of colonial history. According to some conservatives, progressives are out to wage their "woke war" and spread their "woke agenda," and, in the words of Elon Musk, infect others with their "woke mind virus."[32] In Canada, People's Party founder Maxime Bernier has said that media and entertainment have been taken over by a "woke cult with their preachy messages."[33] Conservative Leader Pierre Poilievre claimed that young people were supporting him because they want freedom from the "woke control freaks" in media.[34]

Some journalists have criticized the state of the industry and its conversations about objectivity too. In a 2024 op-ed for *The Hub*, journalist Harrison Lowman claimed that "journalism schools are now developing and encouraging almost exclusively left-wing storytellers, who are most comfortable with progressive storylines, and who often question the value of objectivity."[35] Lowman said that he noticed emerging journalists increasingly prioritizing lived experiences over expertise, first-person accounts instead of data, and pitching stories about the "conditions of victimhood, that were not to be questioned."

What are journalists to do when audiences insist that matters of diversity, equity, and inclusion are a woke conspiracy, or that reporting on race is radical? What are journalists to do when some colleagues believe that stories that contain lived experiences or investigate victimhood shirk data, research, and scrutiny?

Indigenous journalists know attempts to delegitimize their work all too well, with accusations of being preachy or soft when they are the ones who cover Indigenous issues. In a paper published in *Media, Culture & Society*, Indigenous journalists argue that they are still driven by fact when covering issues within their own communities, which promotes Indigenous perspectives, voices, and needs amid mainstream media coverage that denigrates them.[36]

Angela Sterritt, known for her work at the CBC, shared about some of the criticisms she's received as a Gitxsan journalist:

When I'm doing an Indigenous story, I'm an advocate. When I'm doing a non-Indigenous story, I'm told to stay in my lane. That's 2023. Sometimes I give workshops and people ask me how long ago my negative experiences were, and I have to say,

"That was yesterday." I think people of colour who are reporting on our own communities and reporting on underreported
stories are going to be called 'advocates' because again, the
baseline in journalism is white, the norm is white.[37]

It's an exhausting, not to mention offensive, argument: to assume
that racialized journalists covering groups they identify with can't
help but be so overcome with emotion and empathy that they drop
all professionalism, doing away with industry ethics and practices.
Much is to be said of the lived experiences that they possess, which
can help them navigate interviews, research, and reporting in ways
that outsiders cannot. The resulting coverage is valuable to all,
for the groups used to being misrepresented in the news as well
as audiences who might have othering impressions of who they
are. To capture voices missing from coverage, especially those who
are marginalized, is a core part of what journalism is all about.
Criticizing racial and ethnocultural inclusion for being anything
less than journalism is nothing but white gatekeeping.

Who Is "White"? Who Is "Diverse"? Who Is Normal?

Now that we've established what the white gaze is and how it
works, you're probably wondering who exactly counts as white.

Some audiences might consider it taboo for journalists to mention whiteness in their stories. If you are a journalist who has done
this, then I'm sure you've received calls and emails from people
telling you that race isn't real and to please stop talking about it.
You might even get accused, like I have been, of "reverse racism"
(as if racism is supposed to be something that should only happen
to racialized people and not to those who are white). I've been told
that my journalism is "adding more gas to the fire," and that it is

"driven by hate." I've been lectured by readers on numerous occasions about how race is a social construct, and because of that, I shouldn't waste time chasing after this wokeness.

Race might be a social construct, but so are a lot of things. Gene Demby, co-host of the National Public Radio podcast *Code Switch*, countered this argument on Twitter: "It would be great that if, upon stumbling upon the idea that race is not a biological reality but socially constructed, people didn't immediately proceed to presume that that means it can just be waved away. Money is socially constructed. Nation-states are socially constructed."[38]

We live in a world where people classify each other by race, and doing so results in real consequences. It shapes how we treat one another, affecting everything from our health outcomes to our social mobility to which places we feel safe in.[39] So for journalists sitting down to report on just about any topic, they should consider how race might contribute to their source's unique circumstances, especially if it factors into how they experience obstacles that a non-racialized person would be unlikely to face.

Back to our original question. Generally speaking, today we consider white people as those of European origin. It's an evolving definition, and it's expanded over the years to include people who were once racialized in Canada, such as non-Anglo white groups like French settlers.[40]

Even more fraught than reporting on whiteness is reporting on white privilege. Any mention of this by journalists will have some members of the audience howling. I've had white readers send me long histories of how their families endured hardships – surely this is proof, they so strongly tell me, that white privilege isn't real. I know some critics will call me a hypocrite for talking about whiteness while at the same time saying that we shouldn't make generalizations based on people's identities. Yes, treating racial groups as monoliths is problematic, as we will discuss in more detail later on. But at the same time, there is a social phenomenon – one intentionally developed by white people during the colonial era and which persisted throughout the settling of North America – that has given and continues to give white people privileges that others do not have. Our demographic makeup might have shifted, with greater social equality and fewer people who actively support the racist hierarchies of the past, but people who are white, or who appear to be white, continue to have privilege because of the history of settler colonialism in North America.[41] American scholar and activist Peggy McIntosh described white privilege best: it's an "unquestioned and unearned set of advantages, entitlements, benefits and choices."[42]

With the definition of white privilege in mind, we can now have a look at how other things are defined in relation to whiteness. When deciding where to go out to eat, there have been times when friends of mine have said they are craving "ethnic cuisine," to mean food that isn't Western – that is, food that originated in Europe or among white North Americans. It's a sign of how we've been socialized, when we consider that everything that isn't white or Western is different or "other." Take, for example, a series of stories that the *National Post* ran in 2017 called "Multiculturalism Profiles." Featured were a Ugandan Indian refugee, a Chinese Canadian who fought for head tax redress, and a Jamaican Canadian labour leader, among others, as if to say that people who aren't white are "diverse," "ethnic," and "multicultural."[43]

But if you're white? Congratulations, you get to be considered normal! In 2010, a report by the Diversity Institute of Toronto Metropolitan University, then known as Ryerson University, found that footage of people in local "everyday life stories" in broadcast news were overwhelmingly white.[44] There were white workers tired after daylight savings, white tourists on vacation, and white teenagers trying on dresses and being served by white shop owners for a story on "the search for the perfect prom dress." At the time, Torontonians of colour made up 43 percent of the population; however, representations of Torontonians of colour were about half that in the news stories sampled, the report found.

When stories that attempt to portray daily life neglect depictions of racialized people, they reinforce the idea that the average person is a white one.

The Invisible Knapsack

Peggy McIntosh came up with the idea of the invisible knapsack to describe those unquestioned, unearned, and often even unknowing privileges that white people carry.[45] Inside the knapsack are privileges like being able to go into public without mistreatment due to their race, being able to find employment or access healthcare without experiencing discrimination, and being able to attend organizational meetings without feeling isolated or held at a distance.

One of the top privileges on McIntosh's list touches on media. "I can turn on the television or open to the front page of the paper and see people of my race widely represented," wrote McIntosh, who is white. The racialized sources who show up in the news lack many of the privileges on the list. They cannot say provocative things without audiences attributing them to the morals of their race, or having their race put on trial. They cannot speak without risking appearing as a spokesperson on behalf of others who share their racial or ethnocultural identity. They cannot critique the government without being seen by some as cultural outsiders.

I can think of many other privileges. People of colour cannot expect mainstream English news outlets to cover and investigate the events and topics that concern their livelihoods. They cannot expect journalists from those outlets to report on their lives with accuracy, not even when it comes to the spelling of their names. They cannot expect journalists to speak their languages. They cannot experience tragedy without audiences suggesting that they might have deserved it or that such suffering is natural. They cannot obtain assistance from the government without audiences raising the issue of fairness and criticizing the cost. They cannot express their culture without worries that audiences will say it's backwards, immoral, or weird.

White people are simply not subject to the same level of racial scrutiny. Some of these harms ultimately come from audiences and are outside of journalists' control; however, journalists can avoid adding fuel to the fire of discrimination and stereotypes by being mindful of how they report on people of colour. Good reporting focuses on people's humanity and avoids othering portrayals and suggestions that race is behind all behaviour.

"Mainstream" versus "Ethnic"?

Do you fight the system? Or do you go your own way?

Working in a white-dominated industry, some racialized journalists have opted for the latter. Rather than put in tireless labour to try and diversify legacy news outlets from the inside, they've built up their own.

This is something that Indigenous journalists in Canada have been doing since Peter Edmund Jones, one of the first status Indians to obtain a medical doctor degree from a Canadian university, founded the short-lived Hagersville-based newspaper the *Indian*. In its prospectus, the publication called itself "a paper devoted to the interests of the Aborigines of North America, and especially to the Indians of Canada."[46] Some Indigenous-centred outlets today include the Aboriginal Peoples Television Network (APTN), the world's first national Indigenous broadcaster, which launched in 1999 and is a registered charity;[47] and, with the rise of digital publishing, *Media Indigena* and *IndigiNews*.

They're not alone. Digital journalism start-ups that cater to a mass audience on a range of topics have been founded in response to problems with legacy media, in a bid to "repair and reform."[48] The nimbleness of these start-ups allows them to, according to journalism scholars Candis Callison and Mary Lynn Young, "experiment with economic models, partner with non-journalists, collaborate with communities, hire non-white journalists, and privilege underserved, feminist, and diverse perspectives." The *Tyee*, where I've spent the most of my career, was founded in 2003, and there has been an increasing number of successful start-ups since, including *Canadaland*, the *Narwhal*, and the *Local*.

Diasporic media, however, is different in that it caters to a specific audience. They share a "by us, for us" mission, consisting of English-language news outlets and those in a third language – that is, a non-official language spoken in Canada – specific to immigrant groups.

My grandparents have never consumed English-language news media in Canada because they've never had to – they've enjoyed a bountiful diet of Chinese-language Canadian content instead. For print, they read the local versions of *Ming Pao* and *Sing Tao*, filled with ads that show the vastness of the diasporic economy, from doctors to tutors to importers of the latest rice cookers. On weekends, these newspapers come as hefty bundles with glossy magazines on cooking and entertainment news. For broadcast, there are the radio and television offerings of the Fairchild Group, based in Vancouver and Toronto, with local news, dispatches from China and Hong Kong, and even contests that have launched the careers of singers and actors from the diaspora.

Reading, listening to, and watching this media with my grand-parents led me to notice whenever there was another diasporic group with their own media. At Indian supermarkets, I heard the local Punjabi news. At Korean supermarkets like H-Mart and Hannam, I encountered an impressive collection of newspaper racks by the shopping carts, with free publications on local news, Christianity, and real estate going strong even when English-language alt-weeklies began to vanish.

Augie Fleras credits Canada for having an "energetic and possibly unmatched ethnic media," with news outlets that cater to new immigrants in their mother tongues as well as long-time immigrants and diasporas in English.[49] The Canadian Radio-television and Telecommunications Commission has played a part in encouraging and guiding the growth of diasporic media through the Ethnic Broadcasting Policy.[50] Some started in Canadian basements, while others are projects of long-running outlets overseas. They function as "alternative media institutions," says Fleras, reaching audiences who cannot access English-language media, reporting on issues neglected by English-language media, and offering content that helps migrants integrate to life in Canada.[51] This gives these outlets dual roles: as a buffer against white gaze–focused portrayals of immigrant groups, with their own perspectives and reporting; and as a bridge between immigrant audiences and the society they've settled in. This makes them "simultaneously insular and inclusive," says Fleras.[52] Whenever I tune into Fairchild during tax season, the host and expert interviewees assure newcomers that taxes aren't meant to punish them, offering tips on how they can set up investments through their RRSPs and TFSAs – a perfect example of "news you can use."

English-language diasporic media shares these goals of filling the coverage gap on their respective ethnocultural communities.

The outlets are equally varied, from the Asian Canadian literary magazine *Ricepaper* to *Darpan,* which publishes lifestyle and edit-orial content for South Asian groups and runs a prestigious annual awards ceremony for achievers in areas such as business and social causes.[53] Some outlets that have emerged in the online space are more youth-focused, such as the RepresentASIAN Project, Cold Tea Collective, and *5X Press,* with articles on the experiences of children of immigrants of colour that touch on the intersections of race, culture, gender, sexuality, health, and more. There are also those that take a topical approach, like *New Canadian Media,* which calls itself "The Pulse of Immigrant Canada," with coverage intended to represent "all Canadian immigrant communities."[54]

Translating Canadian issues into the many native languages of its residents is important enough. But diasporic media, speaking to an in-group as the primary audience, also offer a rare and much-needed refuge in the media landscape, for racial and ethnocultural groups to safely and sensitively explore issues that are important to them.

Fleras notes one key difference between diasporic and legacy media: institutional power. Diasporic media outlets are "largely powerless" outside of their own communities, while official language media possesses a "legitimacy" that allows them to define public discourse and advance national interests.[55] Academia and the public view the media landscape as a binary made up of diasporic media and the so-called mainstream media, according to Sherry Yu, a leading scholar on the subject in Canada.[56] "Ethnic media have been considered as an 'add-on' at best rather than part of the broader media system," she says, "and the discourse they produce is considered 'valuable' and worthy of 'monitoring,' but not worthy of wider distribution in the broader public sphere."[57] Yu also warns against what she calls the "instrumentalization" of diasporic media, when parties such as politicians use such news outlets to serve their own interests rather than the public.

In her book *Diasporic Media Beyond the Diaspora,* Yu imagines an "intercultural media system" in which both worlds are made more accessible to wider audiences, with joint productions and language translations: third-language outlets offering English and vice versa. I've seen news outlets try this over the years, but such projects have repeatedly been dropped after a short period of time.

That being said, I do not believe that diasporic media are immune from the white gaze entirely simply because people of colour are involved in their production. They are still located in Canada, a country with a Eurocentric media landscape, and can fall victim to stereotypes about immigrants and racial and ethnocultural groups as defined by the white gaze.

Inside Out and Outside In

You'd think that realizing the white gaze exists would make it easier to do journalism.

By learning to see what Toni Morrison called the "little white man that sits on your shoulder and checks out everything you do or say," you can get rid of him, right? "You sort of knock him off and you're free," she said. In one video interview, she pretends to flick him off from her left shoulder. "Now, I own the world. I can write about anything, to anyone, for anyone."[58]

But recognizing the white gaze can mean overthinking the white gaze. American author L.J. Alonge experienced this when writing his series *Blacktop,* about teenage misfits who find each other through basketball. "I'd try to write a scene about two kids trying to dine-and-dash, something I'd done, and stop to wonder if I was playing into narratives about 'black criminality,'" he wrote in an op-ed for NPR. "I'd try to write a scene about a kid getting into a fight, something else I'd done, and feel like I was fueling ideas about 'black-on-black violence.'"[59] For me, when reporting on ethnically Chinese people who own homes, I always worry about readers who hold stereotypes about "crazy rich Asians." I've debated including details about how hard they worked to afford their property, in order to placate audiences who might think they were overseas billionaires or earned their money through illicit means.

But should I really be providing answers to questions or criticisms I predict audiences might raise before they even share them? That's a lot to worry about. Rather than simply reporting a story, I've felt like I'm playing chess, having to anticipate how the opposing side might react. It's caused to me to abandon stories or fill them with unnecessary details in hopes of preventing outrage from white readers.

There's also the issue of journalists intentionally pitching and reporting stories that cater to the white gaze because those are the ones being assigned by editors. For her master of journalism thesis, Jiaxuan Wu of the University of British Columbia interviewed several racialized early-career journalists who mentioned the dilemma of pandering to the gaze in order to make a living. The scarcity of opportunities in the industry puts pressure on these journalists to just give in. One said:

> I always had to make myself marketable. So whatever stories, even if I didn't personally believe in them, or I wasn't necessarily interested in them, I knew they wanted and if that was going to pay the bills, that's what I was going to do. So there wasn't really a relationship where I could speak my mind. It was more like, I know what you want, I think I have what you want, and I'm going to give it to you.[60]

W.E.B. Du Bois describes a feeling called "double consciousness." Black Americans are "always looking at one's self through the eyes of others, of measuring one's soul by the tape of a world that looks on in amused contempt and pity," he writes.[61] It's a feeling that I and other racialized people can relate to, and I wish I had Morrison's resolve to just flick off that little white figure on my shoulder.

That might be her solution for her literary writing, but it's trickier for journalists. As the code of the Canadian Association of Journalists says, our job is to report the truth, encourage civic debate, and serve the public interest – and this means writing for a diverse audience that includes white people.

One year, when Nowruz approached, I remarked to a white editor that all the coverage in Canada about its traditions was catered toward white people. He didn't buy it. What if white people who didn't know about Nowruz wanted to learn about it? Or Zimbabweans, or any other group in Canada who genuinely didn't know anything about Nowruz? These are fair questions, but my problem with the coverage wasn't that it existed. My problem was that it didn't look as though someone with an insider's gaze was covering it. Instead, it looked as though someone was reading about the holiday in a Lonely Planet guide.

The literary theorist, filmmaker, and writer Trinh T. Minh-ha critiques anthropology as a discipline of a white male "us" talking about "them," the distanced other. The othered "them" doesn't get a chance to speak and are only presented "when accompanied or introduced" by the white male "us."[62] The same goes for journalism under the white gaze, with journalists holding the power to publish the representations of people of colour as they see fit.

I see a two-pronged challenge for journalists addressing the white gaze. Yes, we need to make sure that our stories are in the public interest. But racialized peoples should also feel as though they're being covered accurately and authentically by someone who knows them deeply, whether that's because a journalist shares the same background or because a journalist has worked hard with community insiders to ensure that the coverage is representative.

While that perspective from the inside out is the one that's usually missing, I don't think journalists should focus on it so intently that they dispose of the view from the outside in. To serve the public interest, journalists need to learn to bridge the two. Double consciousness can be a burden, but it can also be a tool to ensure that white and racialized audiences are on the same page. Keeping the white gaze in mind allows journalists to have a conversation with it and challenge it, but not cater to it. Morrison might not have been a journalist, but she has some advice on this that applies nicely to journalism: "The point is not having the white critic sit on your shoulder and approve it."[63]

Of Darlings and Deviants

Being a reporter is a bit like being a movie director. Once you decide on a topic to report on, you go looking for a source who embodies what you think your story will be about. If your story is about evictions, you're going to need a troubled renter. If your story is about urban sprawl, you're going to need a worker with an exhausting commute. Just like a director, you're going to want to cast the perfect actor for the part.

A pernicious problem with stories about people of colour is that journalists keep on pitching the same stories and casting the same characters in them. We've all read the ones about immigrant successes and elders sharing their exotic cultures. This problem of pigeonholing is one that Hollywood suffers from, too. Women of colour, for example, are frequently cast as "slaves, nannies, and maids," and the Oscars have been accused of rewarding these repetitive representations.[1] The *Guardian* once published an interview with actor Djimon Hounsou, who was born in Benin but immigrated to France at age twelve. Within a five-year period, he was cast as a slave three times: in *Amistad, Gladiator,* and *The Four*

Feathers. "You can see that some people's vision of you, or what you represent, is very limiting," he said.[2]

Stereotypes aren't unique to people of colour. They are a shorthand used for all subjects in journalism, whether referencing a marginalized group or not. They are "normal and intrinsic to the operational dynamic of an industry that must simplify information by tapping into a collective portfolio of popular images," says Fleras.[3] "In the same way that people depend on stereotyping to simplify everyday reality, media rely on stereotypes to codify reality and process information. Limitations in time and space prevent complex interpretations." Think of the stories that stereotype all Canadians as being nice, or those that make sweeping generalizations about what the lives of millennials are like.

According to Fleras, the problem with stereotypes of people of colour is a pattern of bias that "miniaturizes" their identities.[4] Rather than multidimensionality, audiences are served simple tropes, like people of colour being either heroes or villains.[5] Race plays an outsized role in defining their personalities. Gone or glossed over are deeper issues such as systemic inequality. Instead, journalists might portray people of colour as falling into a predicament because of some flaw of their ethnocultural identity, avoiding narratives that examine power and privilege. As bell hooks, a foundational figure of Black feminism, writes:

> Stereotypes abound when there is distance ... Like fictions, they are created to serve as substitutions, standing in for what is real. They are there not to tell it like it is but to invite and encourage pretence. They are a fantasy, a projection onto the Other.

Othered groups sometimes struggle to refute the roles that journalists cast them in. Immigrants of colour, for example, are more vulnerable to misrepresentation if they are not yet familiar with Canadian media and how to interact with local English news outlets, said journalist Haroon Siddiqui, who spent many years as an editor of the *Toronto Star*.[6] "When they do make feeble attempts at attracting attention, their accents, or lack of journalistic vocabulary and lingo, get in the way," he once wrote. "When they vent their frustrations at street demonstrations, they often end up playing into media hands, fitting into a 10-second stereotypical clip or a photograph, confirming their worst caricatures."

It also doesn't help that journalists are generally bad at sharing the voices of the unorganized, added Siddiqui. Journalists gravitate toward sources with readily available emails and phone numbers, those who appear to speak with authority on behalf of official groups and can summarize complex issues with sprinklings of snappy quotes. But if an immigrant group isn't organized in a way that puts forth these easy-to-find spokespeople, journalists end up recycling familiar tropes.

Admittedly, if a reporter only has five minutes or five hundred words to tell a story, the character development is not going to be like that of a Russian novel. But stereotypes have power in even the shortest of news hits through word choice and imagery, reinforcing or challenging the audience's impressions of the people being reported on.

In *Seeing Red: A History of Natives in Canadian Newspapers*, Anderson and Robertson show how Indigenous peoples have been subject to stereotypes in newspapers since before Confederation. They came up with the "Rule of Three": Indigenous peoples are commonly portrayed as being depraved, innately inferior, and stubbornly resistant to progress.[7] Stereotypes are often "regurgitated" by journalists from society, they write. And if journalists don't challenge stereotypes, they feed them back to audiences in a vicious cycle:

Duncan McCue, CBC journalist and journalism instructor, has his well-known "Five Ds," which contains some elements of the Rule of Three. McCue has shared them as part of his training on reporting in Indigenous communities with CBC bureaus and young journalists across the country,[8] and they are detailed in his useful (and very funny) book *Decolonizing Journalism*.[9] An Elder once told McCue that Indigenous people only made the news if they were one of the Ds. McCue felt it was simplistic to reduce Indigenous representation to a handful of letters, but the more he looked at the news, the more the Ds showed up.

There's *drumming,* or depictions of culture without context. There's *dancing,* depicting Indigenous peoples as frozen in a bygone era. There's *drunk,* used as an explanation for Indigenous suffering. There's *dead,* like the words of an infamous BC judge who once echoed the words of Thomas Hobbes: Indigenous lives before colonization were "nasty, brutish, and short."[10] McCue threw in a fifth D: *defiant*. It's when journalists repeatedly cover Indigenous people marching, protesting, and occupying, as if they're in the way of Canadian progress. Headlines hunger for drama, so journalists give audiences stories of showdowns. Defiant stories also come with dramatic images. There's the famous photograph "Face to Face," taken during the Oka Crisis of 1990, a land dispute between the Mohawks of Kanesatake and the municipality of Oka, Quebec. It depicts a Canadian soldier on one side, and an Anishinaabe student in support of the Mohawk claim, masked and dressed in camo print on the other as they stare each other down.[11] Stereotypes function like shortcuts, says McCue. They're codes that give an audience an "instant, common understanding" based on some aspect of their identity.

I kept an eye out for these kind of shortcuts in Canadian journalism, to find patterns like McCue's Five Ds. While each ethnocultural group is subject to its own racial stereotypes – from geniuses to gangsters, nannies to nurses – I narrowed down a few that applied to people of all colours. Some of these tropes are problematic because they depict people of colour as problematic, though others that depict them in a positive light can be problematic, too. I came up with a mnemonic of my own to capture them, not to replace McCue's but to stand alongside his analysis of Indigenous representation.

Here are my four Ds of diversity in Canadian journalism, when it comes to race, ethnicity, and culture:

- "Darlings" – model minorities who are celebrated;
- "Deviants" – people of colour who have their behaviour racialized, whether the behaviour is bad or perceived as bad;
- "Damaged" – sad and suffering people of colour; and
- "Delicious" – cultures for consumption.

Chapters 2 and 3 will dissect the diversity Ds, from their appeal and their shortcomings to how to evolve beyond them and tell more representative stories.

This chapter will focus on the first two Ds, which feed off of each other. The heroes and the villains, the good guys and the bad: the darlings and the deviants.

DARLINGS

The Fungs, a Chinese Canadian couple who own a greasy spoon on the city's Downtown Eastside called Master Chef Café, showed up in a 2013 profile in the *Vancouver Courier*. The café has all the familiar vintage trappings: bar counter seating, red vinyl stools, wood-panelled walls, and a cash-only menu.

In the profile, it's noted that Mr. Fung does not speak English. He apologized to the journalist – and by extension, the audience

– about this. He and his wife, both in their eighties, had already retired once. But they decided they wanted to work again, "because I like to make the friendship," said Fung. He's proud of the four children they raised in the city, rattling off their accomplishments and university degrees. "I get a life no trouble," he said. "All the people no fight, all the friendship, how good, how excellent."[12]

You don't have to look far to find characters in the news like the Fungs. They are a classic example of the "darling."

Darlings encompass every mould of model minority you can think of, from hardworking newcomers to the brilliant next generation. Stories about darlings are often success stories, told with the intention to inspire. Journalists linger on their toil and romanticize their struggles, making them seem noble and invincible, as if they can weather any and all hardships that come their way. Their endurance and sacrifices yield amazing accomplishments, and they may be quoted by journalists expressing how it was all worth it. Expect positive mentions of the Canadian immigration system and the Canadian dream, with journalists indulging in portrayals of model minorities' big hearts and deep love of country, spelling out what it means to be an upstanding citizen.

— Blood and Sweat —

The Fungs are an example of those sacrificial survivors, darling immigrants, and refugees who've undergone epic journeys and lived tough lives to establish roots in Canada. I've written my share of stories about sacrificial survivors, profiles of those who toil at humble jobs, from barbers to janitors to night-shift taxi drivers. Like the Fungs, many shared pure motives about wanting to serve their community. These darlings are portrayed as dutiful, intent on earning their keep.

Remember the cobbler from my neighbourhood? I interviewed Henry Ng, originally from Taishan, China, when he was eighty-five. He had been fixing Canadians' shoes and skates since he immigrated half a century earlier. He slept four hours and worked twelve hours a day, seven days a week. He, too, insisted he would never retire. How's that for a model minority?

— High Achievers and Trailblazers —

In 1987, a *Time* magazine article featured Asian Americans who outscored their peers of other backgrounds in high school and entered top universities. It was titled "The New Whiz Kids."[13]

Journalists are still writing stories about whiz kids, the amazing children of newcomers who've emerged from challenging starts to secure bright futures for themselves. Every generation seems to break new records to make their parents proud. Take the example of a 2020 CBC story about Harbin Kaur, a nine-year-old from Surrey, BC. English might not be her first language, noted the journalist, but she was on her way to a national spelling bee only two years after moving to Canada from India.[14] The founder of the spelling bee was also quoted, sharing how these young people "recognize that what it takes is discipline."

Trailblazing firsts are also difficult for journalists to avoid, stories about individuals who are the first person of [insert ethnicity/national origin/immigration status] to accomplish something. (We throw in a gender marker, too, if it's noteworthy.)

Considering the current and predominately white makeup of many of our institutions, journalists will be writing about these firsts for years to come. There's the world of entertainment, with Chinese Canadian Simu Liu becoming the first Asian lead of a Marvel film. There's the world of politics, with Jagmeet Singh making headlines over his career for *multiple* firsts. He was the first turban-wearing Sikh to sit as a provincial legislator in Ontario, and later, when he became leader of the NDP, the first person of colour to head a major federal political party.

— Wise and Quirky —

There's a seventeenth-century literary stock character called the "noble savage," an other with a sense of goodness that hasn't been corrupted by civilization. Tonto, the American Indian sidekick to the Lone Ranger, is one famous example. This stock character has persisted to the present day and is the predecessor to another trope, the "magical negro," a Black person with special insight or abilities who enters a narrative to come to the aid of a white protagonist. Filmmaker Spike Lee has cited the appearance of the magical negro in films like *The Green Mile* (in which a Black convict with healing powers teaches white Tom Hanks about life) and *The Legend of Bagger Vance* (Will Smith, the titular character, is a mystical caddie who doesn't age and teaches Matt Damon how to golf).[15]

I've noticed heartwarming stories in Canadian journalism that focus on a person of colour who hasn't quite assimilated – someone struggling to speak English who makes cultural faux pas when interacting with white people, often portrayed as amusing – but possesses something they wish to share with them, often cultural or timeless wisdom. With similarities to the stock characters of the noble savage and magical negro, this character functions like a "magical minority."

The role of the magical minority in a story, marginalized to that of a sage or a sidekick, educates white protagonists who often function as a stand-in for a white audience. Compared to the white protagonists, magical minorities are not well-rounded characters and may even lack biographical details. An editor would consider this limited information inadequate for a primary character in a work of journalism, but because magical minorities are supporting characters, it lends them an air of mystery that supports the framing of the story.

In Vancouver, many of the magical minorities that show up on the news are seniors with immigrant or refugee backgrounds. In 2019, the *Toronto Star* published a story about five English-speaking housemates, described as "hipsters and rockers," who befriended an elderly Cantonese-speaking woman who showed up as if out of nowhere, "wandering the patio and yard." There were culture clashes between the two parties – the senior found it "bizarre" that unrelated people might live together – but they bonded over gardening, with the woman, who they called auntie, passing on her knowledge. She shared tips like putting Safeway bags on cucumbers "to make them heat up and grow enormous," said one of the housemates.[16] Is this magic?

Another example comes from a *Vancouver Courier* story on the "angel of East Hastings,"[17] a woman named Gia Tran who arrived from Vietnam in 1980. Tran searches through dumpsters, garbage cans, and recycling bins for cans and bottles that locals have disregarded to refund for cash. She makes regular treks across the city, seventy blocks at a time, lugging her recyclables. When the journalist asked about the effects of this work on her health, such as handling garbage, the angel laughed and said, "I don't care. I do what I want!" The journalist explained that the angel does this because she is a devout Buddhist, and she donates the majority of her earnings to local charities, with over $15,000 to the BC Cancer Foundation. "She simply wants to help people," wrote the journalist, who quoted her saying, "I see people, no food, no money, sleep outside, they need money, I give them money." The story is accompanied by a photo of the angel standing inside a giant dumpster with a big grin on her face – the magical minority with something wild about her, teaching Canadians about the true value of their waste while embodying generosity.

— Happy, Healthy Representation? —

The appearance of all of these model minority darlings in news media might seem like helpful and much-needed representations of people of colour. They are, after all, positive portrayals – no demonization in sight. Journalists reporting such stories often forego hard notions of objectivity and insert moral language, praising them for their work ethic. The journalist who wrote the story about the angel of East Hastings used words like "devout," "faithfully," and "hard-earned" to describe her work. These stories can stir up audience empathy for racialized people who have experienced discrimination because of their identities. These depictions, for both journalists and audiences, can be hard to resist, showcasing the Canadian dream in action and what people with origins from around the world are doing to fit into our multicultural mosaic.

And why shouldn't they have wide appeal? They stoke pride in being part of an inclusive nation for both white Canadians and racialized Canadians alike, the latter who can point to others who've had similar experiences, those who've fought through poverty and marginalization, and see the results of their struggles recognized in a public place like news media. I was in this camp growing up, marvelling whenever a person of colour showed up in an English newspaper or on TV. It signalled worth and prominence. When I began writing these stories myself, I'd hear from long-time immigrants who thanked me for writing such inspiring tales and waxed poetic about the value of sacrifice.

The term "model minority" was first used in a 1966 *New York Times Magazine* article by sociologist William Pettersen, to describe the Japanese American "success story" of being able to overcome racial barriers to do well academically and socio-economically.[18] Later that year, he used the term again to describe Chinese Americans. The idea of the model minority snowballed after that, furthering the myth that any racialized group has the ability to succeed as long as they pull themselves up by their bootstraps. Asian American scholars noticed the myth's prominence during the civil rights era. There was the implication by well-to-do white Americans that if Asian Americans could make it, surely Black and Indigenous people could too.[19]

This comparison has been called a "racial wedge"[20] for pitting racialized people against one another. The myth leaves out how different groups experience systemic racism differently, with their own unique histories of discrimination. The myth also leaves out how governments like Canada's play a role in selecting who gets to come into the country, such as through immigration policies that target certain countries, incomes, labour, and education. The case has even been made that model minority stories that promote happy, harmonious ideas of multiculturalism uphold settler colonialism, because what they suggest is that all racialized people just want to be included in white society. "While Indigenous peoples do form important alliances with people of color, Indigenous communities' concerns are often not about achieving formal equality or civil rights within a nation state, but instead achieving substantial independence from a Western nation-state," argue Maile Arvin, Eve Tuck, and Angie Morrill.[21]

By reporting stories about model minorities without taking these contexts into account, journalists paint a romanticized picture of how racialized people are able to assimilate into Canadian society while being seemingly immune to power structures at play. Assimilation is also presented as a natural trajectory for racialized others. Such stories, as uplifting as they might appear, can function as false positives when it comes to goals of representation.

— Dealing with Darlings —

In 2021, CBC interviewed newcomers who'd settled in Ottawa for messages to share with those hoping to come to Canada. One individual who arrived as a refugee from the Congo said, "There's nothing that could stop Canadians from doing whatever they put their mind to."[22] That same year, CBC interviewed some darlings for Asian Heritage Month in a special feature called "Meet Metro Vancouver's Inspiring Asian-Canadians."[23] "Canada is a highly hospitable country," said one immigrant from India. "The country treats every person as its own." These are garden-variety stories about darlings. The quotes these happy interviewees offer make for effective "kickers," what journalists call the catchy display copy and endings of stories.

In a country like Canada, with a legacy of migration that continues to the present, it's inevitable that there will be many stories about darlings to report on. But if their lives contain elements that play into the model minority myth, how can journalists ensure that their reporting isn't reductive? Well, they can ask themselves what they're communicating to audiences about what it means to be a darling.

Does the story imply that hard work is all it takes to lift people out of poverty and free themselves from marginalization? Does it equate the main character's experience as universal to all people of colour? Or does it go into nuance about how their particular journey has led them to where they are? Does the story offer a fair accounting of the help they received or the struggles they experienced along the way? Are systemic factors taken into account? Is the story overly produced with the intent to inspire the audience and have them leave with a feel-good message?

To answer these questions, journalists aren't required to grill their sources in tough interviews, prodding them until they crack and reveal the overarching factors that have facilitated their upward mobility – how many interviewees are likely to share, or even know, such things? However, that doesn't mean journalists should only publish quotes from those darlings who truly believe that all people of colour can succeed in Canada if they work hard and call it a day.

For years, the story of the angel of East Hastings remained on my mind. There are many immigrant and refugee seniors from East and Southeast Asia who collect stray cans and bottles in large quantities in Vancouver. They're a common sight – every Vancouverite has seen them hobbling to the depot with carts and trolleys in tow, to sell trash for cash. Surely they're not all darlings who donate their profits to charity?

Years later, worried that low-income seniors were being presented to audiences as archetypal darlings, mysterious figures spiriting away garbage from the streetscape, I wrote my own story on the topic. A social worker told me that a number of these seniors live alone, have not lived in the country long enough to have a pension, do not have family to support them financially, and survive on thin margins. As a result, they work. Selling recyclables is one kind of work they can literally pick up, either as their sole means of income or in addition to another job, because they are unable to make ends meet. "I know some do it to pass the time or as a social aspect," said the social worker. "But at the same time, I think we can grow a stronger social service support network so that seniors don't have to work."[24] Her words shed light on the important fact that many darlings endure hardship to survive in an unforgiving system in which they've become trapped. It's important for journalists to report such important context, and it doesn't make these darlings any less newsworthy.

When journalists promote a myth like the model minority, they are misinforming rather than informing their audiences. They need to be careful about implications of invincibility, when people of colour toil but come out seemingly unscathed and are able to find success. Reporting on darlings who are sacrificial survivors tends to include details about their hard work to impress audiences, from long hours to intense physical labour. Stories like this may treat precarious labour, poor working conditions, and scarcity of resources as normal, inevitable, and experiences for building character. Hardships are even romanticized, perhaps in a story about how someone who skipped lunch for years was able to afford a car, or how a single immigrant mother who worked three jobs was able to support a child through university as well as her family back home.

Implications of invincibility make invisible the abuse, disadvantages, and discrimination experienced by people of colour. Journalists should not neglect the personal costs of being a darling. For example, how do long hours affect one's family life? How does physical labour affect the body? Do all newcomers love the work that they do, or do they put up with it because it is a means to an end? Sure, sacrifices will sometimes lead to success, but they also come with consequences. If these consequences aren't communicated, audiences will be fed the impression that good darlings who want to earn their keep in Canada must accept, without question, whatever hardships come their way, and smile while doing so.

It's not enough for journalists to simply introduce their characters. They need to show how their characters fit into society.

Aside from a single story, journalists should step back and look at their own body of work, and that of their news organization. Are there lots of stories about model minorities? Are they all told in the same way? Are there also stories about newcomers who work just as hard but have a tough time finding their footing? Is there representation of people of colour aside from the darling?

DEVIANTS

If we have darlings, then we must also have their opposite: deviants. Reports of deviance are rarely one-offs and are about more than a person of colour doing something that audiences view as bad. There are many sociological theories that attempt to explain deviance. When it shows up in media regarding racialized people, deviance is often connected to a larger moral panic about how they're engaging in unacceptable behaviour that threatens the well-being, basic values, and interests of society.[25] A solution might even be presented, such as limiting immigration or cultural expression.

While the darling trope offers an example of what people of colour should be, the deviant offers up people of colour to make an example of. The "beating heart" of most moral panics can be found in the media, according to sociologists Erich Goode and Nachman Ben-Yehuda. "The media are an expression of panics as well as their *spark* or *cause*. They set agendas, focus attention on issues, and turn up the heat of concern in all sectors of the society – the public at large, politicians and legislators, social movement activists, and law enforcement."[26] Moral panics require crackdowns, and journalism on deviants often calls for one. While you're not likely to find racial slurs and openly white supremacist views in the news anymore, moral panics give journalists cover to target racial and ethnocultural groups in ways that verge into racism.

So, who's considered a deviant? Criminals of colour are of course included. But so are those portrayed by news media as what Fleras calls "problem people."[27] They don't need to break any laws to be framed as a problem. They only need to burden, threaten, or inconvenience the so-called average Canadian. White voices are often included as the stand-in for that exemplary Canadian that deviants are offending.

Deviants are often portrayed as the "perpetual foreigner" or the "forever foreigner"[28] – putting them at odds with those "'real' Canadians."[29] This is fuelled by a racist belief that people of colour can never truly belong to Canadian society, whether because of real or perceived loyalty to their ancestral country of origin, real or perceived cultural practices, or simply because they are an other who isn't white.

Richmond, BC, just south of where I live in Vancouver, features prominently in headlines about deviants. The city is known for its large Hong Kong, Taiwanese, and mainland Chinese diasporas, with immigration and settlement taking off in the 1980s and continuing to this day. The city also has a large number of residents with roots in India and the Philippines. You might think that Richmond, with its "majority-minority" population, would be a picture of multicultural harmony. International media frequently call it "North America's most Chinese city."[30] The *Guardian* even wrote about Canadian cities like it with the headline "Everybody Fits In."[31] However, Richmond's makeup has resulted in a number of battles that played out in municipal politics and news media, with ethnically East Asian locals portrayed as threatening to white locals and their way of life. A number of deviant examples that follow come from Richmond's unique setting.

You will also notice age-old narratives lurking between the lines in stories about deviants. The invasion narrative is one that has persisted since the beginning of Canada's history, with newspapers drumming up the fear of racialized people outnumbering white people in a country they believed to be for the white race.[32] Rather than explicit racism, you'll find references to Canada's British and French roots as its defining culture, and stories that use demographics to show how white people are being "replaced" by people of colour in parts of the country. This kind of framing is worrisome against the backdrop of the modern far-right spreading a conspiracy theory called the Great Replacement or white extinction, which claims that immigrants are being welcomed by governments in a plot to shift demographics, and therefore influence and power, away from white people born in the country.[33]

Journalists and audiences alike should be on alert when they come across information on deviants or deviance put forth by politicians and institutions, also called "authorized knowers."[34] Relying on such sources can turn journalists from society's watchdogs to the "guard dogs" of those in power.[35]

You might wonder what's unique about this since the news is known for featuring acts of deviance. Journalists are frequently accused of having a negativity bias, with outsized coverage of crimes, violence, and people behaving badly. However, stories about deviants of colour are different because of what journalists imply is the cause of said deviance: their identity. Some stories about deviants of colour do contain newsworthy information. The problem is when they are made targets of racialization, making their racial and ethnocultural identity the crux of the story.

— Racializing Crime —

I grew up in the 1990s watching television coverage of "gang wars" between "Indo-Canadian gangs" in Vancouver and its suburbs. The camera would zoom in on bullet holes in the sides of cars, crime scenes with yellow tape, first responders carting away bodies. Journalists would interview gangsters, broadcasting challenges between rivals on the evening news.[36]

News outlets seemed overly fascinated by the fighting and their ethnocultural dimensions. In a column titled "Keep Your Head Down in Vancouver These Days," a *Globe and Mail* columnist asked why there isn't more coverage of the conflict.[37] "If this were New York or Chicago or the City of Angels, this story would have long ago achieved international notoriety," he wrote. "[The city] is in the grip of a gangland war that reads like the script for one of the Godfather movies or *The Untouchables*."

A number of racialized groups are overrepresented when it comes to news reporting on crime and violence, Black and Brown people in particular. Stories examine the backgrounds of racialized perpetrators in great detail or showcase their identities prominently. Are the backgrounds of white perpetrators under the same scrutiny? Looking at a news outlet's body of work, are certain racial and ethnocultural groups predominantly featured in stories on crime and underrepresented in stories about almost anything else?

A number of studies analyzing news media in Canada show that Black people are overrepresented in coverage of crime and are portrayed as "crime-prone social threats."[38] The majority of the stories in which they appear are related to street crime, entertainment, and sports (with the latter coverage sometimes reinforcing the stereotype that Black people are good athletes because of their "natural talent").[39] In the criminal coverage, sociologist and criminologist Scot Wortley draws attention to the role of police in such coverage, as they decide which crimes and details are presented to the media.[40]

Muslims of various racialized backgrounds have also been singled out in stories about deviance. In 2015, a Toronto-based consulting firm analyzed twenty-five years of *New York Times* headlines that mentioned Islam and Muslims and found that 57 percent of them were negative portrayals. Islam and Muslims were portrayed more negatively than myriad other subjects, including alcohol, cancer, and cocaine.[41] Muslims were also overrepresented in stories about crime, particularly as part of the moral panic that followed after 9/11, with journalists associating them with terrorism while employing less evidence than is usually required when giving such a label.[42]

While there is a wealth of literature that critiques orientalist and Islamophobic representations of Muslims in Western media, legal academic Azeezah Kanji noticed that there were no Canadian studies that compared the coverage of violence by Muslim perpetrators with non-Muslim ones. So, in 2018, Kanji did it herself. She analyzed reporting by the CBC, the *National Post,* and the *Globe and Mail,* and found that acts of Muslim violence, with stories that focus on Islamic extremism and liberal uses of the word "terrorism," received one-and-a-half times more coverage on average than non-Muslim ones. That ratio jumped when discussing thwarted Muslim plots (preparations for violence), which received five times more coverage than non-Muslim ones. On top of this, incidents that concern Muslims are more likely to be labelled terrorism, with extensive detail included about the perpetrators' ethnic and religious backgrounds.[43] In 2014, during the fatal shooting of a corporal at Ottawa's Parliament Hill, a number of media stories ran headlines about how the shooter "referred to Allah"[44] and prayed in Arabic, seizing upon his religion "as the most salient, sensational, and sinister detail in demonstrating the terroristic nature of his motive," with less focus on a video he recorded before the assault that condemned Canadian foreign policy, says Kanji. She also pointed to a survey done the same year[45] that showed that Canadians are significantly more concerned about "homegrown radical Islamic terrorism" than terrorism by white supremacists, despite the fact that white supremacist and far-right violence has been far more frequent and fatal in Canada.[46]

— Pathologizing Culture —

Aside from associating crime with race, journalists also make use of cultural pathologies; that is, implying that behaviour is an inherent part of one's culture, often in racist ways. Journalists often frame non-Western cultures as being uncivilized, barbaric, toxic, abusive, hierarchical, discriminatory, and therefore regressive, concluding that they are incompatible with the so-called Canadian mainstream.

In coverage of violence involving Indian Canadians, many journalists have pinned its rise on what they've described as South Asian culture. A scholar who examined seventy-one years of Canadian newspapers found that the violence was portrayed as being "directly linked to cultural difference, notably to their exotic 'Native Rites' or their unmanageable jealousies."[47] South Asian home lives have been characterized as inherently patriarchal, causing the young men growing up in those households to become violent.[48]

In 2013, there was a story from Richmond, BC, that touched on the pathology of peeing. Someone had snapped a photo of a senior holding up a young boy in a shopping mall so that the boy could urinate into a garbage can. The photo was uploaded onto social media and went viral. Both the senior and the boy were visibly East Asian. With this taking place in Richmond, with its large Chinese population, people who saw the photo assumed the senior and the boy were Chinese.

The photo sparked a minor media storm, with journalists from the local paper to the CBC to the *Globe and Mail* covering the incident. Journalists reported on the urinary episode with a serious tone, interviewing everyone from parents discussing different styles of child rearing to expert voices on China. The *Georgia Straight* called it a "culture clash";[49] the CBC said it raised a debate about "Chinese cultural norms."[50] At the heart of the coverage, it was as if Chineseness itself was on trial.

While these journalists did gather an assortment of voices to weigh in, is a toddler peeing in public really news? Or was it just because he was visibly East Asian? Would the incident have made national and international news if the grandmother was visibly white?

Thankfully, the *South China Morning Post,* Hong Kong's English-language daily, had a correspondent covering the incident as well, who zoomed out and framed the racialized furor for what it was: "anti-China vitriol" at a time when local tensions with mainland Chinese newcomers were high.[51]

When it comes to debates like these, communications scholar Yasmin Jiwani says that focusing on culture "neutralizes" and hides the racialization of an issue.[52] In other words, journalists can claim that it's not racist to talk about Chinese people peeing in public because it's not a discussion of race. "By simply pointing out cultural differences, the media can refrain from using the explicit language of race," says Jiwani. "At the same time, they can attribute pejorative connotations to culture that underscore the superiority of the dominant group and the inferiority of Others. Culture becomes a way of talking race by dismissing and erasing the notion of racism."

— The Unassimilable Race —

Unlike racialized criminals, this deviant, the peeing boy, has nothing to do with the Criminal Code. He and his grandmother are newcomers portrayed in news media as sticking to their culture of origin and not assimilating to the culture of white Canadians, implied as the "fixed" way to be Canadian. Examples of this lack of assimilation include people of colour wearing their cultural or religious clothing, speaking languages other than English, and starting a business not directed at the wider white community – all visible markers of difference that make their white neighbours uncomfortable.

Groups are also deemed unassimilable if they live near one another in large numbers. These stories about "ethnic enclaves" frame people of colour as segregating themselves in one part of town, clinging to their cultures of origin, interacting with their own kind but not with white locals. What the white gaze portrays as social segregation is instead people of colour forming community and sticking together for survival. Perhaps that community is the only place where they can find opportunities and access key services. Perhaps that's the only place where they feel safety and freedom from discrimination.

One story that's persisted throughout the 2010s is the controversy over Chinese-language signs in Richmond. In the lead-up to the city's 2014 election, a group of locals complained to politicians about signs having too much Chinese on them and asked for a bylaw to mandate the inclusion of English and to a specific percentage.

The furore received significant media coverage, even in other parts of the country, giving space to locals who were quoted saying the signs were "unwelcoming" and "un-Canadian." The *National Post* began their story with a white woman stating, "We, the new visible minorities, are experiencing exclusion."[53]

To be fair, the journalists behind some of these stories did attempt to gather a variety of perspectives from their sources, saying that the languages on signs should be left to the market; that honest conversation rather than bylaws would better address a tense controversy; and that the complainants were exaggerating the number of Chinese-only signs in Richmond.

But the way they framed their stories made it sound as though showing a sign that doesn't contain English (or French) is deviant behaviour, even though it isn't illegal. A Global News story on the matter ran the headline, "There's Hardly a Word of English on this TransLink Bus Ad."[54] Another story, this time by the *Vancouver Sun*, noted that one organization "admits mistake in posting Chinese-only signs."[55] On the other hand, white complainants are given labels like "activists" and "lifelong" residents of the city, giving an extra air of legitimacy to their comments. One was even quoted as a "ninth-generation Canadian,"[56] as if her deep roots made her comments more valid than those of others.

The City of Richmond ended up asking two geographers from the University of British Columbia to look into the issue. They noted that a city audit found that fewer than 3 percent of signs in the city are Chinese-only, and that at least one-third of the signatures on the one thousand-name petition came from one person who didn't live in the city. As for the media's role, they noted that a small number of people had managed to get quoted and inflate the issue, "frequently and inaccurately" pushing the narrative that the city was a "polarized and competing" landscape.[57]

Much of the coverage framed the creation of these signs as deviant behaviour, giving a small number of white voices prominent space and labels of privilege, and blowing up a controversy that was called a "debate" but proved to be on a smaller scale than expected. Chinese business owners were even portrayed as un-Canadian and uninclusive, but when the city encouraged them later on to include some English, they proved to be 100 percent compliant.[58]

A few questions for when you come across coverage of racially charged debates like this one: Who are the people labelling something as deviant behaviour? Whose voices are privileged in these types of stories? Are journalists questioning the complainants for comments that might be considered racist, or are they quoting them as is? Do the people portrayed as deviants get a chance to respond? And finally, are journalists putting in the effort to verify whether the claims at the centre of a debate are true?

— The Colour of Trouble —

In 2022, Environment Canada issued a special statement for Toronto and the York Region, warning of the "possibility of deteriorating air quality as a result of fireworks for Diwali." The agency went on to say that people may experience symptoms such as increased coughing, throat irritation, headaches, or shortness of breath if they are exposed to fireworks smoke. Some outlets, like CityNews, covered the statement without much additional reporting.[59] The *National Post* ran the headline, "If the Air Appears Smoky Over Toronto Tonight, It's Not the Weather, It's Diwali Fireworks."[60]

The original statement quickly received backlash on social media from individuals who said that singling out Diwali was insensitive, especially when many other Western holidays have fireworks as part of their celebrations, such as Halloween and Canada Day. Environment Canada ended up removing the statement, and a spokesperson told media that they believed it was the first time they'd issued an air quality statement in relation to holiday fireworks.[61] "I've never seen this type of post on Victoria Day," said Twitter user @billsmachine in one viral tweet. "What's your beef with Indians?"[62] Some of the early news reports on the air quality warning made no effort to question whether Diwali was being singled out and reported on the press release as is.

Stories like these give audiences the impression that people of colour cause more trouble than their white counterparts. This happens when there is overrepresentation of stories that involve people of colour and trouble, such as when their festivities cause unreasonable risk or inconvenience. In the case of the Diwali fireworks, the stories framed celebrants as if they were out to make people cough with their over-the-top revelry. Another example is stories on parades and public events for non-Western holidays that cause traffic to be slowed and rerouted, as if non-white groups celebrating their non-statutory holidays are burdening white Canadians.

Journalists often gravitate toward cases of people of colour doing something unsafe or bothersome. There are many governmental authorities that regularly share information on public safety, such as product recalls or failed health inspections; however, journalists report more on the cases that involve people of colour over the ones that involve white people, such as those that take place at herbal shops or ethnocultural restaurants and supermarkets, places frequented by the other.[63] Telling an audience of the white gaze about unclean sushi, wontons,[64] or "potentially poisonous sand ginger powder"[65] provides a much grabbier story than a recall of cheese.

Indian weddings are one topic of coverage that's been frequently racialized. In a 2021 CBC story on a Punjabi wedding in residential Surrey, the headline said that the party sent "Neighbours Into Orbit."[66] The descriptions that tied the piece together said that the noisy reception, which drew complaints to police, was part of a "traditional Punjabi wedding." When this kind of coverage pops up in the news mix, it reads like, "Here we go again, that crazy group of people is up to no good." If you look at the social media commentary, that is exactly how some audiences respond to such stories, calling people of colour and their cultures strange, dirty, or untrustworthy.

When journalists cover community stories about temporary nuisances and genuine problems – be it smoke or product warnings – they should ask whether they are leaning on racial and ethnocultural markers to make a story seem more newsworthy to a white audience.

— Freeloaders and Invaders —

No subtlety here – in stories about freeloading foreigners, the invasion narrative is in your face.

We're back to Richmond with another example: coverage of "birth tourism" from the late 2010s to the present. Back in 2016, local media began reporting on how foreigners, the majority of whom are Chinese nationals, were giving birth in Canadian hospitals, presumably so that their newborns could obtain Canadian citizenship.[67] One Richmond hospital was at the centre of this.

The *Richmond News,* in a story titled "Richmond Hospital Becomes Passport Mill," did not supply information on the visa status of the "foreigners" – the expecting parents at the centre of the story. It did not say whether they were visitors, temporary residents, or permanent residents. There was mention of an industry of "baby houses," which care for foreign nationals giving birth, taking care of everything from paperwork to maternity care. The story framed the houses as "a shadowy, underground practice," and quoted sources talking about them as if they were a "big money-making industry that does no good to society" and "abuses the system."[68] In the words of one MP, "These kids won't contribute to Canada. They're a passport owner but will spend their life elsewhere." A CBC investigation on the subject was published with the provocative headline "'All About the Money': How Women Travelling to Canada to Give Birth Could Strain the Health-care System."[69] It quoted a doctor who said that the children of these so-called birth tourists "get the Canadian passport, and then they leave the country."

While this was an interesting story about Canadian policy and a recent spike in births, illicit language was used to describe a legal phenomenon that is being allowed to grow by governments and elected officials.

Yes, this is a story where the identity and background of those involved plays a role, but check out the comments section of any story about "birth tourism," international students, the intake of refugees, or any other newcomer group that might make white locals nervous and you'll see racist chatter about "freeloaders" burdening taxpayers. In these stories, people groups rather than Canadian policy are framed as deserving of blame. Journalists may also imply through these stories that people of colour have taken something from white locals or sidelined them into a position of being second-class citizens.

Take this 2014 CBC story about an "exclusive" college at the University of British Columbia. The opening paragraph said that it would "house only high-paying international students, most of them from China," and that "Canadian students need not apply."[70] The story also said that international students have been "displac[ing]" some "regular" students from campus housing. This framing minimized the role of universities in allotting who campus housing is for, and it ignored the fact that universities charge international students exponentially higher fees than Canadians. Again, people, not policy, is blamed. This scapegoating of international students for problems like housing affordability has gone on for years, with news media playing a role in promoting such opinions. In 2023, Prime Minister Justin Trudeau spoke out publicly against the blame.[71]

When journalists report on issues that they know will spark racism or xenophobia, they have a responsibility to handle the material with extra care. That goes for such details as headlines chosen, the language used, the sources quoted, and more.

— No Comment, or No Interview? —

There's a bad habit that journalists fall into when reporting on deviants: they don't interview the people of colour at the centre of the story. Maybe it's hard to find representatives of a community if they don't already have the connections. Maybe the story requires the journalist to speak a language that they don't speak. Or maybe people of colour are aware that a journalist might portray them as deviant and refuse to chat with them.

In the early- to mid-2010s, there was a lot of coverage on the role of money from China in Vancouver's housing market. It was another blame game. The players blamed were newcomers buying real estate, with fewer stories about the greater game: Canadian governments welcoming foreign property ownership and ignoring the side effects. Journalists quoted activists, professors, realtors, and angry locals, all talking at length about newcomers from China who were often portrayed as deviant invaders.

However, it was rare to find an actual person from China interviewed for these stories. Local outlets, national publications like *The Walrus,* and even those with global audiences like the *Guardian, Mother Jones,* and the *New Yorker* have published stories on Chinese newcomers buying real estate without the voice of a Chinese newcomer, heavily relying on the commentary of local residents and expert voices instead. "I feel like a stranger in my own country," said one of these residents (not Chinese) in the opening of the *Mother Jones* feature. "Some of the houses ... they haven't even picked up their mail."[72]

It's a basic requirement of journalists to reach out to the people they are reporting on. This applies to any story, but it should definitely apply to stories featuring people of colour – especially groups who don't have much representation in English-language news media and are reported on as engaging or having engaged in deviant behaviour. If journalists go for easily available secondary sources, they're allowing them to speak on another group's behalf, often in problematic terms.

— Suggested Deviance —

Aside from language, watch out for visuals that hint that people of colour are inherently deviants, even if there is little to no mention of them in a story. Journalists often go to neighbourhoods of colour and start snapping.

Speaking of worries about foreign money supercharging Canadian real estate prices, stories on the subject in the 2010s used a lot of photography of ads and sale signs with Chinese characters as if to suggest a culprit. At the onset of and during the pandemic, local and international news outlets, including the *New York Times,* used photos of Chinatowns and visibly East Asian people walking around in public to accompany stories about the spread of the COVID-19 virus in their cities. The trend was criticized by the Asian American Journalists Association, which said that editors who chose the photos were fuelling anti-Asian racism and unfounded, xenophobic fears.[73] Such decisions reveal the racial stereotypes and implicit bias that exists in newsrooms.

These suggestions of deviance can lead to potentially defamatory territory. In 2016, the *Toronto Star* published a story about "extremist" literature in mosques, running a photo of a mosque in Vaughan that had no connection with discussions of extremism in the story itself. A representative of the mosque, the Canadian headquarters of the Ahmadiyya Muslim Jama community, said that its members were upset to see their building "negligently used as a stock image."[74] This prompted the *Star* to run an apology for publishing a "wrong and misleading photo," admitting that the members were "rightly" troubled to see their mosque pictured alongside the original story.

In an interview with NBC, Davidson College journalism professor Issac J. Bailey said that journalists need "deeper thinking about the choices we make in every circumstance, but especially during a time like this, when fear and uncertainty combine to seed the ground for all kinds of biases and stereotypes."[75]

— Deviant Deviations —

Journalists can become so conditioned to report stories of deviance about certain racialized groups that they are unable to report on them in any other way.

In a letter to the *Surrey Now,* a reader expressed frustration about how coverage of the annual Vaisakhi parade – a huge celebration that "fed 100,000 for 12 hours straight ... [with food] from the kitchens of peoples' homes and was all handmade individually, voluntarily" – focused instead on conflict and danger from Sikh separatists.[76] The reader found that the journalist made an irrelevant mention of how pictures of martyrs were shown at events in previous years.[77] The journalist also included a self-described "brief" history of Sikh separatists that ran 345 words. "The fact is," said the reader, "there was not a single police incident."

In an essay for *This Magazine,* journalist and human rights advocate Amira Elghawaby wrote that "When it comes to Muslims, even the good news stories can turn ugly." Prime Minister Justin Trudeau's visit to a mosque on Eid al-Adha was targeted by a *National Post* columnist who used the occasion to call out his feminist "hypocrisy" for visiting a "gender-segregated Ottawa mosque."[78] Elghawaby said it was an untruthful attempt to frame the mosque as embodying un-Canadian values; a female Liberal MP had shared her experience of visiting the same space in that mosque on various occasions. "That not all mosques are the same, or that there are many Muslims working to make these spaces more inclusive and welcoming doesn't always matter when it comes to media coverage," wrote Elghawaby.

Journalists reporting on a group they do not belong to might try to make the story about something newsy that they are familiar with. For example, introducing discussion of alleged sexism and feminist posturing into a story about the prime minister's mosque visit on a religious holiday. They should ask themselves whether the deviance they are introducing into a story about people of colour is relevant. If it is indeed newsworthy, good! But only as long as it's not blown out of proportion. In the case of the Vaisakhi coverage above, an interesting story about a religious celebration in a suburban setting and the cross-cultural connections it fosters was muted in favour of a focus on the media's attraction to ethnoreligious conflict. As Elghawaby says, good news stories are too often tainted.

— Dealing with Deviants —

For journalists looking to avoid the deviant trope, reporting on criminality or behaviour perceived to be "bad" can feel unnecessarily complicated when it concerns a person of colour. We're acutely aware that when there is a dearth of misrepresentative coverage about a group of people, stories about a single bad apple who happens to be from a racialized background can lead audiences into thinking that the whole tree is rotten, and we don't want to be an accessory to such characterization.

Of course, there will be important stories about deviance that involve people of colour, but when reporting on them, journalists need to make sure that their coverage doesn't imply that the person's race or culture is the reason for their deviant activity. As mentioned earlier, journalists need to be aware of the climate they're sending their stories into, whether it's one of general anti-immigrant feelings or discrimination against a specific group due to some current event. They can examine data from pollsters and Statistics Canada for insight into the extent of the problem. For example, a study from the Angus Reid Institute that found that half of Canadians don't believe Islamophobia is an issue[79] contrasted with a Statistics Canada tally depicting a 71 percent jump in hate crimes against Muslims in 2021[80] should alert journalists to the fact that insensitive framings of stories that concern Muslims and Islam can fuel apathy or hate held by their audiences.

In her *This Magazine* essay titled "Canadian Media Sucks at Representing Muslims in Canada," Amira Elghawaby showed how even one story can be damaging and difficult to rein in once it is out in the world.[81] In 2016, the Canadian Press ran a story with the headline "Islamic Schools, Mosques in Canada Are Filled with Extremist Literature: Study."[82] That study, called "The Lovers of Death?" was self-published, not peer-reviewed, and did not contain any interviews. Instead it based its findings on photos of bookshelves found at mosques and schools.[83] The National Council of Canadian Muslims called the study poor research and said that "such writing only fans the flames of ignorance at a time when vandalism of mosques and hate incidents against Canadian Muslims are increasing."[84]

The backlash prompted the wire's editor-in-chief to write a response admitting that the story was published hastily and needed "more context, background, and the entire range of available opinion."[85] "But it was too little too late," according to Elghawaby, who noted that the story about the study was republished by multiple news publications across the country. It resulted in ugly social media commentary, with readers saying that "It's not a mosque, it's a terrorist command centre," and that it was "Time to demolish all mosques and deport all Muslims back to the hellholes they came from."

When a group underrepresented in Canadian journalism is consistently painted as deviants, why would they trust reporters? In his 2022 Massey Essay titled "Muslims and the Media," Haroon Siddiqui, a Muslim man himself, shared insights from his long career as a Canadian journalist watching coverage of Muslims:

> Regardless of the great diversity of views among them, I find that Muslims are as one in being disappointed, enraged, and estranged from Western media outlets, which they see as anti-Muslim crusaders. The alienated fall into two broad categories: people in the Muslim world and the communities of Muslim minorities in the West. The former have the luxury of criticizing from a distance. The latter have had to deal with the constant fallout of bad coverage and demonization. Muslims don't trust my profession and my colleagues. Indeed, they fear us, especially what they see as our tactics of entrapment. They are petrified that their words will be twisted and distorted if they don't fit the prescribed clichés and stereotypes. "We don't recognize ourselves in your media," I have been told repeatedly over the years, across North America, Europe, the Middle East and the Far East, and Africa.[86]

A tenet of journalism is to minimize harm in the pursuit of the truth. This doesn't just apply to the individuals featured in journalists' stories but also groups featured at large. If journalists know that audiences might see their story and jump to a racist conclusion, they should think about how they can repackage the story to prevent harm, whether that means adjusting the headline, the visuals, how identity is introduced, or the wording in the story itself, so that an entire group isn't vilified.

In many of the examples seen in this chapter, the focus was on how stories about deviants of colour are received by white Canadian audience members. Journalists should also report on stories about racialized deviance with racialized groups in mind. The deviance might speak to a social issue that's affecting their demographic, or to how their social networks are preyed upon. Maybe it's someone running scams in non-official languages that target seniors, or a well-established immigrant making use of a cultural connection to take advantage of and abuse newcomers.

Oh, and don't forget to ask yourself whether markers of identity like race, ethnicity, culture, national origin, and so on are relevant to the story at all. Sometimes they're not, but journalists mention them anyway, unnecessarily racializing an issue. After all, deviants come in all colours.

Of Deliciousness and Damage

DELICIOUS

A big holiday that's not on the statutory calendar? How fascinating! Colourful displays of culture, with dancing and traditional clothing? How exotic! Ethnic restaurants to sample? What an adventure!

Featuring stories about "delicious" racialized cultures is an easy and seemingly inoffensive way for newsrooms to show that diversity is on their radar. But journalists often take on the white gaze when introducing non-Western cultures to their audiences, pointing out things considered interesting or unusual from a Western perspective.

Aside from introductions, these types of stories also focus on opportunities for the out-group audience to participate in non-Western cultural activities, a kind of ethno-tourism with journalists acting as guides. The audience is often encountering the other from within the confines of a charter bus, following a guided path, rather than walking in their shoes. Journalists point out opportunities for the audience to step off that bus to attend a parade, eat at a restaurant, learn a greeting in another language, or buy a decoration to commemorate an unfamiliar holiday.

It might be a bit cheesy, but at the end of the day, it's a good thing that racialized cultures are on display after being under-represented for so long, right?

Well, maybe when representation is done right. Yes, these stories can be great tools for connection, helping audiences get to know cultures they're unfamiliar with and important practices that take place in their community. But when journalists portray racialized cultures from an outsider's perspective, those cultures are often reduced to something delicious, desirable, and daring to consume, rather than existing on their own terms.

There is "orientalism" in the coverage, a term long used by cultural scholars to describe the distorted, distancing depictions of Eastern societies by Western ones. Edward W. Said, who popularized today's use of the term in his influential 1978 book of the same name, says that the Orient is attractive because it is "alien and unusual." But while the West is positioned as sophisticated and rational, the othered Orient is presented as "childlike" and "primitive."[1]

In bell hooks' classic essay "Eating the Other," she talks of how race and ethnicity can be made into "resources for pleasure": "Within commodity culture, ethnicity becomes spice ... The commodification of Otherness has been so successful because it is offered as a new delight, more intense, more satisfying than normal ways of doing and feeling."[2]

British journalist Yasmin Alibhai-Brown called this phenomenon the "Disneyfication" of racialized cultures, a trivializing process that reduces them to shallow elements like "saris, samosas, and steel drums."[3]

Sure, it's important for underrepresented groups to be spotlighted and celebrated in the news, but racialized people and their cultures are more than just something to be savoured by journalists and audiences on the hunt for difference. If journalists overemphasize the perspective of an outsider audience when approaching a specific culture, they can take the portrayal of that culture away from the people it belongs to.

— 'Tis the Season —

Move over, Thanksgiving and Easter! There's nothing like the rush of fascinated journalists covering an ethnocultural group on their holidays and heritage months, with headlines like "What Is Vaisakhi?"[4] "Ramadan: What's It All About?"[5] and "Diwali 101: How To Celebrate The Festival of Lights."[6] Why are these old and hugely celebrated holidays being presented as so foreign that they need an instruction manual?

It's true that "calendar journalism" isn't limited to non-Western holidays. Stories about New Year's Day babies, Halloween shenanigans, and Black Friday consumption madness are common fodder for journalists looking for seasonal coverage. Where it differs for racialized groups is that coverage peaks around these events then plummets the rest of the year. For example, experts in all things Asian Canadian have told me that May, which is Asian Heritage Month, is a hectic time because of the spike in reporters calling them for comment. Journalists have lists of usual suspects to visit, including those working at, say, a local temple or a cultural society, for locations to set their stories. The "ethnic" restaurant is a favourite, all the better if there's a special snack that symbolizes something about the holiday in question or comes with an old legend. Why are there walnuts for Lunar New Year? Why, because "Shaped like a brain, the Amber Sesame Walnut symbolizes intelligence, leading to abundance and wealth," says the *Toronto Star*.[7]

Journalists also tend to include trivia about how a specific holiday came to be ("Bandi Chhor Divas marks the release of the Sikh Guru Hargobindji in the 17th century"). There are descriptions of cultural practices and what they symbolize ("During Nowruz, the Persian New Year, people jump over fire as a purification ritual"). There are definitions of words that might be "new" to some audience members ("Diwali, by the way, means 'row of lights' in Sanskrit"; "A dhol, by the way, is a two-sided drum used throughout the Indian subcontinent"; "Hanbok is traditional Korean clothing"). And there are explanations of phrases, sometimes with pronunciation, to be learned and repeated ("Kung hey fat choi!" "Ramadan Mubarak!").

Am I being too picky about these light exchanges of culture? After all, there are going to be people in the audience who don't mark Eid al-Fitr or Mid-Autumn Festival but genuinely have an interest in learning more about them. And holidays of all cultures are indeed worth covering, to remind audiences that not all Canadians hold Christian holidays and official government public holidays with the same cultural importance. Again, the problem is not whether cultures are covered, but *how* they are covered. Journalists should of course introduce a holiday to audiences who are unfamiliar with it, but they should also cover the holiday for the people who do celebrate it. Too often, the stories that are published offer a collection of fun facts through a white gaze, inviting audiences to stare at the non-Western other.

What about the holidays that don't have any activities for out-group members to participate in? Qingming, the Chinese holiday where people clean the gravesites of their ancestors – "tomb-sweeping," it's called – is seldom reported on, likely because it's a sombre occasion difficult for out-groups to participate in. (Sorry, no stage performances or yummy food stalls on this holiday.) While there is a lot of reporting on delicious holidays, is there enough coverage of important cultural moments marked in private that don't have public displays like parades?

And outside of big calendar events, are journalists covering the ethnocultural groups the other days of the year?

— Race and Taste —

Who doesn't love eating something new?

Food journalism is an especially popular and non-controversial way for news outlets to showcase cultures. Coverage is done by reporters as well as food columnists, who present information journalistically, with research and interviews, though with the added subjectivity of their critiques. Food coverage takes up prominent space on air and in publications, with dedicated sections and expert journalists who are often beloved for being champions of cultural connection.

What better way for audiences to encounter the other than through food! Surely, culinary exchanges like food journalism can lead to acceptance? Racialized food, the fare of non-Western palates looked upon as belonging to the other, might be celebrated in such coverage, but it can still be held at a distance. Just because these dishes are enjoyed by white audiences doesn't mean they are free of the white gaze.

Racialized food is othered by journalists all the time. CityNews called fish balls at a night market "exotic" despite being an everyday protein in many East and Southeast Asian cuisines.[8] The *Ottawa Citizen* said that food trucks serving dal, dosas, and dumplings will make the city "more exciting, ethnic and fun."[9] The *National Post* once carried a story about congee that began with the questions "Want a delicious new way to eat rice? As in, a way that doesn't involve eating it from a little white takeout box?"[10] The writer seemed unaware that congee is three thousand years old, or that rice might exist outside Panda Express. My friend joked that I should write an article about toast, the delicious new way to eat bread.

This coverage raises questions about positionality. "Exotic" to who? "Exciting" and "ethnic" to who? "New" to who? In Canada, Eurocentric foods tend to be the baseline by which all other cuisines are measured. It is from this baseline that journalists hunt for "new" food experiences, and emphasize the crossing of boundaries into the world of the other as an adventure. Think back to what bell hooks said about the commodification and consumption of otherness; it can be presented as a "new delight, more intense, more satisfying than normal ways of doing and feeling."[11]

In other words, audiences are told that the more exotically they eat, the more cosmopolitan and culinarily experienced they are. Feminist scholar Uma Narayan says that racialized foods can be used to constitute a Western eater as a "colonial 'savant,' adding to her worldliness and prestige in much the same manner as 'knowledge' of faraway places she has visited."[12] It might've been exciting once to write about sushi (eating raw fish, what a thrill!). But as restaurants have multiplied, with sushi making its way into Western supermarkets and gas stations, journalists can no longer cover it as something new and exotic. They must turn to other racialized foods unfamiliar to the Western standpoint if they want to satiate their audiences.

Sometimes the othering is obvious. For example, the *Daily Hive* once published a guide to dim sum that introduced chicken feet as "Not everyone's first choice." "It's not the flavour that most people have the problem with," said the writer, "it's getting used to the gelatinous texture." That and "get[ting] over the fact that you're sucking on bird toes." Weird perhaps to a Western audience, but this is a cherished favourite known in Chinese as "phoenix claws."[13]

Othering can be hidden by reverence. Food journalists often express an over-the-top love for racialized dishes. In 2016, the *Globe and Mail* reviewed Walia, the latest Ethiopian restaurant to open among a small handful in Edmonton.[14] The food is described as boasting "exotic fragrances," "enticing scents," and a "raw authenticity that has not yet been whitewashed and distorted." The writer said that Ethiopian cuisine has yet to go mainstream, but that "one can only hope that it doesn't" because it's "best enjoyed when all the trappings of Western expectation are pared away and one is left with the unadulterated joy that comes from good, honest food." Saying that racialized food is better when it is raw, honest, authentic, and isn't whitewashed might sound like a compliment, but it exoticizes the food of the other by confining its identity to something distant and romanticized. In bell hooks' words, the food of the other offers "spice, seasoning that can liven up the dull dish that is mainstream white culture." Also, the title of the article stated that the restaurant is "an Experience Best Shared." It speaks to a Western audience used to eating dishes individually, because the Ethiopian dishes described in the article are always shared.

Distance makes racialized food more delicious and prestigious in the eyes of the white gaze, as it is made rare, different, and seemingly unknowable. The distance the audience has with the people who make the food – chefs from faraway places they've never heard of, or grandmothers employing ancestral secrets in the kitchen – adds to its alluring flavour. There isn't an adventure if there is no distance, meaning that the desire of the audience is rooted in the other remaining othered. A *Vancouver Magazine* article titled "Unexplored Territory" once called Indonesian, Malaysian, and Singaporean food "one of the world's greatest – yet least known – cuisines," while noting in the same paragraph that beef rendang, indigenous to this part of the world, was voted in a CNN poll as one of the world's most delicious foods.[15] This shows how valuable distance is to deliciousness, with journalists emphasizing it even when it's contradictory.

Journalists play a role in brokering that distance between white audiences and racialized food cultures, telling them why it's worth a try by assuaging their fears and using Western reference points to describe the eats. In a *Globe and Mail* article, an Ethiopian meat dish called chacha, which is served on a skillet, is compared to a fajita platter.

"[Not] every cross-cultural meal is an intentional act of colonization or neo-colonial Othering," acknowledge Canadian food sociologists Josée Johnston and Shyon Baumann.[16] But at the same time, they note that "the foodie's search for exotic culinary adventures cannot be viewed in a power vacuum, or solely in terms of an individual's intentions, but must be placed in a larger geopolitical context."

How can journalists ensure that their food coverage goes beyond the white gaze? They can start by asking which local cuisines are being covered and what's the reasoning behind these choices. Is it driven by an ongoing desire to cover local diasporas often left out of news media? Or are journalists letting Western food trends from social media, celebrity chefs, or global publications like *Bon Appétit* dictate which racialized cultures are deserving of coverage? When journalists share their coverage, how are racialized foods introduced to audiences unfamiliar with them? Is the focus on the audience and how they might experience such food? Or does the coverage prominently feature the point of view of the people and culture to whom the food belongs?

— New and Newsy Cravings —

Outside of holidays and heritage months, a news moment can spotlight a culture that the white gaze is unfamiliar with.

When the Korean film *Parasite* won the Oscar for Best Picture in 2020, news outlets like the CBC reported on the Korean instant noodles featured in the film. The two brands, Neoguri and Chapagetti, have been around since the early 1980s and can be found in just about every East Asian supermarket but were experiencing a newfound deliciousness due to Western audiences coming to know them through the film.[17] It's not that such moments aren't worth covering, but the status of racialized food as a discovery by white audiences can overshadow its heritage.

In 2021, a *Globe* recipe for smashed cucumbers openly acknowledged this problem of discovery with the headline "Smashed Cucumber Is All the Rage – But the Technique Isn't New."[18] "[They] seem to be everywhere, from restaurant menus to recipe columns," wrote food columnist Lucy Waverman. "Whether the inspiration is Asian, Middle Eastern or European, the technique is universal – but it is not new. Smashing cucumbers is an ancient Chinese practice, pairing the heady, intense, spicy food of Sichuan province with the coolness of cucumbers to offset the heat." This acknowledgment is an uncommon and welcome touch, helping educate readers caught up in a foodie trend about the history behind what they're making.

A news moment that spotlights food doesn't have to be a positive one. It might be a tumultuous one, like the war in Syria or the Taliban takeover of Afghanistan, causing journalists to take a sudden interest in cultures they've previously overlooked only as they are pulled into global headlines. For international crises that last months, newsrooms will be on the lookout for creative ways to cover them. Editors situated in Canada often ask their reporters to hunt down local angles to piggyback off of the attention of the news moment.

A 2018 *New York Times* headline perfectly described the hastiness: "Toronto Suddenly Has a New Craving: Syrian Food."[19] The author of the feature included some meta commentary on the suddenness of it all, describing the media attention as "overwhelming." One non-profit made up of Syrian women chefs who sell takeout dinners has been "the subject of dozens of news stories around the world, and a documentary film is in the works." Another Syrian chef, recently arrived from Aleppo, said of the attention that there is "almost too much media."

Stories like these – whether it's recent arrivals from Syria or Afghanistan, or groups that settled years earlier during similarly traumatic circumstances, from Vietnam or Cambodia – mingle pain and sorrow with deliciousness. In 2017, *Scout* magazine ran a headline that included the phrase "The Delicious Things That Refugees Bring."[20] One *Province* story about a Palestinian restaurant mentions how the owner, who spent eleven years in the world's largest refugee camp in Lebanon, "Heals [The] World One Dish At A Time" through a menu "connecting all of the Middle East."[21] The author muses about how chefs have the power to "put aside history and politics and make beautiful food together." Foods like bolani and manakeesh aren't only introduced to audiences with Western tastes who want to feel cosmopolitan but also those who want to feel charitable and humanitarian.[22]

This kind of bumper coverage of delicious culture is complicated. Big global events and local connections to them, especially when life and death are concerned, deserve to be covered, but there's a risk of insensitivity. For journalists reporting on cultures during a time of turmoil, be careful of putting opportunities for consumption at the centre of stories and turning the gravity of a situation into a side dish. Rather than rushing in and trying to hang a frame on a story to tie it to events unfolding abroad, listen.

— Aged Products —

Yum, round rice cakes to symbolize coins for prosperity![23] Ah, the sacrifice of an animal to represent Ibrahim's willingness to sacrifice his son![24] Here come a Korean couple wearing traditional hanbok on their wedding day as they bow to their elders![25] These details make for colourful journalism, whether it's an exciting sound bite of songs or prayers, an action-packed video clip of some cultural performance, or a sensory opening sentence that invites white audiences into worlds they're unfamiliar with.

Journalists and audiences love these depictions of culture because they feel authentic – that is, rooted in the distant past and places far away from Canada. Portrayals of racialized culture in Canadian journalism are often dusty and dated. Culture is ever changing, but you wouldn't know it from stories that revere and romanticize all things ancient. Practices that take place in Canada will have diasporic twists. It's important for journalists to report on how traditions have evolved or taken on geographic variations. Perhaps it's difficult for an ethnocultural group to practice their culture where they live, whether because they have a small population, because it's hard to find the right ingredients to cook dishes, or because of discrimination. These are all important ways of covering culture. If journalists cover culture as people practising a tradition exactly as it's described in a history book, they'll miss how it's practiced in reality.

Grounded coverage of culture is admittedly going to be less delicious to a white gaze that wants to see the exotic and the theatrical. Hearing about adults beaming Lunar New Year money via WeChat is going to appear less exotic in a sentence or photo than an image of children bowing before elders to receive an envelope. The CBC once covered seven thousand Muslims celebrating Eid al-Fitr at Vancouver's BC Place, a stadium where concerts and football games take place, greeting one another in the middle of the big grassy field.[26] It showed how a non-Christian holiday was being celebrated in a big way at a mainstream venue, eschewing more run-of-the-mill coverage depicting the holiday at mosques. Another story, this time in the *North Shore News,* showed images of young Iranian Canadians jumping over bonfires for Chaharshanbe Suri wearing North Face jackets on a popular beach where people swim and surf. It was representation of people participating in cultural traditions, but with a Canadian setting. Such details help situate a culture in the present and in a specific place, to show how the culture and people can adapt and localize. This too is part of representation and avoids the misrepresentation of racialized people as being out of time and stuck in a pre-modern existence. Coverage doesn't always look like ethnic people doing obviously ethnic things on big ethnic days wearing very ethnic clothing.

— How to Make an Introduction? —

With all of these potential pitfalls, how do you introduce a culture to an audience through journalism?

Culture is indeed a delicious thing to cover. But journalists can get carried away emphasizing the novelty of a culture that they or Western readers are unfamiliar with. This results in essentialist, exoticizing, and othering portrayals.

Journalists need to be wary of the inequalities at play with respect to which cultures are considered delicious and which are deemed not delicious enough to be reported on. There will always be holidays and heritage months, social movements like Black Lives Matter, and global trends like K-pop. But covering racialized and ethnocultural groups is more than just a flavour of the month. The white gaze of newsrooms can develop a taste for a handful of cultures, especially when they're in the media spotlight, while ignoring and stigmatizing others if they're out of the zeitgeist. Journalists have a responsibility to ensure that racial and ethnocultural groups that live within their markets don't get ignored.

There is always room for those crash courses on culture to create connection, to build familiarity, to educate, and to foster acceptance. But don't forget about the importance of showcasing racialized and ethnocultural experiences from the inside out. The worst kind of journalism puts out-group audiences on a tour bus to react to people different from them. If reporting caters to the tourists but is of no interest to the very people whom the story is about, what's the point?

DAMAGED

Understanding darlings and deviants requires unpacking model minorities and racialized behaviours. Deliciousness is complex, too, and helps us analyze how cultures can be turned into objects of consumption. But stories about damaged people of colour? This isn't a difficult D to comprehend. It follows that old saying in journalism: if it bleeds, it leads.

The news is filled with people of colour as victims: refugees fleeing oppression, immigrants targeted by predators, vulnerable workers under the mercy of their employers, or marginalized individuals in Canada and their experiences of racism in daily life. Such coverage is usually tied to a newsy hook that sends journalists after people of colour to collect their experiences related to some big current event, whether it's the war that drove them from their home country or the rise of hate in the face of a pandemic. Some news items like immigration are evergreen, a staple of Canadian journalism as a nation of immigrants, with journalists reporting on the troubles that newcomers experience both during and after their journeys.

Abuse, violence, war, displacement, racism – these are all news-worthy and part of the lived realities of people of colour in Canada. But how do journalists portray those who experience these hardships? Are they victims and nothing more? Are they passive with no agency? Journalists have a duty to inform audiences about the experiences of racialized people, but they must do so without dehumanizing them.

— Victimized —

When journalism only depicts people of colour as suffering, pushed around, and caught in dangerous situations, it creates the impression that they are inherently helpless. This can happen if and when people of colour are portrayed as lacking agency. Rather than having the ability to act, they are acted upon by others. Namelessness and facelessness can further dehumanize them, turning them into anonymous subjects, like in news stories that rely solely on police reports about victims of colour.

With the increase in anti-Asian hate incidents in Canada during the COVID-19 pandemic,[27] there were many news stories about visibly East Asian people who'd been abused and attacked, from being punched in the face to shoved to the ground.[28] These are important incidents to document, but with journalists sharing one story after another, there was overrepresentation of ethnically East Asian people as victims.

This D has echoes of the white gaze's racist dismissal of Indigenous people's lives as "nasty, brutish, and short." Flip through some old news stories and see how many different kinds of victims you can spot.

Many newcomers are preyed upon and exploited. It might be happening because middlemen are taking advantage of them, in stories like "Dozens of Migrant Workers in Vancouver Victims of

Immigration Scam, Lawsuit Alleges."[29] It might be happening because of public policy that paves the way for exploitation, in stories like "Foreign Students Accuse Canada of Exploiting Them for 'Cheap Labour'"[30] and "Jamaican Migrant Workers in Ontario Pen Open Letter Likening Conditions to 'Systematic Slavery.'"[31] Seasonal farm workers from other parts of the world are one group that's been in the headlines over the years, with reports of unpaid wages and poor living conditions. Another group is caregivers from the Philippines, with stories of abuse going unreported because of the power imbalance inherent in the relationship between them and their employer, and worries about jeopardizing their status in Canada.

It's not just recent newcomers who struggle, either. There are stories about immigrants who have lived in Canada for a number of years but are still jobless and without a permanent home.[32] There are stories about immigrants who have long been citizens and Canadian-borns who encounter bigotry, discrimination, violence, and hate.

If there is only representation of nastiness, brutality, and mortality, what else are audiences supposed to believe?

The Dart Center for Journalism and Trauma, a project of the Columbia University Graduate School of Journalism, has identified a problem called "Act I journalism."[33] "If the 'Act I' of journalism is the immediate reporting of what happened and how people were impacted – the blood and pain, the violence and the despair," reads one of their guides on trauma-informed reporting, "'Act II' is the often unreported narrative of what happened next." BBC journalist Peter Burdin is quoted in the guide as saying that reporters often provide a "diet of raw emotion." "We capture the grief, the anger, the tears but there are many more human emotions and a range of feelings which are excluded from our obsession with the immediate. To truly reflect our world we need to report those more discreet human responses as people seek to rebuild their lives and reconcile themselves to what happened to them."

— From Dystopia to Utopia —

While there are journalists who tell complex stories about how life isn't easy for people just because they make it to Canada, there is a category of coverage that takes a more binary approach. In it, migrants are portrayed as having wholly terrible lives in their countries of origin before coming to the utopia that is Canada.

Audiences hear about death, depression, rape, separation, suicide, surveillance, and violence. A family trapped in Syria during the civil war.[34] A young man's father killed by the Taliban.[35] A woman in Iran who fled her abusive husband.[36] From there, journalists chronicle their challenging odysseys to Canada. Starvation. Sleeping on chairs. Forced into sex work by smugglers. Caught in bureaucratic limbo, with fear of deportation.[37]

These stories frame a migrant's point of origin and their Canadian destination as opposites: refugees flee a bad place to get to Canada, a good place. A CBC story described a Syrian refugee as choosing to "start a new life from zero."[38] In another story about a Syrian refugee, she was quoted as saying, "the darkness is behind us and now we can start chasing that ray of hope."[39] More recently, a former Afghan refugee said the latest cohort arriving in Canada is now "free from any form of violence [and] persecution."[40]

It's a black-and-white view of the world: Western countries like Canada are home to stable civilization while chaos reigns elsewhere. Arriving in Canada is portrayed as the ultimate destination for those seeking to heal from past traumas. Journalists quote refugees saying things like, "You'll be safe, you won't go hungry," "You'll find a good country, good people," "If you want to do it, you will do it,"[41] "People are all the same, there is no separation of classes,"[42] and "Thank God we reached here."[43] In a story about newly minted Canadians voting for the first time, one individual said, "Democracy is awesome."[44] Visuals drive home the idea of Canada as a utopia with stories of happy refugees wearing red-and-white face paint or waving the flag of their new country.[45]

The stories also allow comfortable Canadians – whether they're local-born or foreign-born, white or not – to feel good about their country and affirmed about what it stands for. Canada is portrayed as a safe place. Canada is a country in high demand. A benevolent promised land that they're now part of, one that welcomes those from troubled parts of the world. The more damage experienced by racialized migrants from their places of origin, the warmer the image of Canada.

— What's the Damage? —

Journalists tell us that bad stuff happens to people of colour, but why does it happen, and what's next? This D features people of colour who are up against powerful forces, from totalitarian regimes and agents looking to exploit the vulnerability of a populace or a people, to a Canadian government that welcomes them but doesn't offer enough support. What people can do against such forces might be limited, but it's still important for journalists to show how migrants are making decisions about their lives in the face of adversity.

If characters are unable to act, journalists can lay out the systemic and political forces that racialized people are up against so that audiences understand that they're not frozen because of some inherent flaw or weakness, but because they're up against great odds. It's important for journalists to take the time to explain why hardship and obstacles exist in the first place, rather than simply serve up coverage based on raw emotion. What makes racialized people vulnerable? Why are there cracks in our systems? In the story I wrote about the racism experienced by low-income immigrant seniors who recycle bottles and cans, I included quotes from a social worker who explained that these seniors are viewed as easy targets by racists who take advantage of their poor physical condition and inability to speak up to rob them using physical force. Journalists can include details like these that educate audiences about a specific group's unique marginality, rather than conveying the impression that a group is suffering consequences because they are weak.

Context helps educate audiences and shows them where social change is needed. Suffering shouldn't be described as a natural and inevitable part of the lives of racialized people. Rather than showing how workers are being abused at a job site, a story can illustrate the perils of immigration and labour policy that lead to such things. Rather than just show police violence against Black Canadians, a story can illustrate how this is part of a pattern and ask whether anything is being done to remedy it. Rather than just show people of colour caught in the middle of a COVID-19 outbreak, a story can explain how social factors affect health outcomes for different marginalized groups. By all means, journalists should report on the damage that racialized people are experiencing. But they should remember to explain to the audience why it exists in the first place.

A DELUGE OF Ds

Set aside this book for a moment and scan the stories of the day that feature people of colour. How many of them feature one of the four Ds?

As I'm writing this, I had a look myself and here's what I found.

"How Immigrants from Benin Saved a Quebec Town's Storied Poutinerie" is a *Globe and Mail* story about how a couple from the West African nation became the "surprising new owners" of a business that's been around since the 1960s – a tale of darlings taking over the business with "no intention of changing a winning formula" and long-term plans to export the Canadian dish to the place they come from.[46] To describe how integrated they've become, the journalist mentions that they are citizens who use Québécois expressions, including Catholic curse words.

"Police Warn Public to Stay Away from 2 Surrey Men with Gang Connections" is a Global News story that doesn't explicitly mention the race of the two men, but the mention of Surrey and gangs coupled with the photos of two South Asian men places this story against sustained coverage over many years that portrays them as racialized deviants.[47] You can argue that these are just the facts of the story, but you only need to look at the comments on places like Facebook to see how audiences have been socialized to read coverage of crime in a racialized way, chiming in about having the two men "sent back where they came from" and saying they're not real Canadians.[48]

"Gurdeep Pandher is Canada's Favourite Bhangra Dancer and All-purpose Good Vibes Ambassador" is a CBC story about a Punjab-born, Yukon-based teacher who's been dancing with minor hockey teams, members of the Canadian Forces, and combining it with Indigenous drumming and Celtic dance – a delicious tale of cultural connection that could only happen in what is portrayed as pluralistic Canada.[49]

"'I Helped So Many Canadians'" is a CTV story about a former Afghan interpreter for the Canadian military pleading for the federal government to let his family, currently being harassed by the Taliban, into the country. Yet another tale about the damage experienced by refugees.[50]

Stories about darlings, deviants, deliciousness, and damage are a reflection of where we are at this point in time in Canadian history: a multicultural society in a nation with colonial legacies, high rates of immigration, and both fascination and stigmatization of non-Western cultures. Depending on the concerns of the day, the common tropes will shift, says Duncan McCue. In *Decolonizing Journalism,* he notes some newer tropes about Indigenous people that have popped up in recent decades, such as the corrupt financial manager and the noble environmentalist.

Perhaps you've noticed new categories of Ds about people of colour showing up in the news with increasing regularity. One that I've spotted on the rise could be called "disoriented," when the children or grandchildren of immigrants feel like they're caught between two cultures while living in Canada. They talk about how their families and cultures of heritage cause tensions with Western life. They might even blame their cultures for being regressive. (More on this kind of essentialism later.) While these experiences of diasporic disorientation have been felt in Canada for over a century – for a discussion of the experience in America, there is an influential book on the matter titled *Disoriented: Asian Americans, Law, and the Nation-State* by Robert S. Chang[51] – there is an increasing number of venues, from classrooms to online communities, for children of racialized immigrants and refugees to explore issues of identity, as well as works of popular media that reflect them. With the prominence of these discussions, newsrooms have also been running stories that show how cultural pluralism is formed. As such, I believe this D will continue to gain prominence.

It gets tricky when racialized sources embrace generalizations and stereotypes. Some will happily tell media that they're from an intrinsically hardworking culture, wanting to be known as darlings for the struggles they've overcome and the successes they've achieved.[52] One global example of this is the Philippine government calling Filipino workers "bagong bayani" (modern heroes)[53] as if they make better workers – part of a branding exercise to bolster labour exports. Some racialized sources will play up the exotic aspects of their culture when they talk to media, perhaps chefs discussing secret techniques passed down to them by their elders.

There are also common ways in which the Ds overlap. There's the "damaged darling," which is when a newcomer with a traumatic past manages to succeed in Canada – perhaps a refugee who raises hardworking children, or an immigrant who pushes through workplace discrimination to send their earnings overseas to their loved ones. That can become a triple D, the "damaged, delicious darling" cherished for sharing their culture. Audiences especially love hearing inspirational odysseys behind their favourite eats.

Some of the most popular stories I've ever written have had protagonists that fall into this special category of darling. In 2016, I wrote a feature about Vancouver's legendary Duffin's Donuts, a casual 24/7 restaurant serving subs, tortas, tamales, phở, the Fritou brand of Québécois fried chicken, and doughnuts in varieties that you're more likely to come across in Southern California than at a Tim Hortons. There's the angel, dusted with powdered sugar, and doughnuts made with buttermilk. The restaurant is located on the Knight Street truck route, which runs through an otherwise quiet part of residential South Vancouver. A giant red sign with *Duffin's* in cartoony letters rises from the parking lot to make sure passersby don't miss this oasis. The clientele at night and in the early mornings range from weary truckers looking to fuel up to drunk partyers looking for high-calorie munchies.

The long-time owners of Duffin's are a refugee couple from Cambodia who fled to Thailand before making their way to Ottawa in 1983. The husband worked as a hospital cook and the wife worked at a nursing home. Three years later, they visited relatives in Los Angeles who, like many other Cambodian refugees, entered into the doughnut business. There, the couple learned the trade before bringing it over to Vancouver with some of California's Latino eats tagging along. The line I used to describe the extensive offerings: "a map of migration on a mosaic of a menu."

I wrote the story because I love doughnuts, but also because locals like to describe racialized businesses with eclectic menus like Duffin's as "random." Through my story, I wanted to show that as people move around, they take pick up flavours and recipes from each place they spend time in and bring them along with them. Duffin's must've been pleased with the story, because a printed copy, on the cover of the *Vancouver Courier,* is still up on the wall.

This story caught the attention of two scholars of English and geography, who dissected my story in an article for the journal *Canadian Literature* titled "Donut Time."[54] They approached my story with a critical and theoretical eye far deeper than my own profile of Duffin's, examining the cost of 24/7 labour that a generation of refugees has had to pay to become model minorities – a complex analysis of the common ingredients that are the diversity Ds.

— To D or Not To D? —

Is it fair to be so critical about these Ds? As I said, journalists are not fiction writers. We don't make up stories. So, can we really be blamed for stereotyping people of colour when we stumble upon the story of a lovable model minority who loves Canada, or a refugee starting over after losing their family to war?

And how can journalists be expected to counter common tropes by diving deep into inequality, institutional racism, cultural nuances, and other complicated matters in such limited length, while meeting the strict deadlines of today's around-the-clock news cycle? Not to mention the short attention spans of online readers who spend on average only one or two minutes reading an article.[55]

Journalists might be dedicated to the truth through the recounting of facts, but we do select and frame those facts. Duncan McCue reminds journalists that we need to convey accurate facts *in context*. This is something journalists can do whether they have five seconds on a TikTok or a five-thousand-word feature.

Again, there's nothing wrong with covering stories on any of the Ds! There will be many stories that rely on them that are indeed newsworthy. There will be many audience members, white or non-white, who will be interested in them. None of the tropes are inherently good or bad. Rather, it's about how they are used.

Does the audience learn anything new? Are the stories reductive, or do they complexify certain issues? Is the representation of racialized people a sanitized vision of "diversity without oppression"?[56] Are the characters flat or human? Is there information about the worlds and structures they inhabit? Regarding a news outlet's body of work, are journalists writing a variety of stories about people of colour, or are they constantly relying on the Ds? "What happens when a frame breaks with itself is that a taken-for-granted reality is called into question, exposing the orchestrating designs of the authority who sought to control the frame," says American philosopher Judith Butler.[57] In the case of the Ds, myths like racial stereotypes and the model minority deserve to be challenged.

The actor Constance Wu, known for her role in *Crazy Rich Asians* and for playing a Taiwanese American immigrant parent in the television series *Fresh Off the Boat,* has offered an interesting challenge to representation. She was once interviewed about stereotypes of Asian Americans.[58] "Rather than avoiding stereotypes, I think we ... need to sink into them because Hollywood really did them wrong the first time," she said. "So rather than reinforcing the idea that these 'stereotypes' are inherently shameful, I think we need truly great actors who can humanize these stereotypes, so rather than being reductive, they're expansive." In the same way, how can journalists take stories that start off as one of the four Ds and make them reflective of the complexities of reality?

If racial and ethnocultural diversity is reported on in the same ways over and over, the audience will have limited impressions of people of colour. The news needs that diverse representation, but it also needs a diversity of stories.

Of Intersections and Identity

Race, ethnicity, and culture popped into conversations more frequently when I entered high school. How could it not when I lived in a part of Vancouver with a population that was more ethnoculturally diverse than the city as a whole? In the 2000s, people of colour made up half of Vancouver, but in my neighbourhood of Oakridge, we were 75 percent.[1] You didn't need to look at the census to tell you that. You could tell just by scanning the faces of my schoolmates at Eric Hamber Secondary.

As 2010 graduates, we were the first generation of teenagers to play around with Facebook. Someone had made a group on the platform called "You know You Go to Hamber When ..." One of the first entries was about knowing what it's like to be lost in the "sea of black hair." That's how we treated identity at that age, connecting appearances and behaviours to race and ethnicity. The majority of our "minorities" were Asian, specifically with roots from China, Hong Kong, Taiwan, the Philippines, India, Korea, and Vietnam. We were a mix of Canadian-borns and those born overseas. Because of this, there was a generic two-word phrase that we regularly used for a myriad of meanings: "So Asian."

When I was age twelve, a classmate approached me with a business proposition: she wanted to pay me to hack into someone's email account. I told her I didn't know how, which confused her. "But you're Asian," she said. I'm not sure who or what TV show taught her that being Asian meant that we would all be computer masterminds at such a young age.

"So Asian" was used all the time in school to describe how we looked, how we dressed, how we acted, what we liked, and what we believed. You're taking Advanced Placement courses? Playing on the ping-pong team? So Asian! Is that Cup Noodles you're heating for lunch? Writing notes with gel pens? How Asian of you! Your parents won't let you go to sleepovers? They bought you a jacket a size larger because they wanted you to grow into it? How Asian of them!

We Vancouverites in Canada weren't the only ones having these discussions in the 2000s. Other cities around the world with a multicultural mix of teens, from Los Angeles to Melbourne, were having them. They made memes to make sense of it all, like "High Expectations Asian Father," who would say things like "You got 99 problems? Must solve each one." There were YouTube creators who churned out videos like "THINGS ASIAN PARENTS DO,"[2] from saving plastic bags to refusing to turn on the heating in the house on cold days. Subtle Asian Traits, a Facebook group with two million members, would later appear on the scene, sharing content like this for solidarity.[3]

As we grew older, we tweaked our discourse slightly, despite not maturing in our understanding. Instead of saying "so Asian," we started to describe things as being part of "Asian culture." Parents strict about curfews and dating? Parents who never use the dishwasher? Parents who save extra napkins and condiments from the food court? Ah, it's because of their Asian culture. We didn't question how ridiculous it was to assume that something like stashing ketchup and soy sauce packets could be a cultural practice, let alone one shared by the 4.6 billion people worldwide who might be described as Asian.

This way of looking at identity culture isn't just held by teens. It shows up in journalism too.

Tolkien Diversity

The CBC once ran a headline about podcasters: "Calling Out Toxic Attitudes in Filipino Culture" such as body-shaming and colourism.[4] The *Vancouver Sun* ran similar headlines, such as "Ethnic Chinese Groups Protest LGBT Programs Again," accompanied by the caption "Chinese leaders in Metro Vancouver ... have long opposed schools instituting anti-homophobia policies. Now the issue has turned to transgender rights."[5]

But is body-shaming really an intrinsic part of Filipino culture? And is being against queer education intrinsic to being Chinese? Just like the immature understandings of race held by my cohort of high schoolers, Canadian journalism often features these broad brush understandings of race, ethnicity, and culture. This way of framing identity is vague, misleading, and reductive.

If ever you've read or watched *The Lord of the Rings*, then you'll know that Middle-Earth is populated by elves who are graceful and love nature, dwarves who are stubborn and love the earth, and hobbits who are simple-minded and love comfort. Author J.R.R. Tolkien treats race as a marker that defines how its members act, a treatment that has trickled down to much of modern fantasy. It's similar to how journalists treat markers of identity like race, ethnicity, culture, nationality, and so on as catch-all explanations for everything from values to personality. In our survey of the four Ds, you'll have noticed that this kind of "Tolkien-ism" happens a lot, associating Asianness with hard work or Blackness and Brownness with criminality.

Journalists give subjects of colour space to speak generally and authoritatively about their own backgrounds in this way. These sources make definitive statements such as "cooking is how Chinese parents express love,"[6] or how living under a roof without one's parents "isn't an option"[7] in Indian culture, communicating to audiences that everyone within one of these groups acts the same. For the journalists who don't question such sweeping statements, is it because they don't have the education or experience to do so? Is it because they just trust ethnic people to know their ethnic stuff? Is it because the generalizations fit with what they feel is true about an ethnocultural group, and sound true enough to publish? Or is it because they feel like it would be inappropriate, even racist, to challenge someone about an identity they claim?

In 2016, the CBC covered a story about how BC's Fraser Health Authority was working with South Asian institutions within its large service area to encourage people to cut down on fat and sugar in their diets, as part of an effort to reduce rates of heart disease and Type 2 diabetes.[8] The opening of the story reads: "'When you look at South Asian culture, they enjoy their food, they enjoy their sweets, and so people are just used to high sugary food but they don't understand the repercussions of that,' said Deljit Bains, manager of the South Asian Health Institute."

Journalists might not feel that they need to add context around sources speaking about their own cultures, especially ones with dignified titles. But it's important for journalists to ask themselves what race, ethnicity, and culture are being defined as in their stories, especially if the chance for an underrepresented group to be misrepresented is high.

In the story about diets, is the journalist communicating to the audience that it's part of a specific culture to eat sugary food and ignore health repercussions? Does the journalist imply that if a South Asian person does not eat sugary food, they'd lose some of their South Asianness? Ascribing behaviours to race and cultures ignores other factors at play in stories about social issues as multifaceted as health. How might class and education play a role in what people choose to eat? How might geography and finances affect access to fitness and healthy food? When markers of identity are treated as destiny, journalists should be alerted to the need for more explanation.

What's missing? Intersectionality.

A Prism for Identity

Intersectionality can help journalists unpack complicated social issues, go beyond the shallowness of the four Ds, and reveal the humanity of their subjects in their reporting.

If you've only heard this term used by conservatives, you'll have a very different impression of the word than its intended meaning. Like "woke," "intersectionality" has been blasted by right-wingers, particularly in the US, called everything from a "conspiracy theory of victimization"[9] to "really dangerous" by conservative commentator Ben Shapiro. He described it as a "form of identity politics in which the value of your opinion depends on how many victim groups you belong to."[10] As *Vox* pointed out, it's a "highly unusual level of disdain" for a word that was relatively obscure outside of academic circles until recently.[11]

So what exactly is intersectionality? The ideas behind it have been around for decades, but the term was coined and defined by Kimberlé Crenshaw, a Black American legal scholar, in 1989.[12] The theory originated as a way to describe how Black women experienced different forms of oppression, but it has since expanded into a way to understand myriad social identities.

Intersectionality describes the ways in which social categories – such as race, class, gender, sexuality, age, ability, citizenship status, religion, appearance, and more – combine and shape how a person experiences life, from privilege to oppression.

The term came about because Crenshaw was concerned that the law seemed to neglect how Black women were subject to discrimination due to race, gender, and sometimes a combination of both.[13] She reviewed a case from 1976, when five Black women who worked for General Motors in St. Louis sued the company. For years, there were Black jobs available on the factory floor, but they were considered "men's jobs." There were "women's jobs" available, such as secretary positions, but they were for white people only.[14] The company eventually began hiring Black women, but when seniority-based layoffs hit, they were the first to go. As a result, the five women alleged discrimination on the bases of both race and gender.

The courts noted that General Motors did hire women (albeit white women) and concluded that the seniority system could not have been sexist. The courts dismissed the claim about racial discrimination, asking that the plaintiffs consolidate it with another case against General Motors alleging racial discrimination.

The five women were frustrated because theirs was not a claim of racial discrimination: it was discrimination on the basis that they were both Black *and* women. But Judge Harris Wangelin argued that creating a new category for Black women would be problematic because that would put them in greater standing than Black men. And from there, where would it stop? In the judge's words: "The prospect of the creation of new classes of protected minorities, governed only by the mathematical principles of permutation

and combination, clearly raises the prospect of opening the hack-
neyed Pandora's box."[15]

Over four decades later, this argument against intersectionality
still persists, with such critics as Canadian author, media personality, and psychology professor Jordan Peterson. Peterson, in a piece
for the *National Post,* didn't make reference to the 1976 case, but
picked up on the judge's "Pandora's box" criticism that intersectionality would result in endless permutations of identity. Peterson did
some math for comedic effect, starting with the social identities of
race and gender, and going on to multiply it by class brackets and
various disabilities, producing equations like "$30 \times 2 \times 2 \times 2 \times 2 \times 2 \times 2 \times 2 \times 2 \times 2$." He came to the conclusion that there are a min-
imum of thirty thousand identity categories to consider, with the
greater possibility of "endless multiplication of categories of victimization." It's a silly argument that tries to dismiss Crenshaw's
enduring observation that looking at certain issues with a "single
axis" ignores how privilege and discrimination can be compounded
in distinct ways.

Use of the term "intersectionality" has increased over the years,
finding its way into fourth-wave feminism in the 2010s[16] and everyday use as it's been adopted by dictionaries. But the term has also
picked up unintended meanings, in what Crenshaw calls a "very
bad game of telephone."[17] "The way we imagine discrimination
or disempowerment often is more complicated for people who
are subjected to multiple forms of exclusion," she said at a 2017
event. "The good news is that intersectionality provides us a way
to see it."[18]

For journalists, introducing intersectionality helps audiences
understand social issues in multiple dimensions. A story about temporary foreign workers gains new insight if the journalist chooses
to focus on gendered experiences. A story about an ethnocultural
community will be different depending on whether a journalist

gathers perspectives from Canadian-borns, long-time immigrants, or newcomers. A story about newcomers will reveal marginality if it compares those with little transferable education to English-speaking retirees with a lifetime of savings. A story about a refugee who is LGBTQ2S+ will reveal unique persecutions they have experienced on their journey to Canada.[19] A story about racism experienced by a Sikh man will be different depending on how visible his religious identity is, such as wearing a turban. Without intersectionality, we wouldn't understand the multidimensional experiences of the people behind the headlines.

I can understand why someone might feel like the categories are "endless," as Peterson has said.[20] But he views intersectionality as a kind of "multiplication," calculating identities as if they're points to be tallied. Instead, Crenshaw defines it as "a prism for seeing the way in which various forms of inequality often operate together and exacerbate each other."[21]

"Intersectionality is simply about how certain aspects of who you are will increase your access to the good things or your exposure to the bad things in life," she explains.[22] "We've got to be open to looking at all of the ways our systems reproduce these inequalities, and that includes the privileges as well as the harms."

Down to the Essentials

Without intersectionality, journalists gravitate towards "essentialism," which is the belief that a category of people possesses a set of fixed characteristics intrinsic to their existence.[23]

Essentialism can apply to negative stereotypes ("All women are bad drivers"), but also seemingly positive stereotypes ("All Black people are musical") or seemingly neutral descriptions ("All gay men love shopping"). Whatever the intention, using a single axis of identity to make generalizations about behaviour can be discriminatory, dehumanizing, enforce bogus views of biology, cover up causes of inequality, and deny differences within a group of people.

One especially egregious example of essentialism in journalism is a cover story published by *Maclean's* in 2010, originally titled "Too Asian: Some Frosh Don't Want to Study at an Asian University."[24] The story is still referred to with infamy in Asian Canadian studies. Its thesis was that white students were avoiding universities that were "too Asian." These schools, according to the semi-anonymous main sources, were a "bit of a killjoy." The two journalists who authored the story described supposed differences between white and Asian students on campus. (Never mind that they use the descriptor "Asian" loosely when they really mean East Asian.) Ethnically Asian students are described as "strivers, high achievers and single-minded in their approach to university" who "risk alienating their more fun-loving peers" and prefer being part of "segregated, self-selecting, discrete communities."

To support these claims, the authors quoted a former admissions officer at Stanford University who said that "there's a long tradition in Chinese culture, for example, going back to Confucius, of social mobility based on merit." As a result, the value of education has been "drilled" into Asian students by the parents, explain the authors. They included a brief quote from a retired professor of education who added that Asian immigrants to Canada are highly educated, resulting in highly educated children. The authors summed up their evidence with the phrase, "That Asian students work harder is a fact born[e] out by hard data."

The story resulted in tremendous backlash from readers, campus groups, Asian Canadian scholars, and prominent journalists, to councils of cities with large East Asian diaspora populations,[25] even prompting them to pass motions in condemnation. While such action might give elected officials a boost in popularity for speaking out against the story and for taking a stand on behalf of their constituents, it's highly unusual for a piece of journalism to spur such formal action from a civic government.

There were numerous criticisms of the piece. The framing was accused of being racist,[26] from use of the invasion narrative to presenting racialized students as unassimilable "forever foreigners" who self-segregate. (Well done if you guessed that a title like "Too Asian" would mean that deviants make an appearance.) The reporting methods have been criticized too, with the former chair of the journalism school at Toronto Metropolitan University[27] calling out "horrendous journalism no-nos." He noted that the story's claim that a "growing cohort of student [is] eschewing some big-time schools over perceptions that they're too Asian" has no evidence to back it up – only the two main anonymous sources referred to as "Alexandra" and "Rachel."

Racial essentialism is a problem throughout the story. A coalition of groups from across Canada, ranging from scholars to labour to activists, signed a letter in response to the story's portrayal of the vague "Asian" student.

The media often portray Asian Canadians in homogeneous ways and fail to account for diversity within the group. They do not distinguish among Asians who are Canadian-born, naturalized citizens, newcomer immigrants, or international students. They neglect to consider the varying educational circumstances of Asian Canadians based on income, class, gender, religion, and language. They lump all Asian Canadians together regardless of their ancestral background, whether they are from China, India, Japan, South Korea, the Philippines, Vietnam, or Sri Lanka ... [t]hey failed to acknowledge the various structural roots of the academic and social struggles that many Asian Canadian students experience. They also missed seeing how community groups are addressing barriers that hinder their goals and pathways for genuine settlement, integration, and well-being in this country.[28]

In other words, alongside the story's biased reporting, it also lacked intersectionality.

As for *Maclean's* response, the magazine added a question mark to the story title, so that it read "Too Asian?" After that, the piece was retitled "The Enrolment Controversy." In a statement, *Maclean's* rejected claims that the magazine held a "negative" view of Asian students,[29] which critics viewed as a non-apology.[30] In 2020, ten years after the story was published, a number of professors at the University of British Columbia held an event to examine its legacy, with one of them reflecting on the "remarkably resistant" stereotypes employed.[31] "Too Asian" is a testament to the power of essentialism in journalism.

Lessons from the Pandemic

Thanks to COVID-19, I received a crash course on intersectionality.

BC's Provincial Health Officer Dr. Bonnie Henry said early on in the pandemic that "we are all in the same storm, but each of us is in a different boat."[32] I thought it was a poignant way of explaining how our individual health is made up of social determinants. However, journalists who avoid going into intersectional detail about what those boats look like may instead point to race, ethnicity, and culture instead as the only explanations of why one group is harder hit than another.

In April 2020, Alberta's then-Chief Medical Officer of Health Dr. Deena Hinshaw spoke about the alarming outbreak of COVID-19 at the Cargill meatpacking plant in High River, Alberta.

A large percentage of the workforce is of Filipino background, and they were overrepresented among the cases. According to the *Edmonton Journal*,[33] Dr. Hinshaw mentioned that there's a strong ethic in the Filipino community not to let the sniffles get in the way of a hard day's work.

The journalist did include some other factors mentioned at a press conference regarding the spread of the virus: that the ethnically Filipino workforce live in large households, carpool to work, and have partners who work in health care. This leaves the audience to wonder what it is about identifying as Filipino that led them to be more exposed to risk. Is it really something to do with their inherent ethic, as Dr. Hinshaw stated? Or that living in large households and carpooling to work is a Filipino cultural practice?

Intersectionality is missing here. How does the visa status of workers from the Philippines affect the power dynamic with their employer? Is it easy for them to speak up about working conditions? Is it easy for them to take sick days? Is it even possible for them to switch jobs? How does their identity and income affect what housing options are available to them? For those with dependents, whether in Canada or overseas, how does that affect their decision to work in spite of the dangers of COVID-19? How does the pandemic affect how they experience their role as providers? How do their identities affect how they're treated in the community?

A number of journalists did break down the intersectional reasons behind the overrepresentation of Filipino workers in risky frontline work. *Ricochet* reported that "migrant workers now face even more stress, as their essential jobs force them to choose between their own health and work."[34] An organizer with a women's centre highlighted the intersection of age: "Unfortunately, a lot of workers are also our older generation and the concept of mental health is not really something that's talked about because as a community we're on survival mode."

The *Calgary Herald* reported on the discrimination experienced by meat-packing workers, who were subsequently banned from entering banks and grocery stores. A representative from a Filipino migrants' support organization explained that while carpooling and living in large households is often thought of as a lifestyle choice, it's actually a survival tactic for many temporary foreign workers: "We should start reconsidering how we look at these workers, because this issue is a community and workplace issue. It is not the fault of the foreign workers or the racial backgrounds they represent." A spokesperson from a food-packing union also shed light on the bigger picture: "The very fact that a person's status in Canada is tied directly to their employment is one of the defining features of our immigration system but what we're seeing, with respect to COVID-19, is a heightened sense of fear amongst a number of workers."[35]

Without this context, audiences might read about the Cargill outbreak and lament what meat packers have to go through. But using Crenshaw's prism of a theory to examine the many facets of their identity helps audiences understand exactly why a particular demographic – many of whom were vulnerable as temporary foreign workers – was overrepresented when it came to health risks.

A *Huffington Post* story[36] focused on the role of remittances in the lives of Cargill's Filipino workers. "If they get sick, they jeopardize their capacity to be in Canada legally," said a geographer quoted in the story. "Filipinos aren't hard working by virtue of their culture, it's because they have to be."

Yes, it's true that anyone is susceptible to catching a virus. But every crisis and disaster has social dimensions to it. Just as the first wave of COVID-19 was tearing through senior homes and plants like Cargill's, American writer Rebecca Solnit reminded us that the coronavirus discriminates "because that's what humans do."[37] "Some of us are financially devastated, some are gravely or fatally ill or have already died; some face racism outside the home or violence within it," Solnit wrote in the *Guardian*. "The pandemic is a spotlight that illuminates underlying problems – economic inequality, racism, patriarchy. Taking care of each other begins with understanding the differences."

Pandemic reporting fascinated me as a journalist because there were times when effects were felt along ethnic lines but required intersectionality to explain why. Without it, people would be treated as if they were indeed elves and dwarves with essentialized behaviours, and that some cultures are inherently superior or inferior when it comes to staying healthy.

In 2020, there was a story about Richmond having far fewer cases of COVID-19 per capita when compared to neighbouring Vancouver and the rest of Canada during the first wave of the pandemic.[38] Richmond, as I've mentioned, is described as North America's "most Chinese city." But is this another issue of ethnic ethics? Are there inherently Chinese behaviours possessed by all Chinese people that allow them to evade the virus? (If yes, this would also imply that there are ethnocultural groups on the opposite end of the spectrum, with inherent behaviours that make them weaker and more prone to catching the virus – kind of racist!)

The *South China Morning Post*'s Vancouver correspondent reported on this data, alongside the fact that locals had already been taking action before Canada declared lockdowns and a state of emergency in 2020. A Buddhist monastery had closed its doors, some Lunar New Year celebrations had been cancelled, many of its Chinese shopping malls and restaurants were largely deserted,[39] and masks were already a common sight. A virologist and Canada research chair told the publication that he "absolutely" believed that Chinese Richmondites' early adoption of social distancing had to do with the low infection rate, and that their behaviour "needs to be applauded and recognized."[40]

Rather than it being Chineseness that protected them, the newspaper's reporting noted that residents who had experienced East Asia's SARS outbreak back in 2002, either first- or second-hand via friends and family, helped build a "grassroots" response when COVID-19 came around. The virologist interviewed also noted the comfort and familiarity in East Asia when it comes to wearing masks. A CBC story on Richmond's low infection rate[41] mentioned that Vancouver residents with ties to China were already paying close attention to the virus's devastation there in January, prompting them to take early action in expectation of what would soon spread overseas. These are all important details to note, otherwise audiences might think that the coronavirus avoided Richmond because its Chinese residents had a "careful" gene.

Another big story was about people of South Asian descent experiencing more COVID-19 transmission. BC's Surrey and Ontario's Peel Region were both hotspots for the spread of COVID-19 in the early waves of the pandemic.[42] Both are home to large South Asian populations – an important detail for health authorities investigating why these regions might have been hit harder by the virus and how to protect them, such as through multilingual messaging. After English, the most common language spoken in both places is Punjabi. Both are suburban communities, home to newcomers who work in essential sectors such as trucking, food production, and health care. Both are home to a high proportion of people who live in large households, from students and immigrants sharing accommodation to multi-generational families that include children and grandparents under one roof.

BC's Dr. Henry said that people might live in multi-generational households for "cultural reasons" and that the virus can "exploit" crowded situations.[43] But a comment like this makes it sound like a group's culture is inherently risky. "We don't talk about white culture that says it's perfectly normative to put your elders in an extended care facility where the risk is really high," said Satwinder Bains, director of the South Asian Studies Institute at the University of the Fraser Valley, in an interview with CBC. "You know, people question why we live in large homes, why we have extended family units without really understanding the social, the cultural, the economic support that happens to families." By including intersectional explanations beyond just culture, journalists can help audiences outside of an ethnocultural group understand why they live the way they do.

Over the course of my pandemic reporting, I interviewed health geographer Valorie Crooks who told me, "One of the strongest determinants of health is freedom over the choices in your life." It reframed how I viewed our public health recommendations during the pandemic, because actions we took for granted like physical distancing or working from home were not available to everyone. What if someone holds a job that requires them to be in close quarters with others? What if a senior shares a home with working adults on the frontline?

Cracking open Canada's censuses, one finds a dizzying amount of data that can help journalists with intersectional stories: on race, on gender, on income, on housing, on language, on immigration, and even on how people get to work. Applying the right data can help audiences understand social problems more accurately, pinpoint who's affected, describe what they're experiencing, and detail possible fixes.

One Big Happy Family

Aside from "culture," there's another C-word that journalists love to use when reporting on people of colour: "community." When journalists say that the "Nigerian Canadian community is outraged," does that mean every single person with that respective identity feels the same way?

It's important for journalists to be specific when describing who's at the centre of a story. Do they mean to describe a group as functioning in thought and deed as a single unit? That there is no difference in opinion within? Such a big umbrella of a term can hide important intersections. For example, in coverage of cannabis legalization, Glacier Media reported "largely negative sentiment towards cannabis among those in Asian communities," and that the "Chinese-Canadian community has been among the most hostile to cannabis legalization" due to lasting stigma from the Opium War. Journalists need to specify divides, like whether politics, religion, generational differences, or where a person was raised play a role, so that audiences aren't led to believe that people of colour function like a hive mind.

Journalists aware of the vagueness of the "community" label and its ability to mislead might even craft a story around the diversity within diversity. In 2022, the Canadian Press tried to challenge the myth of the monolith with a story on the political differences among Vancouverites of Chinese descent.[44] The journalist reported on how Chinatown stakeholders were split in their support for the city's new mayor, Ken Sim, who was known for being pro-police and was the first Chinese Canadian to hold office. In 2023, the CBC published a thoughtful story about how queer Muslims were upset with a Muslim association in Canada that wanted Prime Minister Justin Trudeau and schools to apologize for their pro-LGBTQ2S+ stance.[45] "They don't represent me," a gay Muslim interviewee said of the association. Such stories challenge the white gaze's perception and depictions of all racialized groups being the same.

When journalists report on controversial issues that concern racial and ethnocultural groups, they might describe them as being "divided" in opinion. It's important to stress differences, but journalists should avoid implying that groups should be united simply because they share an identity. Indigenous peoples share this frustration. "Indigenous people are not 'divided,'" Angela Sterritt once wrote. "We have different opinions. We are not homogenous. Even within our own nations we have different politics, opinions, ways of being and interrelations of traditions."[46] Imagine how ridiculous it would be if every time white people disagreed with something, journalists told their audiences that the white community is divided.

There are times when racialized people *do* like to identify as a monolith. One example comes from Korean Canadian actor Sandra Oh. During her Golden Globe acceptance speech in 2019, she declared, "It's an honour just to be Asian."[47] Diasporas felt empowered, and Oh's viral words were even printed onto T-shirts. But does this play into essentialism?

It's the ongoing work of journalists to find interesting perspectives that shed light on what claiming and expressing identity means, whether people are relating to a big label like being Brown or something more specific like being a Pakistani Muslim in Canada. Writer Beth Hong shares her thoughts in *Schema Magazine*, saying that "instead of rallying all Asians around a false flag of ethnic solidarity, I would prefer to see, read, and hear more voices about what being Asian in Canada actually means."[48] It's a struggle that Indigenous peoples face as well, with media scholar Candis Callison explaining that "the long labour required and important intervention of defining indigenous people rests on indigenous peoples both having much in common and so much diversity at the same time."[49] One of the problems with the diversity Ds is that they limit what it means to be a person of colour, preventing journalists from being open to complexity and contradiction. There will always be many voices from a variety of intersections to report on as people express their identities in different ways, and that's okay.

Too Much Intersectionality and Difference?

At the onset of the pandemic, I visited taxi dispatch centres to chat with drivers and managers about the drop they experienced in passengers.[50] Many taxi drivers are immigrants, Hafiz Khan, the general manager of Garden City Cabs, told me. He was a lawyer in Bangladesh before he immigrated to Canada. But once he arrived, he opted to work in the taxi industry because he encountered too many barriers to transition to practising locally as a lawyer. Stories like his are common among drivers, he said. Driving is a skillset many newcomers have, and the business model offers a stable ladder for them to climb: make enough money, buy your own taxi, make even more money, and then maybe move on to something else.

I shared this story with another long-time taxi driver and asked if he had a similar experience as an immigrant. To my surprise, he challenged me, asking whether he's still considered an immigrant if he arrived forty-five years ago and has been a Canadian citizen for forty of them. He made a good point.

For stories where identity or culture aren't front and centre, how do journalists know whether or not to include them? We all hold many social identities, but that doesn't mean everyone's full resume of demographic data should be included with every media appearance. Ultimately, whether identity and culture should be ignored, sprinkled lightly, or explored in depth in a story depends on the story, and whether the inclusion is othering or misleading.

The answer is simple if a source's identity or culture is not relevant to the story at hand: journalists can ignore it. Imagine attaching someone's annual salary or sexual orientation to their quotes if the story has nothing to do with such topics. In my early years on the job, I asked every non-white person about their ethnocultural background and migrant history (or family migration history), because I thought that their inclusion in news outlets dominated by white characters was a good thing, not understanding that this representation could open the door for more misrepresentation. Let's say I'm reporting a story on modern parenting and I introduce a source named Steve Fernandes as a second-generation Indian Canadian parent. If there are white parents in the story whose identities are not mentioned, Fernandes is suddenly othered. And whatever comments Fernandes makes about cellphone use or afterschool activities, the audience might be misled into thinking that such things have something to do with his diasporic identity.

Then there are stories where identity and culture don't need to be mentioned front and centre, but journalists can sprinkle in little references for out-group audiences with the intent of normalization and familiarity. When profiling a source, it could be a mention of a dish that they had for lunch, or a culturally specific item they have at home. When reporting on a neighbourhood, it could be a mention of how the local community centre offers a wide range of programming from sepak takraw to Arabic calligraphy. A *Globe and Mail* feature on five students across Canada going to prom does this sort of sprinkling well, briefly mentioning in one of the profiles that the student was not eating at the banquet due to fasting for Ramadan.[51] Photos and video have an advantage in capturing cultural details visually in homes and streetscapes. But whatever the medium, the key is to avoid drawing too much attention to cultural details that aren't central to the story. If hijabs are not the focus of a story, don't spend a few paragraphs talking about hijabs or lingering too long on them with the camera. In pursuit of representation, news outlets should run stories where racialized identity and cultures simply exist as part of daily life.

However, if identity or culture is or could be relevant to the story, then this should be explored. Let's say the assignment is to report on parents volunteering at a local school, and the journalist notices a significant number of parents of colour, many of whom appear to have grown up in Canada. "My parents worked multiple jobs and didn't have time to show up to school events," the source named Steve Fernandes might say. "I'm fortunate to have a stable job, so that's why I want to show up when I can." In this case, it would be relevant for the journalist to include Fernandes's background as well as those of other parents. There is a layered story here for a journalist with an intersectional lens to dive into, on how factors like class, migration, labour, and likely gender and language as well all shape which parents get to volunteer at their children's schools.

Going back to the taxi driver who was tired of being characterized as an immigrant decades after arriving in Canada, I believe he made a good point; however, I also believe that immigration was key to the labour aspect of the taxi story. In the end, we came to a compromise: he talked about immigration from his position as an industry expert, but I did not identify him as an immigrant because he did not want to be – raising the importance of communicating with your source.

Back to School

The other day, a friend of mine posted a photo on Instagram of her hot pot dinner. Her caption: "Just being a good Asian."

If only I had a time machine! I could return to my high school days and educate my peers on intersectionality. See someone complaining about "so Asian" tiger parents harping on them about homework? Hey, I could tell them their parents' attitude has less to do with Asianness and more to do with being blue-collar immigrants who want a different future for their kids, and that because Vancouver has a lot of immigrants from East Asia, they're associating this with all "Asians" and adopting an essentialist belief that all Asians are militant about educational achievements! I'm sure I would've been very popular.

Of course loose phrases about race and culture will be thrown around lightly among friends or in casual conservation, but putting out journalism for the public is different. That might seem obvious, but it's easy to let essentialist phrases or frames of homogeneity slip into reporting. It might come from the journalist's neglect of intersectionality, the desire to condense information into a story, or even from the sources themselves.

Journalists may invoke identity at the wrong times, treating it as a kind of tribal membership used to explain away behaviours and outcomes. Journalists may also ignore identity at times when it's crucial to unpacking privilege or oppression. Building up literacy in intersectionality is crucial in order to help audiences get a better understanding of the people and the systems in which we all live.

Of
Maps
and
Monsters

I once pitched a story about how an artisanal ice cream shop was making a neighbourhood cooler. It was at my first internship, and while I did not yet possess any formal instruction in journalism, I still feel embarrassed now that I wrote one of those boosterish stories about hot, hip, happening areas. It's not that I don't love ice cream; it's that I didn't pay attention to the bigger picture of what was going on in this neighbourhood.

The shop in question was called Earnest Ice Cream. It couldn't have been more emblematic of the hipster Vancouver of its day – they starting off selling treats out of a tricycle at farmers' markets and were known for their signature pint-sized mason jars. Preceding Earnest's launch in 2012, Vancouver had a reputation as a "gelato town," a point noted by sources as far away and as respected as the *New York Times*.[1] As a result, Earnest's hard ice cream was a welcome palate cleanser for the city.

Pedalling forward from the tricycle sales, Earnest opened its first location on Fraser Street on the city's east side, in an area that "doesn't have an established name," I wrote in my article. Earnest and the other businesses I interviewed agreed, sharing about how they were "scared" but decided to take a "bit of risk" to move to the "kind of sleepy, really kind of beautiful" area because they "believed" in it. And because the rent was cheap.[2]

I wasn't the only one to write this story about Fraser Street. The *Georgia Straight* floated the idea that it could've been called "Little Portland," thanks to the tide of other hip new businesses sprouting up.[3] It was more than a place for a scoop of ice cream, with a burgeoning scene of artisanal coffee shops and downtown restauranteurs emigrating to this part of the eastside to make their mark serving cocktails, pretty pastas, and experimental dishes like foie gras torchon and chicken liver parfait. One of those restauranteurs said the openings had brought a "distinct bounce" to the area. Another said it was "a little bit edgy ... a little bit rugged, but that gives it character." *Vancouver Magazine*'s guide to the area also commented on its transformation. This was a "boggy" place, a "no-man's land" that was "off the beaten path" until these adventurous creatives came along. A realtor interviewed said that people "used to joke about needing passports to come this far east."[4] Somewhere in the thick of all these arrivals, a name was given to the "up-and-coming" area: Fraserhood.

One day, long after my piece was published, I was strolling down Fraser Street when I noticed banners hanging from the lampposts overhead. On those banners was a name: "Mountain View." Eek! I had ignorantly written that the area did not have an established name. And now I was learning from banners that had been there for years that it did indeed have one.

Years later, with more journalism experience, I was determined to revisit Fraser Street. At that point, I had my own reported column called Urban Scrawl in the commuter daily *Metro*, which chronicled snapshots of urban life. It was the perfect place to publish my penance: a piece on the Mountain View I had ignored.[5]

Mountain View began as a working-class streetcar suburb not too far from downtown. After the world wars, it developed a rich history as a landing place for immigrants, mostly from Poland, with a scattering of those from Germany and Austria. In the 1980s came Vietnamese newcomers, followed by those from the Philippines. Somehow, I missed all of this: that the Vietnamese newspaper *Thời Báo* had its newsroom in the neighbourhood and that a number of Filipino businesses – from remittance centres to turo-turo cafeteria-style restaurants – dotted the Fraser Street strip.

The Polish society building, completed in 1959, was still around. Its president, who arrived in Vancouver in 1979, told me he loved the multicultural mix of his street: "We'd run across the street from the society to grab a coffee or sandwich from the Polish deli, then go next door to have a soup from the Vietnamese place!"

How did I miss all this? I was no stranger to strolling Fraser Street, but somehow, I had ignored the elements of the Polish, Vietnamese, and Filipino communities because I'd never had a reason to visit them as an outsider. On top of that, I was too caught up in the excitement during my first attempt at spotlighting what I thought to be the "new" that I did not bother to consider what was there before.

Here Be Minorities?

Everyone has their own mental map of the community in which they live. My mental map of a place is not going to be the same as yours. We each have some fog over the different areas we're unfamiliar with. If I don't like to shop, I likely wouldn't know where the cool shops are. If I'm not Muslim, I likely wouldn't know where the mosques are or which halal butcher sells the best meats. If I'm a tourist, I'd be able to point you to the city's manicured attractions, but not the haunts frequented by locals.

The white gaze plays a role in these mental maps too. Just as it shapes journalistic representations of people of colour, it also shapes representations of places of colour. A journalist unfamiliar with a particular ethnocultural group is likely to be oblivious to, ignore, or misrepresent the places that are important to that group. For example, there is an overwhelming number of stories on immigrant neighbourhoods like Chinatowns and Little Indias, because they are the historic and obvious places for journalists to gather coverage for their outlets on people of colour. However, this leaves out less touristy and more contemporary places where diasporas have clustered to live and set up hubs of business. Even for journalists who do know such places frequented by insiders, they may feel pressured to represent them for outsiders, exotifying difference and filtering out anything that white audiences might not consider newsworthy.

Of course, it's not just journalists who craft narratives of place. There are politicians promoting opportunities for transformation, tourism boards who curate attractions, condo developers who drum up desirability, and social media influencers with cameras at the ready. Whatever images these people and groups imprint upon a place, journalists might wind up replicating them. And that includes the stereotypes and stigmas attached to racialized places: the walled enclave, the dangerous ghetto, the exotic destination. All are othering representations that don't capture how these places function and what they mean to the people who spend their lives there. Like Edward W. Said describes in *Orientalism,* discourse produces understanding. The more that racialized places are othered in journalism, the more that audiences will believe what they see, hear, and read.[6]

Mental maps with fog over these racialized places might as well have the label "Here be monsters." Or rather, "Here be minorities."

Everything and Everywhere

Doreen Massey, the feminist geographer known for her ideas about place and power, taught me that stories are everywhere. I know a lot of newly minted journalists see the world this way, believing that every human being they encounter has deep insights about life. But that's not what I'm talking about. I mean this in a literal way.

"I would say that space is not a flat surface across which we walk," Massey once said in an interview, sharing an image that she attributes to cultural theorist Raymond Williams. "You're taking a train across a landscape – you're not traveling across a dead flat surface that is space: you're cutting across myriad stories going on. So instead of space being this flat surface it's like a pincushion of a million stories: if you stop at any point in that walk there will be a house with a story."[7]

Editors and reporters make decisions about the dimension of place every day, whether they're consciously thinking about geographic representation or not. Are they ensuring that their stories cover a variety of settings? Are misrepresented and underrepresented places sought out, helping to disperse the fog that exists in the minds of people in their audience? Or does coverage just focus on the same locations that are well-trod by journalists?

There will inevitably be those places that receive more journalistic representation than others, such as big cities, government centres, main streets, and public squares that host parades and protests. But newsrooms should be regularly thinking about whether they're leaving any settings out, and how their positionality might play a role in that neglect. Many of the Vancouver journalists I've met all live in the same few urban neighbourhoods, leaving me to wonder how they know what's going on elsewhere unless they make a conscious effort to venture farther afield.

Like the train that Massey describes, I worry about journalists skipping the places they don't deem newsworthy. Are cities hogging the headlines or is there also coverage of suburban and rural communities? Are journalists reporting on high-, middle-, and low-income areas evenly and without prejudice? Are places only spotlighted when some big drama explodes, or do the long-standing stories behind everyday routines also get reported on? Do journalists only report on the trendy places that audiences like hearing about, or do they also make room for places that have less of a cool factor? Are white places overrepresented, or do racialized places get to be in the news too, and not just when crimes or celebrations occur?

Places as Constellations

Massey warns us that places can be essentialized too.[8] And racialized places have been the victim of a variety of news frames that have essentialized them as being inscrutable and unwelcoming, enclosed and unassimilable, abnormal and troubled, dangerous and uncivilized, exotic and foreign, and more.

Forget facts – places can be essentialized based off of impressions. In 2007, *Toronto Life* published an infamous feature titled "The Scarborough Curse."[9] The subtitle: "How did boring, white-bread Scarberia become Scarlem – a mess of street gangs, firebombings and stabbings? Portrait of Toronto's unluckiest suburb." The journalist honed in on "the spectre of ethnic gangs, of sectarian tension" in the diverse city, despite the fact that Scarborough's per capita crime rate was lower than much of Toronto's.[10] In a reflection on the city's so-called curse published in the *Globe and Mail,* author Omer Aziz said that the piece "crystallized what many people thought of Scarborough in those days ... There was violence in Scarborough, yes, but unlike other places, Scarborough was defined by it."

Racialized places are often measured up to white places, home to white people and white businesses, which can be essentialized too. White places have been described in stories as the natural and healthy way for a place to be, with paragons of neighbourliness, vibrant community life – a perfect setting for raising a family, complete with descriptions of unlocked doors, festive holiday celebrations, and neighbours who know one another's names down to the family dog. By positioning whiteness in this way, people of colour can be framed as disturbing this harmonious norm.

In 2016, the *Walrus* published a feature titled "The Highest Bidder: How Foreign Investors are Squeezing Out Vancouver's Middle Class." The foreign investors are from one specific place, according to the article: "When we follow the money, it leads primarily to the city's newest wealthy class: buyers from mainland China." The story romanticizes the "reassuring displays of domestic life" that have been lost on the city's whiter west side, such as "a neighbour mowing the lawn or waving hello, screen doors slamming, children playing."[11] And in a nod to the invasion narrative, a source in the feature who grew up on the west side compared it to the Michael Crichton sci-fi novel *The Andromeda Strain*, which was about an alien microorganism "where everybody has died from a mystery virus, and we're the only survivors."

There is an important story about housing here, but many journalists have racialized the issue. The *South China Morning Post*'s Vancouver correspondent Ian Young shared some wise words in an interview:

What defines those people in terms of their behaviour here in Vancouver, and in terms of their impact on affordability, is not [their] Chineseness; it's their millionaireness. You know, the idea that there is commonality to be found in the Chineseness, I find that kind of insulting. Why would you think that someone was better defined by the colour of their skin rather than the colour of their money?[12]

By racializing this housing crisis, journalists turn this into a battle of us versus them – with the white "us" pitted against the Chinese "other" – that blames people rather than public policy.

Heritage of place can be manufactured, according to Massey, and in these stories, Chinese invaders are portrayed as eroding an idyllic heritage of neighbourhood life. But who's to say that they don't have vibrant lives in the neighbourhood that their white neighbours cannot detect because they are newcomers who speak different languages and have different social networks? The few journalists who've bothered to document their lives in the city reveal how they've been putting down roots, raising families, and making connections and contributions for years,[13] far from the standoffish impression that many stories suggest.

When it comes to place, how do journalists avoid becoming gatekeepers that prioritize the narratives of the privileged? How do they avoid a politics of resentment against people of colour othered as deviant? Massey challenges us to move beyond a "reactionary" sense of place that puts too much stock in nationalism and manufactured heritages, with antagonism toward anyone deemed an outsider. Instead she champions a more "progressive" sense of place, which offers criteria that I believe can help journalists portray places more accurately and holistically.

Firstly, explains Massey, places aren't static. They aren't rooted in a singular history. Places are processes, and they are ever-changing and not frozen in time.

Secondly, places don't have strict boundaries. They do have borders that define the area they cover, but these borders allow for interaction between the inside and outside.

Thirdly, places don't have single identities. They have multiple, which may be a source of richness or a source of conflict.

Massey explains that places are a "constellation of social relations." Journalists can and should strive to describe the relationships behind a place as best as they can, but they shouldn't allow their loudest sources to dominate stories with opinions on who the outsiders are in a particular place. That only adds monsters to audiences' mental maps.

In Fear of Enclaves

As pockets of Canada diversify to include more people of colour – a product of both migration and children of diasporas moving into areas where they would not have been welcome in the past – let's have a look at how journalists have been reporting on places of colour.

In sociology, a geographic area where a large population of people of colour live and work has been called an "ethnic enclave." The term has percolated into everyday use and remains a well-used term in journalism on the topic. It refers to urban neighbourhoods like Koreatowns and Little Jamaicas, but also the suburban cities at the edges of urban cores that have become newcomer destinations. Geographer Wei Li has labelled them "ethnoburbs,"[14] and they contain a much larger presence of a specific ethnocultural group than any Chinatown or Japantown of old. Richmond and Surrey are the best-known examples in BC, while Ontario has many outside of Toronto, from Brampton, Markham, to yet another Richmond in Richmond Hill.

In reporting on ethnic enclaves, there is a danger of reinforcing that rigid sense of place Massey has warned about, as if enclaves have strict boundaries and identities with no deviation, functioning as if they're separate from Canadian society and not subject to its laws. Some ethnic enclaves have become so racialized in the popular imagination that audiences may end up racializing news stories on their own accord – regardless of whether or not a person of colour shows up in the coverage by name or appearance. A shooting in Surrey? It must be those Indian Canadian gangs who live there! Yet another car crashing into the window of a Richmond business?[15] The city is filled with terrible Asian drivers!

Social media chatter in response to news stories is filled with such comments. Journalists aren't the only ones distressed by them; sources are too. I once wrote a story on feral rabbits, a piece that at first glance doesn't seem like it has anything to do with race at all.[16] I spoke with the head of a charity that rescues feral rabbits in Richmond, where rapid reproduction has become a serious and expensive problem, with rabbits burrowing and feasting in public and private grounds. Richmond's rabbits frequently make the headlines, so much so that people from other cities have told her explicitly that the rabbit problem is "because there's all those Asians." Half of the charity's volunteers are visibly East Asian, and they've been asked whether they eat rescued rabbits. Because of this stereotype, the head of the charity has also been questioned about whether it's really a good idea to adopt rabbits out to families of East Asian background.

In the 2000s and 2010s, a wave of stories sounded the alarm on these enclaves and what they meant for the country. These geographies of the other were portrayed as geographies of deviance and unassimilation, as if people of colour had established a patch of foreign soil in Canada. In 2012, CBC's Vancouver show *On The Coast* held a public forum on the subject titled "Choosing Segregation: Ethnic Enclaves in Metro Vancouver."[17]

Journalists relied on studies as evidence for such claims. A headline from the *National Post* read "Ethnic Enclaves Weak Link, Study Finds."[18] Another from the publication simply used "Our Chinalands."[19] One Statistics Canada study,[20] quoted by the *Toronto Star*,[21] used the language "rapid replacement." A headline from the *Vancouver Sun* asked the question, "Are Growing Ethnic Enclaves a Threat to Canada?"[22] Also using a study as a springboard, the story talked about how these "self-chosen ghettos are an expanding phenomenon to be taken seriously," and how "when immigrants alleviate their worry through ethnic enclaves, they're also less likely to feel loyalty to Canada."

Adding fuel to the fire was research by prominent American political scientist Robert Putnam, who concluded that immigration and ethnocultural diversity in the short run can reduce social solidarity and cause residents of all races to "hunker down"[23] and "pull in like a turtle."[24] His work was countered by scholars who analyzed the same data and found that the distrust was expressed by white people uncomfortable living near people of colour, but not vice versa.[25] Nonetheless, Putnam's research was picked up by Canadian media and referenced in critiques of ethnic enclaves and multiculturalism.

The federal minister of citizenship, immigration, and multiculturalism at the time also fanned the enclave fear with his comments. Jason Kenney, who would later become Alberta's premier, served in the ministerial role under the Harper Conservatives between 2008 and 2013. During that time, he said that there should be more "focus on bringing communities together, to make sure that we don't experience the kind of ethnic enclaves that we see in parts of Europe and elsewhere."[26]

But what exactly are the people in ethnic enclaves doing wrong? Have a close look at the stories of the day and see if you can figure out what journalists are including as examples of deviance. The "rapid replacement" of white residents is a common one, particularly in stories about immigration. Once whiteness is established as the norm for a place, people of colour can then be portrayed as invaders while alarms are raised about "white flight." There was also no mention of the fact that enclaves could in fact be white, and that journalists were implying that white enclaves were a good and natural thing.

Segregation and the perceived inability to assimilate is another example. In a *Vancouver Sun* story titled "Ethnic Enclaves Hurt Canadian 'Belonging,'" it was reported that newcomers who live in such places don't "feel healthy patriotism, send their children to diverse public schools, move beyond ethnic loyalty in the voting booth or find common ground with others, to protect the environment or supporting the United Way."[27] A story in the *Province* talked about the "harmful ethnic isolation" in such places and the pressure to "avoid contact with other races."[28] As a result, white people may be "ostracized" as "outsiders" in communities they grew up in. In turn, questions are raised about whether they're the ones facing "discrimination and exclusion" against growing populations of people of colour.

Then there are the stories about how newcomers are causing an extra burden on Canadian services in ethnic enclaves. A *Toronto Star* story discussed "the transformation of schools in affected neighbourhoods into front-line settlement agencies," and how "schools [have] so many Mandarin-speaking students that students are having a hard time learning English from their classmates."[29]

Some stories, whether through framing or quoted sources, have floated the idea that ethnic enclaves are bad for Canadian multiculturalism itself: there's a lack of a "shared purpose,"[30] a shared language,[31] and a concern that this might even cause racism. According to a *Globe and Mail* story, "while many newcomers disappear willingly into ethnic silos, some Canadians are starting to reject diversity."[32] That story also talked about how ethnic enclaves, with their non-Western cultures, keep children from blending into Canadian society. One source has "never been to summer camp, taken in a Blue Jays or Maple Leafs game or a rock concert."

In these stories, Canadian culture is solely defined as what white people deem acceptable. There are also suggestions that cultural pluralism is not possible, and that diaspora groups in Canada cannot be Canadian and hold their cultural heritage at the same time.

Modern enclaves are described as a product of self-segregation. Some journalists acknowledge the difficulties of "disorientation"[33] when coming to Canada as an explanation for why newcomers might form communities with others of the same background. The *Vancouver Sun* once concluded from census data that the "most popular Metro region for blacks is the Whalley area of Surrey."[34] By focusing on how racial and ethnocultural groups find an area "popular" and are "choosing" segregation, this ignores how barriers like discrimination, exclusion, and hate might play a role in the establishment of these so-called ethnic enclaves.

In 2016, journalist Noreen Ahmed-Ullah wrote a reported essay about Brampton, in Ontario's Peel Region.[35] In the "mostly brown" city, Ahmed-Ullah discussed fitting in in a special community and not needing to worry about being judged for wearing her hijab, white people lecturing her about her behaviour, or full-throated racist comments. There are cultural conveniences too. "I love that I can walk to the Asian Foods grocery store down the block when I've run out of coriander or turmeric, or just craving some samosas. Who needs a neighbourhood 7-Eleven when all my favourite comfort food is a stroll away?" Quite simply, Ahmed-Ullah enjoys not being the other: "I love that I don't stick out like a sore thumb."

Brampton's large population of South Asian diasporas has earned it nicknames like "Browntown," "Bramladesh," and "Singhdale." But, as Ahmed-Ullah noted, it has also been given an uglier one: "ghetto." "It's naïve to think race doesn't play a role in what gets labelled a ghetto," said Sikh activist Pardeep Nagra in the essay. "The negative is only associated with brown skin, whether it be blacks or South Asians." Here, Nagra refers to the racist idea that people of colour are "forever foreign," as are the spaces they imbue with their identity and culture. "At what point do I get freed and get to be seen as Canadian?" he asked. "Is it being born here? Is it having citizenship? Is it cheering for the Leafs? Is it playing hockey? Is it having some maple syrup? Doing the Terry Fox Run? ... My existence here offends people because of what I choose to wear. They can't exist in my space. They're offended that I exist in their space."

What places do journalists other? What places do journalists portray as ghettoes? Are out-group perspectives privileged in stories over in-group ones? Are there strengths of places of colour that journalists have ignored in favour of surfacing what they believe to be weaknesses?

Home Improvement?

In journalism that upholds invasion narratives, you will find white voices criticizing people of colour for hogging local resources, like school seats, or for altering the landscape of their community, such as by introducing signs in other languages.

But what happens when white people move into places of colour? Looking back at the Fraserhood stories, there appears to be an underlying message that it's a good thing. Journalists framed these stories as a celebration of new residents, businesses, and culture moving in as the neighbourhood sheds its "boggy" roots. These stories might have focused on commercial activity, but the upscaling of the area was connected to the fading of its racialized roots. I participated in that myself by writing an ice cream shop story that implied to audiences that Fraserhood's racialized histories did not exist.

This kind of reporting is erasure and downplays displacement along the lines of racial and class marginality. If journalists are upholding the idea that Fraserhood's past is boggy, wouldn't audiences believe that whatever change comes will be better than a bog? And by circulating a brand-new name for the area, one used by foodies and real estate marketers, it's as if someone hit the reset button on the neighbourhood's history, allowing a new one to be written from scratch.

If racialized places are portrayed as foggy territory on a map, it's no wonder that journalists portray the white people who move into these places as explorers. *Vancouver Magazine* once featured a craft brewery that opened up in the city of Burnaby, taking over what was once an auto shop. The craft brewer interviewed talked about how risky it was to move into the "middle of nowhere," how their success was based off of his ability to recognize the area's "potential," and how he wanted to be the "first in" and "really put our stake in the ground."[36]

But this so-called middle of nowhere is chock full of stuff. There are industrial kitchens that make tofu, noodles, phyllo, and kimchi, the lifeblood of retailers in the region. Then, sprinkled throughout the houses, are a gurdwara, a Hindu temple, a Buddhist temple, dozens of immigrant churches, and the Nikkei National Museum and Cultural Centre, which is a hub of Japanese Canadian history and activity. The closest main thoroughfare is Kingsway. By day, it's where residents stock their kitchens with Korean, Chinese, and Iranian staples at the well-curated local supermarkets they'd rather give their business to than the big box stores. Even the big box stores here are responsive enough to start stocking non-Western cultural goods. By night, Kingsway is where karaoke bars blast K-pop hits past midnight and roadside signs ask drivers to pull over for hot pot, bubble tea, and flame-grilled skewers.

If a journalist isn't familiar with the place they are writing about, especially a place home to many different ethnocultural groups, it's important to avoid solely relying on the claims of a source who is new to the area; in the case of the craft brewery, a source who makes the claim that the "deepest throes of South Burnaby" are where a "lot of people in the area" have "no amenities whatsoever." Once again, this erases the importance of places of colour in the news and signals to people of colour that their narratives of place are easily bulldozed.

All-Access Pass

While some racialized places are portrayed in journalism as exclusive and problematic, others are deemed authentic and attractive. Under the white gaze, accessibility to white audiences is the line between deviance and deliciousness. Shannon Sullivan, a critical philosopher of race, coined the term "ontological expansiveness." It's an unconscious habit of white privilege, which she defines as when "white people tend to act and think as if all spaces – whether geographical, psychical, linguistic, economic, or otherwise – are or should be available to them to move in and out as they wish."[37] Ethnocultural places in Canada that are made accessible to people outside of the group tend to get covered in a more positive light.

You will know by now that Richmond and Surrey, BC's "ethnoburbs," are frequently singled out in news coverage for each being too much of an enclave. To help visitors get to know them, the tourism boards of both cities have decided to use food. They cooked up a cartographical solution to help out-group visitors explore the cities' non-Western restaurants: food maps with hand-picked destinations. Richmond, known for its Chinese cuisines, got a Dumpling Trail. Surrey, known mostly for its South Asian cuisines but also for its Caribbean and African fare, got a Spice Trail. Media ate it up. The trails garnered coverage from the *Toronto Star,* the *Globe and Mail,* and many local news outlets that set out to gobble everything these trails had to offer.

In the coverage, journalists quoted encouragement from their interviewees, to make their news audiences more comfortable: "Don't be afraid to try us out," said the owner of a Caribbean café.[38] There was instruction from the *Vancouver Sun* on how to consume the culture of the other, such as eating a soup-filled xiaolongbao: "Hold it by the nub on top ... You can bite off a bit of the skin, take sips of the soup and then eat it."[39] Audiences were told exactly where to go, what dishes to order, and what to expect. There was even a dash of orientalism, with the newspaper calling Richmond's offerings an "exotic treasury."

While it is the job of journalists to inform their audiences, too much exposition can be a turn off for in-group audiences. A person from the Caribbean who reads coverage on the Spice Trail might wonder why someone is telling them "don't be afraid" to try Caribbean food. When coverage is white-centred, everyone else is left out.

The Adventure of the Hidden Gem

There's nothing like the thrill of a hidden gem. The more difficult it is to access a restaurant, the more exciting it is. The more different it is from Western tastes, the more exotic it is. Both physical and social distance add to the deliciousness of a hidden gem.

A hidden gem is a place that's portrayed as a diamond in the rough, something delicious and off the beaten path that only those with an adventurous spirit will dare to seek out. Audiences hunger for such content, especially with the rise of visual social media like

Instagram and TikTok. A steakhouse or a French restaurant doesn't have the same adventurous allure to the white gaze as a strip mall off the highway where Nepalese aunties are making momos by hand. If you're wondering about ontological expansiveness and the desire of white accessibility, that's still at work here. But with hidden gems, racialized places have to be novel or a wee bit harder to reach – whether by long commute across the city or by language barriers – in order to feel valuable.

Scout, a Vancouver magazine about food and culture, carries a column called "Never Heard Of It" that surfaces such gems. Like the name of the publication, the column's name embodies the act of seeking and spotlighting "informal hole-in-the-wall eateries."[40] The column has echoes of the work of Jonathan Gold, the Pulitzer Prize-winning food writer who reviewed global eats that were brought to his home of Los Angeles. "Never Heard Of It" takes Gold's anthropological approach in unpacking how the Ghanian meat pies you can find in Vancouver's suburbs are the product of colonialism, or how a Vietnamese restaurant's dishes come from the cuisine of the former imperial capital of Huế.

Food journalism will inevitably introduce audiences to new dishes. But does it imply that someone from Ghana or a specific city in Vietnam would have "never heard of" their own food or one of the few places in town that serves their cultural food? The imaginary reader that such coverage is catered to is an outsider encountering foods from foreign cuisines that might be new to them. Virtually all of the restaurants reported on under the "Never Heard Of It" label are non-Western.

In journalism about hidden gems, there are common descriptors like "unassuming,"[41] "unglamorous," and "nondescript." Places are called "worth finding" while simultaneously being critiqued for their settings, with descriptions like "plain and mousey." Service is also critiqued, recording such observations as an owner falling asleep for laughs and as a signal to the audience that such a place is a dive.[42]

Audiences are affirmed that the food of the other is authentic because it lies in the land of the other. The *Merriam-Webster Dictionary* defines a hole-in-the-wall as "a small and often unpretentious out-of-the-way place,"[43] but journalists have come to use the term liberally. It doesn't matter whether a hole-in-the-wall is a big restaurant or on a major thoroughfare or is very popular with the ethnocultural group that it caters to – it's a hole-in-the-wall because it's far from of the ethnocentric familiarity of the Western palate. This distance allows journalists to emphasize the everyday as exotic and sell cornerstones as hidden gems.

As bell hooks writes, "Encounters with Otherness are clearly marked as more exciting, more intense, and more threatening. The lure is the combination of pleasure and danger."[44] Authors will include disclaimers, warning audiences that such places are only for "adventurous eaters."[45] Foreign territory has to be travelled and certain expectations lowered if the audience wants the good stuff. There might even be a joke about getting lost.[46] Descriptions of eateries' locations might be played up for curiosity and drama, like the *New Yorker*'s Toronto coverage of "a two-year-old Syrian bakery wedged between a Subway and an adult-video store."[47]

The *Globe and Mail,* in its review of the food court of a suburban Chinese mall, instructed readers to travel down "a sleepy hallway flanked by herbalist shops selling shrivelled lizards and travel agencies that never seem to be open," where "tiny, unglamorous mom-and-pop gems" are waiting. The *Georgia Straight,* which also took to the immigrant suburbs to spotlight a samosa shop,[48] emphasized rewards of prices "far lower than what you would pay in the grocery stores." The *Edmonton Journal,* in a review of a Korean Chinese restaurant titled "Out of the Way and Out of This World,"[49] noted the "unlikely" industrial location that "looks more like a 1950s-style mechanic's garage than an eatery," a building that's "yellowed, as if it's been smoking cigarettes for a long, long time" – but the food is so good the author doesn't want to tell anyone about it. Journalists often put down these places while praising them at the same time, stoking their status as explorers with a penchant for risk, inviting daring audience members to take a chance, too, if they want to taste the really good stuff.

In Vancouver, there is a restaurant that's been reported on so many times as a hole-in-the-wall that I don't know how journalists can maintain their credibility if they keep describing it as such. This "hole" is constantly in the media spotlight and has been acclaimed Yelp's number one restaurant in Canada in 2023.[50] The Northern Café is above a hardware store in Vancouver's industrial south and is run by a Chinese Canadian family. It's been covered by everyone from the *National Post* to the *Daily Hive* to countless food Instagrammers, as if they've found the El Dorado of greasy spoons.

The *Post*'s coverage used language like this: "Prepare to be staggered: by the uneven floor"; "visual confusion"; "random drawings"; "might seem like it's falling to pieces"; and likened it to a "funhouse at a summer fair." The headline proclaimed it as "Canada's oldest and most rundown restaurant," and "the best of the oldest, most decrepit eateries in the land." Admittedly, news on food – whether by reporters or columnists – allows for some colourful language. But such coverage too often strips restaurants down to objects of discovery and consumption.

Yes, a label like hole-in-the-wall may very well refer to a place's physical location. Indeed, many of them are sparse, small joints. But the coverage can essentialize people of colour as hiding in stark spaces because they're just weird like that. They're often portrayed as delicious darlings, but bumbling ones who don't know what it takes to run a proper restaurant and have no sense of hospitality.

What's missing? Failing to ask why these places are the way they are. To take the metaphor of a gem even further, what are the pressures it experienced that caused its formation?

In 2020, a *Toronto Star* story about eateries in strip malls took the time to explain *why* they're out of the way: because the rent in desirable spaces like the downtown is too high.[51] The fact was driven home in another story about the affordable stalls in North York's Downsview Park Merchants Market, with offerings that range from Salvadoran to Jamaican to Basque.[52] By highlighting the economic realities that racialized food business owners face, journalists communicate that racialized entrepreneurs aren't choosing far-flung locations just for the heck of it. It's because they're squeezed out of hot, high-traffic areas, leaving them with real estate that might not be the most conducive to running such a business.

In another *Star* story, a sushi restaurant at the border of North York and Scarborough was described as being easily "missed with its shades drawn and located in a tiny plaza where the busiest tenant is a KFC (it's one of the few locations that still has the giant bucket on a pole)." The sushi chef was given space in the story to explain his situation: "Ultimately it's the rent. My job is calculating food costs. Fish prices are very high. If I opened downtown, everything would be more expensive for the same quality."[53] Rather than a throwaway line that hidden gems can be found uncovered in "unlikely" locations, this is a helpful explanation of why there is actually a high likelihood that such chefs would open their restaurants in locations off the beaten path – because of budgets. This context gives popular hidden gems even more reason to be commended, because they are able to thrive without the advantage of high traffic.

Being transparent about these realities gives audiences an understanding of the lives they are encountering and the geographies they are stepping into when looking for a bite to eat. The owner was spotted falling asleep? Perhaps they're working long hours seven days a week to make ends meet. The decor doesn't look like an interior designer had any part in it? Perhaps the restaurant is a vehicle for survival rather than an attempt to score a Michelin star. The menu is difficult to navigate for a first timer? Perhaps the food is catered first and foremost to a diaspora rather than to foodies seeking new flavours.

While we're on the subject of transparency, I hope journalists will stop pretending as if they're Columbus discovering the New World every time they find a new restaurant. I noticed that a *Daily Hive* writer has tried to remedy this by being open about places being new to some and old to others, stating that she covers the "hidden (and not so hidden) gems."[54] In one review of a Korean supermarket, she wrote, "The funny thing about living in a city is that one person's hidden gem is another's regular spot. What may seem off-the-beaten-trail and undiscovered to one person is part of someone else's daily routine – a place they've known about and have been visiting for years." In her write-up about the Northern Café, she acknowledged its history and heritage: "The attention it's now receiving may seem delayed and out of touch ... And we get it – this place has been around since 1949 and already has a steady roster of regulars and other folks who warm its booths on a regular basis."[55]

How refreshing it is for someone to report on the reputation of a restaurant as it exists in reality, rather than to pretend that it only exists because they're reporting on it.

"A Pincushion of a Million Stories"

Other than being critical of outside actors, like savvy marketers or xenophobic locals trying to take control of narratives of place, what are journalists to do when telling stories about places of colour?

I learned by making a mistake that it's important to fact check before writing down sweeping characterizations of places that I'm unfamiliar with.

Think about the point of view that a journalist adopts as a story opens. Where do those first scenes take place? If the story caters to the white gaze, the audience will be hanging around the doorway of a racialized place, but awkwardly not invited in. Authenticity hinges on access to underrepresented places, and that's different from places being made accessible to white audiences. Does the story bring the audience into a community and allow them to witness events that hold deep meaning? Is the place rendered with telling details? Are there characters that feel real? Is there context about this community's place in the wider world? Watch out for language that distances such a place, telling the audience that they have to "make a trek" to get there because it is located "far out" or "at the edge" of places within their understanding.

When reporting on racialized places, there may be room to confront records of misrepresentation directly. You can talk about it in the story itself, adding context kind of like a literature review. I often do so in my stories, sprinkling in hyperbolic, stigmatizing, or out-of-touch quotes from media, marketing materials, public reports, and prominent figures to show how they've gotten an impression of a place all wrong. Similarly, in 2022, *Maisonneuve* published a feature about the importance of the Scarborough RT, a light rapid transit line. The author unpacked the city's "Scarberia" slur, which is associated with stigma and inequality in a place home to many immigrants and people of colour who are low-income, and explained how that stereotype of desolation has roots in an underfunding of services.[56] The *Squamish Chief* published an entire piece dedicated to understanding the roots of the city's "Squampton" moniker.[57]

Sprinkling in history helps, so that audiences understand that no place is really "new," and that a space might have or have had multiple identities. Journalists can look for opportunities to include Indigenous histories of a place, to avoid implications that colonization is when a place began or that the land was *terra nullius*, empty and ripe for the taking, until some white settler founded a city or village there. Not only does the inclusion of Indigenous histories offer audiences broader and more accurate contexts – contexts that were wilfully erased – it also offers revealing insights that shed light on culture and geography. The *Burnaby Beacon* wrote about the history of local major roads like Kingsway,[58] which connects Vancouver with New Westminster, the former capital of the Colony of British Columbia, and is dotted with a number of immigrant communities.[59] The story reports that these were roads used by local Salish peoples long before any contact with European settlers. Kingsway even had temporary villages along the route. After contact, settler engineers imposed their first roads over the long-existing Indigenous ones. T'uy't'tanat-Cease Wyss, an artist and ethnobotanist with Skwxwú7mesh and Sto:lo ancestry, brought together past and present Kingsway with this quote: "What began as a trail that connected many villages and many people continues to actually do the same thing."[60]

Even in racialized places that appear to be monocultural, there are, as Massey explains, a "constellation of social relations." In my interviews with sources, I've been surprised many a time by histories that I did not expect, from the Chinese migrants who once farmed land on the Musqueam reserve at Vancouver's edge to the Indian migrants who made regular shopping trips to Little Italy because that was the only place where they could buy lentils in bulk. These relationships challenge the stereotypes of enclaves as walled places and diasporas as anti-social. Journalists alert to investigating such relationships are able to reveal the dynamic realities of place to their audiences.

So how can a journalist get to know a place as omnisciently as possible? By doing everything they possibly can. Walk the streets, yes, but also the alleys. Get there by transit to see if it's well served. Explore it by car to get to those places you can only get to by car. Visit at dawn to smell the bakeries and see who's headed out or coming home. Visit during rush hour to feel the full bustle. Visit at night to see what comes alive. Go there on a normal day, but also on a day of celebration.

Have a peek at the census to see who lives there. Who's rich? Who's poor? What's the ethnocultural mix? What does the average household look like? What languages are the linguas franca? What jobs do people work? Data is helpful, but it's important to talk to people – everyone from the kid who grew up there to the family that just moved in, from the people running a business to the politicians they elected. What makes them angry? What are their dreams?

Check out the main street, the strip mall, the subdivisions, the towers, the schools, the offices, the industries, the parks, and the wilderness. Are there things there that can't be found anywhere else? Do things that cost money and things that are free. Stop for a bite to eat. Get a haircut. Peek into the local church or temple. Is there a place that makes you uncomfortable? If so, why?

Read the bulletin boards, social media posts, books, all the news coverage you can find. See if it matches up to the reality that you see. Turn back time on Google Street View and see how the area has changed.

This is a lot of work and not what a general reporter can do in a day. But it's something they can do over a period of time, to get to know the communities they're reporting on and to dispel the fog from their mental maps. As Massey says, places are pincushions of millions of stories. Don't be like me, swept up by the promise of an up-and-coming neighbourhood just because there's a new ice cream shop.

Of Silence and Shutdowns

Whenever I file a story on race, I can guarantee that a handful of readers will comment and email me the day that it's published to tell me that I've done a bad job. On one occasion, someone even took the time to send me a long, handwritten letter via post. No topic has generated more criticism from my audiences than when I write about race. It doesn't matter whether it's the subject of the story or not; even a passing mention can rile them up.

Many of my fellow journalists have had similar experiences, with some going through awful cases of doxxing and harassment. While less extreme, it is far more common to receive messages from the subset of our audiences who are so incensed by the presence of race in a news report that they feel the need to take a few minutes out of their day to let the journalist know their thoughts.

The content of these messages can vary widely. There are indeed a few commenters who spout white supremacist views about the inferiority of racialized people or groups while praising the superiority of Western civilization. More common are those who fancy themselves authorities on race, lecturing us journalists about what they insist is the correct position and how we've gotten it wrong in our stories. But I've noticed that the vast majority of commenters are those who are upset that the topic of race is being reported on at all. Most of these commenters don't hesitate to tell me they are white. They have sarcastically said that they know I won't listen to them because they are "just another old pale guy." Others I can confidently guess are white, from their last names, their profile pictures, and how they talk about their relationships with people of colour. Which leads me to conclude that it's mostly white people and not people of colour who are upset when race is reported on.

Is this "white fragility"? Robin DiAngelo coined the term in her book of the same name, a bestseller of the anti-racism genre. A doctor of multicultural education, she documented the reactions she encountered during her twenty years as a diversity trainer for businesses. "I was taken aback by how angry and defensive so many white people became at the suggestion that they were connected to racism in any way," she wrote.[1] "The very idea that they would be required to attend a workshop on racism outraged them. They entered the room angry and made that feeling clear to us throughout the day." I've noticed the same with white news audiences, refusing to accept that racial inequalities exist in society and that some people have benefited and continue to benefit from racial privilege. They believe that only bad people could be racist and that structural or individual acts of racism could not possibly be carried out by people with good intentions.

DiAngelo defines white fragility as "triggered by discomfort and anxiety" but "born of superiority and entitlement."[2] It arises when attempts are made to connect white people to structural racism, something so unsettling that it can feel morally offensive. DiAngelo argues that white fragility upholds white privilege because it prevents racial inequality from being discussed and confronted.

Some people simply aren't emotionally prepared or intellectually equipped to learn about how people of colour are disadvantaged by discrimination while at the same time white people benefit from often unacknowledged and unearned advantages.

It makes me realize that Canadians, for all our trumpeting about multiculturalism, still have a long way to go when it comes to talking about and tackling issues of race. Comfort is preferred over having to confront difficult truths. Journalists attempting to increase the racial awareness of their audiences through reporting on privilege and inequality still meet resistance.

There are those occasional commenters who drop F-bombs, racial slurs, and offensive stereotypes in response to such reporting. Among them are a nasty bunch who like to criticize the journalist personally. I've received many "go back to China" comments when my reporting challenges Canada's welcoming multicultural image, as if I'm not a journalist but a whiny customer asking too much of the country, and that someone with my ancestry should know their place. I often think of McIntosh's invisible knapsack, as white journalists don't have to deal with these racial attacks.

This chapter does not bother addressing bigoted responses because they come from a place of unreason. Instead, this chapter focuses on those audience members who attempt to dismiss journalism on race and racism using what they believe to be reason.

One of my go-to sources on issues of race is Andy Yan, director of Simon Fraser University's City Program. He's come across such dismissals in his urban planning work and calls them "shutdown commands." Like how pressing control-alt-delete on a keyboard will initiate the shutdown of a computer, there are social shutdown commands intended to end discussions of race and racism. Shutdown commands can be a difficult thing to wrap one's head around: audiences using what appear to be positive reasons, such as claiming to be on the side of real journalism and multicultural harmony, in their bid to ask journalists to stop reporting on racial difference and inequality.

This paradox of conflicting priorities is a kind of made-in-Canada racism. Frances Henry, one of Canada's leading scholars on race, famously diagnosed the problem as "democratic racism." Canadians often call for justice, equality, and fairness while dismissing and discriminating against racialized people. "As modernity commits itself to these liberal ideas and to the moral irrelevance of 'race,' there is a proliferation of racial identities and an assortment of exclusions they support and sustain," Henry says.[3] In other words, the belief held by some Canadians that our society is "post-racial" plays a part in allowing discrimination and inequality to fester.

There's an online maxim that goes, "Don't read the comments." Online comments, particularly anonymous ones, are a far cry from the letters to the editor that run in news outlets, which are typically approved by a real human being before they are published. Full names, addresses, and phone numbers are often disclosed as a way of verifying identity and lending weight to the commentary.

But online? It can be a hellscape. Reading the comments on an article or a social media share can expose you to all kinds of harm, hatred, and horrors left by anonymous trolls. It's telling how bad things can get that the CBC made the decision to disallow comments sections for their stories that involve Indigenous people due to the sheer amount of hate they received.[4] News outlets like the *Tyee* and Global News occasionally do the same with their comments for stories that concern marginalized people and groups.[5]

As both a journalist and a news consumer, I can't deny that the maxim is good for one's sanity, especially when seeing racialized people get attacked. I've avoided looking at them for stories of my own that I know attract bad faith commenters, asking my friends to have a peek for me instead to preserve my own mental health.

The negative impact of comments has led one web developer to create a browser extension called "Don't Read the Comments!" that hides comments sections, allowing internet users to consume the news in peace. It's demoralizing when I read an original piece of journalism that highlights the experiences of racialized people, only to scroll to the comments section and see it teeming with bigots intent on tearing down the work, denying discrimination, and spouting stereotypes and hate.

It's not just the comments sections that upset me. In 2016, after Facebook released the ability to react[6] to links beyond a simple like, with emojis like hearts and sad faces, I noticed that many stories that featured people of colour sharing details about their racial and ethnocultural experiences were tagged with laughing emojis. Clicking through to see why, I found users ridiculing the people in news stories for crying wolf about racism.

The "Taking Care" report, conducted by the Canadian Journalism Forum on Violence and Trauma in 2022, asked journalists whether they had experienced online harassment or threats in the past four years. Fifty-six percent of them said yes. When you look at the racial breakdown, 54 percent of white journalists answered yes, which was much lower than their racialized counterparts. Those who identified as Arab, 83 percent; as South Asian or Filipino, 75 percent; and as Black, 71 percent.[7] A CBC journalist surveyed in the report shared this about the impact of such toxicity against media workers: "I believe in what we do and that has always carried me through, but when it feels like so many other people no longer believe in us, it's discouraging."

But nestled within the comments lie widespread assumptions about race that deserve to be challenged because they are harmful and in many cases untrue. The reasoning behind shutdown commands shares similarities with what Henry calls "discourses of domination" – narratives that uphold the white dominance of

Canadian culture. These are a part of democratic racism, using progressive-sounding excuses to further regressive views.

Some of the logic wielded by commenters might give you a headache. For example, did you ever consider that trying to stop racism can cause more racism? These shutdown commands might sound rational on the surface, but they are rife with logical fallacies and arguments that lack evidence, contain contradictions, or are based on irrelevant points.

It's important for news audiences and journalists to be aware of the faulty reasoning behind shutdown commands so that they can counter it. I've selected a number of the most common ones for examination. Rather than let anyone who uses a shutdown command have the final word, here are some ways to challenge them – whether you're a journalist or someone in the audience – to keep the conversation going.

"Reporting on race is racist."

How's this for a paradox of a shutdown command? When I wrote my first essays on how the white gaze shapes portrayals of people of colour in journalism, I received the following email: "interesting how you chris will start to promote more Racism in our country rather then be part of a solution [sic]." Another told me that I should "get past this identity politics bullshit and accept that we are essentially the same."

But what exactly is the behaviour that these commenters are calling racist? Well, they're defining racism as simply mentioning race, and pointing out the way that it manifests in societal divisions. As a result, they believe that anyone who talks about race is racist.

There is a fallacy called *tu quoque,* which means "you also" in Latin. It is an attempt to discredit a speaker by pointing out their own behaviour. In this case, commenters accusing a journalist reporting on racism of being racist, according to their definition.

If journalists do as these commenters suggest – ignore race and "accept" that we are all the same – then they'd be ignoring the very real divides that exist in every aspect of Canadian society. It's no wonder that stories about darlings and delicious cultures are so popular: they allow audiences to indulge in Canadian narratives of opportunity and plurality without having to confront unequal realities. As DiAngelo says, "unequal power relations cannot be challenged if they are not acknowledged."

There is a slightly milder version of this shutdown command: "Reporting on race divides us." This blames the reporting itself for dividing people. But race by definition is a way of dividing people, and it exists whether or not it is talked about. Unless we know how groups of people are privileged or oppressed because of their racial or ethnocultural identity, we won't know the ways in which we should be striving for equality.

Anyone who uses either of these shutdown commands should be challenged with the following questions: Are you uncomfortable learning about how some groups have privilege because of their racial identity? And about how other groups experience discrimination and oppression? Are you trying to avoid stories that share ways that our country is racist because you prefer hearing about stories that focus on unity? Also, if these shutdown commands imply that journalists should cease reporting on any topic that could or might be divisive, then following this logic, we should forget about covering everything else that could potentially be divisive, from politics to hockey.

"Reporting on race shouldn't be done because we are all part of the human race."

In his famous "I Have a Dream" speech, Martin Luther King Jr. shared his hope that his children "will one day live in a nation where they will not be judged by the color of their skin but by the content of their character."[8] According to DiAngelo, many white people misread and embraced this as a "simple and immediate" solution to racism: all they have to do is focus on merit, not race.

The extrapolation of King's words popularized the idea of "colour-blindness." Never mind that King also talked about the need to reconcile with the "manacles of segregation and the chains of discrimination" – all we need to do is treat each other equally. "I don't see colour" has become a proud declaration of enlightenment and what some believe to be the correct approach to racial issues. But the line hearkens back to Henry's democratic racism: it suggests equality, but actually encourages erasure.

A former premier once uttered the line during a debate. British Columbia NDP candidate John Horgan was running for re-election in 2020. After he was asked to comment on white privilege, he shared a story about his youth playing sports with friends who were of Indigenous and South Asian backgrounds, concluding with "I don't see colour."[9] People were quick to challenge Horgan (he would later apologize), including journalist Sunny Dhillon.[10] "If you don't see colour, you don't see us," he tweeted. Psychologists say that adopting a colour-blind ideology of race leads to "power evasion," denying the existence of structural racism.[11]

In 2023, the *Globe and Mail* published a story about Black artists sharing Black experiences through opera.[12] The director and librettist of one production talked about the importance of telling authentic stories: "This is not a white opera about a Black subject. This is a Black opera."

Two days later, the publication's link to the story on Facebook had garnered over 350 comments. Predictably, many of the responses said that talent is more important than skin colour and implied that the artists were only given opportunities because of diversity quotas. The top comment, with over 100 reactions, blasted the coverage: "Focusing on someone's skin color and saying their story matters more than others [sic] stories is racist. Sorry but it's true. If you really cared about racism you wouldn't be dividing people by race, period. You would be telling the stories that are profound to human nature, no matter their skin color."

Let's see what this commenter is trying to define as racism. According to them, one criterion is "focusing on someone's skin colour." The commenter ignores the significance of what it means for a marginalized group to be able to share their own stories. Instead, they suggest that highlighting Black experiences is racist because we should be highlighting "stories that are profound to human nature." Did they mean to imply that that racialized experiences aren't profound? Or even human?

This is "All Lives Matter" ideology, which promotes "racial dismissal, ignoring, and denial," according to critical race scholar David Theo Goldberg.[13] Of course we're all human, but Black people and other racialized groups deserve to be recognized after their experiences have been kept out of journalism for so long in favour of racist misrepresentations.

"Reporting on race makes racism worse."

I once received an email from a reader that told me my essays on the white gaze in Canadian media were prompting "garden-variety racism and stereotyping of white people."

Yes, I've heard this one before. But then the commenter went on to say that such work "may actually help provoke the formation of a defensive white consciousness that will lead to the very kind of white nationalism you think you are challenging." According to the commenter, I was "shaming" whiteness, and that the "beneficiaries of increasing race consciousness among whites will, of course, be the Conservatives."

This is one heck of a shutdown command, with the commenter claiming that reporting on race, and whiteness in particular, would strengthen the cause of white nationalists. What a backfire for journalists! There's a false cause here, also known as a causal fallacy, which assumes that one event produces the effect of another. In this case, the commenter is warning journalists that reporting on race will result in an eye-for-an-eye situation, and that white people made aware of their racial identity will lash out in response.

The commenter is also blaming journalists for the issue of racism. According to the authors of The Myth of Racial Colour Blindness, "By claiming that the discourse is the problem, people are able to evade the real culprit – that is, racist acts or behaviour ... What is made worse in such situations is the comfort level of Whites who want to ignore race."[14] That applies to institutions too, giving them an excuse to avoid investigating why certain inequalities exist.

To my fellow journalists, ignore the foolish commenters who use this shutdown command. Who honestly believes that racism is remedied with silence? Just keep on reporting.

"Reporting on race should be ignored in favour of more important issues."

There are commenters who accuse journalists of wasting airtime and print space reporting on race because it's a "fringe" issue belonging to "special interest" groups trying to push their "identity politics" and "woke agenda."

Instead, journalists should be reporting on the "real" and "bigger" issues, the ones about life and death, they say. While audience members suggest global capitalism and wealth inequality, climate change is the one I notice that gets brought up the most. These audience members cite facts like the damage to ecosystems, the speed at which the global temperature is rising, and the effects it has on human health. I don't doubt that they genuinely care about climate change, but they wield these tallies of destruction as a kind of indisputable evidence to belittle the value of reporting on race and to smother what they believe is frivolous reporting on identity politics while our planet is in peril. There's a bit of the relative privation fallacy in this shutdown command, pointing to worst case scenarios to avoid the subject at hand.

A reader once wrote to me about climate change with the note that, "it will matter little if the victims are white or Asian, LGBTQ or otherwise, whether we experienced intergenerational trauma, or were raised in loving, tolerant, liberal, racialized families. The ultimate outcome will be extinction for all of us, without distinction." Comments like this show a lack of intersectional understanding, ignoring how "bigger" crises have systemic and social dimensions, with the vulnerable and marginalized being hardest hit. It's ignorant to assume that inequality is purely about class, that a pandemic is purely about health, and that climate change is purely about the environment. Race has ways of intersecting with them all.

Those who follow climate change closely should know that its impacts are felt unequally, a point raised by United Nations experts. A 2022 report warned about the creation of "sacrifice zones" around the world, within and between countries, with the burden of contamination falling "most heavily upon communities that are already vulnerable or marginalized because of race, poverty and other socioeconomic factors."[15]

There's another problem with the suggestion that journalists should not report on race because there are supposedly bigger issues in the world. If we take this suggestion to the extreme, should we forget about reporting on art, culture, and sports? Instead of race, perhaps those commenters who use this shutdown command should protest book reviews, travel articles, and any other coverage where human extinction is not a direct concern. I never see commenters picking on book editors and sports announcers. Picking on race for being unimportant to them is just racism.

"Reporting on racism in Canada is false because the country is not racist."

There are commenters who seem genuinely offended that a journalist would dare produce journalism that suggests there is racism in this country. They say, look at our legislation, which enshrines multiculturalism as something to be preserved, enhanced, and shared! Look at our good works, welcoming immigrants and refugees to a land of opportunity! Look at our diverse population, with people of colour in significant numbers who are free to practice their cultures!

A retired university instructor once shared this last point with me. He was upset with my journalism on race and refused to believe that racism was still alive and well in Canadian media. His proof?

The fact that he walks past lots of happy people of colour every day in Vancouver. People who take this view mistake presence for power. They see people of all colours around them and believe that the fight for equality has been won. But racism isn't a numbers game. Just because there are a lot of people of colour strolling the streets doesn't necessarily mean that they are also in positions of power.

There are conservative voices who think we are past racism as well. In 2020, commentator Rex Murphy wrote a controversial opinion piece entitled "Canada Is Not a Racist Country, Despite What the Liberals Say" in the *National Post*. (The publication later updated the online article with an apology, admitting that there was "failure in the normal editing oversight.")[16] Mantras like "Canada is not a racist country" are part of the country's four-century-old amnesia and collective denial, argues Henry. Because racism is frequently invisible to everyone but those who experience it, it's all the more important for journalists to document racism in their reporting, to challenge these powerful mantras.

There is another version of this shutdown command: "Canada is not the *most* racist of countries." Commenters employing this command especially like to compare Canada to the US. But are they seriously suggesting that Canadians should do nothing about the problems in our backyard if it's believed that we have it better than other places? Again, another example of the relative privation fallacy, using worst case scenarios as a distraction from the issue at hand.

"Race has nothing to do with the story."

Let's say there's a story about how people of colour are overrepresented among COVID-19 patients. Long-term care homes with a significant percentage of people of colour making up the staff have been particularly affected. In the comments, you see someone claim that this story has nothing to do with race, and that it shouldn't be surprising that health care employees working in-person jobs have a higher likelihood of catching the virus.

Say there's another story, about housing discrimination against racialized families in the city. The families reported on have been contacting landlords about listings and have been invited enthusiastically to come view them. But once the landlords see what these prospective buyers look like, the families are told that a particular listing might not be available. Noticing a pattern, they contact housing advocates and decide to speak to media. In the comments, you see people exclaim that this is not a story about skin colour. Landlords usually don't like renting to families because children are noisy, they say, insisting that journalists are trying to spin this into a story about race.

Remember the judge who presided over the case of the Black women who claimed discrimination at General Motors? The company stated that it wasn't discriminating against Black people because they had hired Black workers, and that it wasn't discriminating against women because they had hired women. Commenters who employ this shutdown command are no different than that judge: they are unable to see the intersectionality at play.

In the stories above, the commenters mention the vulnerabilities faced by front line workers and the housing discrimination set against families – both important factors key to understanding the positionality of the main source. But supplying these definitions doesn't refute the fact that race might play a role. Are journalists supposed to dismiss the dimension of race just because another factor is present? There are audiences who'd rather grasp at all other factors in an attempt to explain the issue at hand without having to accept the uncomfortable truth: that race might play a larger role than they wish to believe.

"The reporting is incorrect because my experience of race is different."

In the comments sections of just about any piece on race, you will find people arguing about how the findings are false. The proof that they offer? Experiences from their own lives.

The fallacy of anecdotal evidence should need no explanation. "It can't be true that people of colour are overrepresented among police street checks because I'm white and I've been street checked many times," one might say. Or, "It can't be true that white people have an easier time finding work in their fields of study because my doctor in Canada just arrived from Taiwan a few years ago." Or, "It can't be true that people of colour say that this city is racist because I live there too and I'm great friends with people of all colours." Comments like these might be followed by an accusation that the journalist is over-generalizing racial issues – never mind that using personal anec-data might be over-generalizing too.

Commenters who use such a shutdown command seem to mis-understand how journalism works. Journalists don't write stories by documenting the first thoughts that pop into their heads. Journalists are professionals with shared practices and ethics on how they gather and share information. This doesn't mean that the stories they produce are perfect (as this book attests!), but it does mean that they strive to produce coverage that is informed by real people and backed up by research.

Generalizations are sometimes made, but it's no different from the work of social scientists. DiAngelo says that she's comfortable generalizing because "social life is patterned and predictable in measurable ways ... There are, of course, exceptions, but patterns are recognized as such precisely because they are recurring and predictable. We cannot understand modern forms of racism if we cannot or will not explore patterns of group behavior and their effects on individuals."[17]

In *White Fragility*, DiAngelo does recognize that generalizations can cause white people to be defensive. To that, she offers this advice: "Try to let go of your individual narrative and grapple with the collective messages we all receive as members of a larger shared culture. Work to see how these messages have shaped your life, rather than use some aspect of your story to excuse yourself from their impact."

Fighting the Silence

Journalists serve the public interest, and some engagement and healthy debate with audiences is part of the job. But it's hard when there are audience members who stand up and reject race as a topic worth reporting on, going so far as to question the integrity of journalists and newsrooms that engage with it. What's in the public interest, like issues of race, might not be interesting to all members of the public.

An article published by media institute Poynter captures the problem faced by journalists: "When writing about race, abuse follows. Especially for journalists of color and women. It leaves reporters in a no-win situation: Either write about important subjects and face hate, or leave crucial subjects unexplored." This abuse is bad for everyone, said Gina Masullo, a media professor quoted in the article. "If journalists can't do their job effectively because they're being attacked so much, that isn't good for democracy because their job is to hold power accountable."[18]

Abuse and shutdown commands don't just have an effect on the life of stories after they air or are published; stories can be aborted in the brainstorming and pitching process. Journalists might avoid or tiptoe around topics they fear will aggravate their audiences, muting their frames and language to avoid backlash. Words like "genocide" and "white" – not to mention "white privilege" or "white supremacy" – are particularly triggering to audience members who might instantly turn off coverage that contains such language. I've self-censored many times, like when trying to write about racism without mentioning the word "racism" itself, worried that the R-word would outrage and frighten away readers unprepared to confront uncomfortable truths about privilege and inequality head-on.

But should journalists really be trying to anticipate audiences' shutdown commands, tailoring and toning down their coverage to make it more palatable? On one hand, you could argue that it's the job of journalists to make information digestible for the masses. Perhaps audiences will come to greater racial understanding if the coverage is free of language that has come to be viewed as "politically charged." But on the other hand, you could argue that this is catering too much to that fragility, and that it's important for audiences to confront racism for what it is.

As a journalist, especially a journalist of colour, it can be incredibly distressing and depressing to see that there are people in your audience in denial about the racial problems you have spelled out in your story, telling you that they don't exist. I once wrote a story about language discrimination and how immigrants and refugees have a hard time finding employment, reading their own health information, and accessing city services. It's something I've witnessed first-hand as an interpreter for relatives who were ridiculed at medical offices for not knowing English and asked to go away.

Readers came after the story with the shutdown command that this has nothing to do with race and is not racism. They also denied the existence of language discrimination in Canada. These challenges are simply part of the newcomer experience, they said, and blamed newcomers for making plans to move to Canada without taking the time to learn an official language. The commenters also wielded their own experiences as proof that it could be done: If they could learn Spanish after spending some years in Spain, why couldn't others learn English or French after moving to Canada? I was awed by the privilege expressed by some of the English-speaking commenters. They compared their own experiences of picking up Romance languages abroad, on trips undertaken for leisure, with that of one of my sources, a refugee from a fishing village in Vietnam who had little formal schooling and struggled to learn English after moving to Canada because he was working multiple jobs to provide for his family.

Behind many shutdown commands is the idea that any discussion about race – and whiteness in particular – should be off limits. It reminded me of the adults of my childhood who hushed me whenever I used the word "white." I suppose this was my first experience with a shutdown command, and the belief that delving into race was, in the words of the grown-ups, "not nice."

Journalists need to be prepared to cut through the shutdown commands and communicate to audiences why a racial dimension is needed for a holistic understanding of the social factors behind the daily headlines. Yes, audiences will experience discomfort. But it is necessary for journalists to challenge audiences through their reporting if they are to learn how racial differences, divides, and discrimination impact the lives and livelihoods of people of colour.

7

Of Words and Worry

One of the most agonizing parts of being a journalist is choosing the right words. I know what you're probably thinking. A journalist struggling to find the right words? Isn't that the job? Yes, but the stakes couldn't be higher with the representation of an under-represented group in your hands. Choose the right words and your audience will become more familiar with people whose experiences are often left out of the news. But choose the wrong ones and you risk falling victim to the white gaze, losing a chance to inform your audience, and reinforcing negative racial stereotypes.

The derivative diversity Ds introduced earlier show common story frames when it comes to journalism on people of colour, but those frames are held together by language, which is the nuts and bolts of representation.

Nobody wants to sound out of touch. There are myriad evolving style guides out there to keep people up to date on inclusive and non-stigmatizing language, from those found at individual workplaces to ones used by scholarly institutions and professional associations. The Associated Press was mocked for a tweet that recommended avoiding "general and often dehumanizing 'the' labels such as the poor, the mentally ill, the French."[1] Twitter users joked about the alternative being "people experiencing Frenchness." *Washington Post* columnist Megan McArdle tweeted that "the people experiencing journalism at the AP have their work cut out for them."[2] Not even the illustrious Associated Press could avoid being teased for a poor example of what was otherwise a good point about style.

The best of style guides don't stay fresh forever. It's no exception for journalism, with Canadian newsrooms having to purchase new *Canadian Press Stylebooks* every few years. It may seem strange for a book we all have to have, but it's not the fault of the writers of these guides for being unable to publish a lasting document. Words expire and new ones are ushered in all the time, all the more so with language related to race and culture. Not that long ago, people wouldn't have batted an eye at a descriptor for non-white people as clumsy as "ethnically diverse individuals."

Code Switch, NPR's race and culture outlet, examined the phenomenon of our evolving language on race in an article titled "Why We Have So Many Terms for 'People of Colour.'"[3] They explored how labels like "minority" fall out of use due to inaccuracy while others become too saddled with negative usage like "coloured." It's a bit like a treadmill, but this is how language works: "It reflects the relationships between speakers and groups," wrote the author. "These descriptors will be in flux as long as our orientations to each other keep changing." The *New York Times* ran an article about the racial terms that "make you cringe"[4] but are still in use, recognizing that many acceptable terms are still far from perfect.

Both the Canadian Press and its American counterpart, the Associated Press, offer some helpful foundations for journalists on the language of race in their respective style guides. However, these sections are short.

A number of other style guides have been created to help fill in these gaps, from the Conscious Style Guide to the Radical Copyeditor, both of which also cover language around gender, sexuality, disability, and more. In Canada, Gregory Younging, the late publisher of Theytus Books, the country's first Indigenous-owned publishing house, adapted many of their lessons on countering the language of white ethnocentrism into *Elements of Indigenous Style: A Guide for Writing By and About Indigenous Peoples*. During the COVID-19 pandemic, Elimin8Hate produced a timely style guide (which I advised on) called "Reporting on Asian Canadian Communities," to highlight how media can avoid reproducing anti-Asian racism.[5] Many major news outlets have in-house style guides too, to cover challenges their own journalists commonly run into.

Some style guides are just a list of words to use and words to avoid. You won't find such an A to Z below. Rather than supply a cheat sheet that will eventually expire, I've picked out some common challenges that journalists encounter when it comes to the language of race, ethnicity, and culture. How to talk about people the way they talk about themselves? How to translate racial and cultural experiences for a mass audience without sounding cheesy or exoticizing? How to avoid journalese, the hyperbolic over-abbreviated language of news media?

People who believe they are under siege by the armies of "woke culture" might take one look at such a journalistic guide on language and cry, "Censorship!" It's not about policing language, though; it's about using language that is accurate and avoids unnecessary harm. As the Canadian Press style guide says, journalists "must reflect and showcase the ethnic diversity of the country in a natural, organic way that is free of bias, whether it be explicit or unconscious."[6] It starts with choosing the right words.

Whatever the vocabulary of the moment is, here are a few lasting lessons to keep in mind:

Be specific. Journalists should avoid homogenizing groups.

Avoid othering language. Journalists shouldn't imply that whiteness is the baseline of normality.

Go easy on the colour. Journalists might find it irresistible to exaggerate markers of difference, especially in display copy like headlines. Don't allow it to lead to racial stereotypes. Also, be on the lookout for times when race is not relevant at all.

Let's dig into these a big deeper.

More Than a Monolith

Journalists reporting on people of colour love using the word "community," as mentioned in Chapter 4. It's vague, but denotes a sense of belonging that makes a story easier to cover. Journalists report on how "the Asian community" is worrying about something,[7] how an artist is "popular with the South Asian community,"[8] how the "national Korean community has waited for [a] moment for decades,"[9] how institutions want to build trust with "diverse communities,"[10] how this community "stays united,"[11] how that community is "excited" about something,[12] protesting this, and mourning that. But because "community" suggests unity, does this language imply that every single person with that respective identity feels the same way? When journalists use these all-encompassing labels, it gives audiences a homogenous impression of racialized and ethnocultural groups.

This is why it's important for journalists to be specific when describing who's at the centre of a story. Do they seriously intend to describe a group as functioning in thought and deed as a single unit?

Journalists often use the word "community" to combat the vagueness of standalone descriptors. It has a pleasant air to it and sounds definitive, lending weight and authority to their stories.

Adding the word to a singular pronoun like "Asians" so that it reads "the Asian community" seems less othering, avoiding the aforementioned blunder made by the Associated Press. But such a label is still vague. It would be better to specify who are the "Asians" talked about in the story, and who the community is made up of. Is this story about a group of national origin, or is it about everyone who identifies as a particular ethnicity? Does it concern newcomers or long-time residents?

One place where it can be useful to use the word "community" is when describing an ethnocultural group within a specific geography, such as "The Jamaican community in Toronto" or "The Vietnamese community on Victoria Drive." The marker tells the audience that journalists are talking about a specific population in a single community.

One small improvement to prevent the audience from viewing a group as a monolith is to use the plural: "communities." For example, the makeup of people with South Asian backgrounds in Canada is incredibly diverse. "Canada's South Asian community" is absolutely flattening. "Canada's South Asian communities" is a little better, though journalists shouldn't allow that little "s" to do all the heavy lifting. They can add subsequent details so that the audience knows who's included. Depending on the story, a journalist might include notes about linguistic diversity, religious diversity, or geographic origin. In CBC's coverage of Diwali, journalists noted that it is the biggest holiday of the year for "many South Asian communities" and is celebrated by "several major religions around the world and, for each faith, it marks different stories and histories." The story goes on to note those differences for Hindus, Jains, and Sikhs,[13] allowing the pluralization to pave the way for further descriptors of plurality.

"Diaspora" is a less loaded word than community. It doesn't carry the same rosy connotations of harmony and has more clearly defined boundaries, which can help audiences understand that the "Japanese diaspora" in places like Canada is different than Japanese people living in Japan.

That being said, a diaspora is still a very big group. Canada, with its long legacy of immigration, is made up of newcomers as well as long-time migrants and their children. A story might require a journalist to be more specific about status or generational details. Is the story talking about the diaspora as a whole? Or does it need to hone in on foreign nationals, newcomers, or Canadian citizens?

If an ethnocultural group does seem to share a monolithic opinion, what then? Journalists, don't put your intersectional lens away just yet. It might be the case that the group has something in common, such as being predominantly working class, having all left the same point of origin and arriving in Canada at the same time due to immigration policy. If you encounter a monolith, you could educate audiences about how that monolith might've come to be.

And as pleasant as "community" might sound, don't forget you can also use the word "people." Rather than generic, homogenizing singular pronouns like "whites" and "Blacks," there's nothing wrong with using "white people" or "Black people." It's simple, and doesn't create an artificial community where one might not exist in your story.

Members and Leaders

Just as the word "community" sounds like an official unit, the word "member" sounds like an individual who is officially part of that unit.

Let's say we have an election story about how "members of the Taiwanese community" supported a particular candidate. Does it mean that all people within that ethnocultural group are a united force that adheres to strict rules and bylaws about their political leanings or how to express their shared identity? Maybe this candidate is popular with Taiwanese newcomers because of what she said about creating job opportunities, but not so much with well-established immigrants who already have jobs. Maybe this candidate is popular with young people with Taiwanese roots because of her social media campaigning, but not so much with seniors who are offline. Journalists need to explain this. Taiwaneseness or any other marker of identity is not an explanation for why people vote a certain way, and suggesting that it is or could be pushes the racial stereotype of an ethnic voting bloc. Even if the candidate was born in Taiwan, the journalist needs to explain why they might be popular with Taiwanese Canadians. (Imagine if there was actually such a thing as an "Asian community," which news outlets like to reference. I could be a card-carrying member. We could have dinner, the many millions and billions of us.)

With "community" also comes the word "leader," which signals that a person is well-respected and has formal or informal power. People of colour often show up in stories framed as though they were elected democratically and are speaking on behalf of all those "members" who share their identity, whether they're claiming the label of leader or had it bestowed on them by the journalist who spoke to them. I can't help but imagine audiences with a white gaze viewing the people described as leaders of racial and ethnocultural communities as tribal chiefs, universally revered and respected.

Rather than just acclaiming leaders, journalists need to be clear about who these people are. If such a person is an activist, a religious figure, a prominent businessperson, or the head of an organization, why not say so? That way, audiences know exactly who these supposed leaders are representing and where their priorities and sense of importance comes from. Someone who has power because they have a lot of money is very different from someone who is respected for their social contributions.

Of course, the word doesn't just appear in stories about people of colour. You'll no doubt have come across stories on the news or in newspapers about the "hockey community," the "arts community," or the "local business community." But what's different about grouping people of colour into a community is that it has the potential to make a misrepresented group into a monolith, connecting people together who don't always belong. Do journalists lead audiences to assume that all "members" of a community share the same stance, especially when it comes to politics or a controversial issue? And in their stories, do journalists refer to groups like the "Black community" or the "Pakistani community" as if they're forever foreigners and not truly Canadian, separated from society at large?

Not White? What to Write?

What to call people who aren't white? "Ethnic" and "visible minorities" are terms that are on their way out. So is the successor "people of colour," "racialized people," or "non-whites"? The right term depends on the context, so committing to using only one and ignoring all the others won't do.

"People of colour" works when talking about all groups together as a whole.

"Racialized people" can be used in the same way. Because the term "racialized" refers to how whiteness has othered everyone else, there are stories in which "racialized people" would be a more descriptive term than "people of colour." For example, it would be better to use "racialized employees" over "employees of colour" in a story about workplace discrimination because there is an action taking place.

As for "non-white," who would want to be known by such a label? People want to be identified by what they are, not what they are not; however, in stories that compare or contrast white people with everyone else, the label can be useful.

The term "visible minority" has generally been retired as a term for people of colour, but there are institutional settings in which it is clinging to life because of its status as a legal definition. Canadian employment law uses the term as a basis for discrimination,[14] which means you might see it in reports that you draw from for your journalism, such as Statistics Canada data. But it can be swapped out in stories for "people of colour" and "racialized people."

Because of migration, Canada has communities where the term "visible minority" is inaccurate due to white people being the minority population. The term "majority minority," despite being a paradox, has been used as a catchy term to describe these communities. However, it's also led white people who live in them to say that they are the new minorities. Because the term "minority" has historically been used to describe marginalized groups, white people have claimed marginalization and victimization simply because they have become the minority when it comes down to the numbers. Think back to the coverage of the Chinese signage debate in which a white woman said that "We, the new visible minorities, are experiencing exclusion,"[15] without considering which privileges they – white people – might have over new immigrants of colour.

"Ethnic" is also retired, but it appears in terms that still show up in journalism, such as "ethnic groups," "ethnic hatred," and "ethnic violence." Ethnicity is defined by anthropologists as people who identify as a group based on "perceptions of shared social experience or ancestry ... sharing cultural traditions and history that distinguish them from other groups."[16] Someone could be ethnically Japanese and a Canadian national, or ethnically Malay and a Singaporean national. The problem is how journalists often use the word to describe anyone or anything that isn't white, as in "ethnic food" or "ethnic cultures." Foods considered Western, like pasta and baguettes, would fit the definition of ethnic foods, but they're not commonly described as such. Journalists who use this word should double check whether they are reinforcing whiteness or the Western world as the baseline of normality, othering everything else as ethnic.

"Ethnic enclaves" is another term that has stuck around and is still used by both sociologists and geographers. But over the years, it has been burdened with stigma, treating enclaves as if they were rundown ghettoes. Journalists should try to find other ways to describe a place that has a large population of people of colour.

Rather than "ethnic," "ethnocultural" has been adopted by social scientists and government agencies like Statistics Canada to emphasize that these groups are not only defined by shared attributes but also shared practices.

And with all this discussion about what to call people who are not white, it is also important for journalists not to shy away from using "white" in stories where it is an important distinction. If journalists commonly use the terms "racialized people" and "people of colour" but not "white people," it implies that white people are the norm and that they don't need an extra label. For example, whiteness would be relevant in a story on crime where race is a factor, stories on racial inequality, and of course, stories on racism.

Distilling Diversity

Too often do journalists report on diversity while fudging the use of the word "diversity." There are stories about governments wanting to hire "diverse people," and stories about those diverse people bringing "diverse perspectives."[17] There are spotlights of "diverse cultures" in a city serving "diverse foods." There are data reports about how "diverse groups" and "diverse communities" are on the rise in Canada.

Rather than being used to refer to people and elements that are different from one another, the word "diversity" is used to describe things that are different from a supposed norm. In the cases above, which refer to race and culture, "diverse" is used to describe anyone and anything that isn't white or Western. As someone who isn't white, this rationale would mean that I am an inherently diverse human being who has diverse views and eats diverse foods at every meal.

Alex Kapitan, who runs the website Radical Copyeditor, explains the problem like this: "If you follow this thinking to the root, it's based on the idea that there is a neutral, majority, dominant way of being, and that diversity is the addition of non-normative elements to that supposedly 'default' environment. This is a falsehood. The truth is that diversity is what humanity inherently contains – we all differ from one another."[18]

No person, place, or thing can be inherently diverse. And the word should not be used as a stand-in for anything racialized because it then promotes the idea of whiteness as normative. Instead, the accurate way to use the word is to describe variance, as in a "diversity of cultures," or the need for people from a "greater diversity" of backgrounds.

The word "mainstream" can be problematic in the same way, used as a stand-in for "white" in phrases like "mainstream Canadians." It is also used to talk about assimilation, with people of colour adapting to a "mainstream Canadian identity." Journalists should avoid this language, as it implies that there is such a thing as a mainstream Canadian identity, and that such an identity is a white one. I've interviewed many people of colour who have become so used to employing these frames that they practice self-othering, describing themselves as being outside of the mainstream. Which begs the question, does that mean they can never belong?

Endonyms and Exonyms

An "endonym" is a proper name used internally by a group of people to describe themselves, a place, or their language. Endonyms are all about self-identification by a native group. An "exonym" is the opposite. It is a name used by non-natives for a people, a place, or a language. Endonyms and exonyms are a useful way to distinguish between names used by people inside and outside of a group, and I like to use them to describe other aspects of culture that are often reinterpreted for western audiences.

For example, "Chinese New Year" is an exonym because Chinese people don't go around saying "Happy Chinese New Year." English speakers came up with it to differentiate from the Gregorian New Year. In this case, the endonym used by Chinese people is the "agricultural new year." (Of course, nobody goes around saying, "Happy agricultural new year." They just say, "Happy new year," the same way that English speakers don't wish each other, "Happy Gregorian New Year.")

I was introduced to endonyms and exonyms at an early age thanks to my mom, who tried to interpret Chinese foods for my Canadian-born palate. I was hooked on Chinese desserts with red bean paste, which she told me was "Chinese chocolate."

Journalism is filled with endonyms and exonyms. "Pajeon" has been called a "Korean pancake." A "gurdwara" has been called a "Sikh temple." A "kirpan" has been called a "ceremonial sword" or "ceremonial dagger." "Mithai," the word for sweets in a number of South Asian languages, has been changed to "Indian sweets." "Bánh mì" has been called a "Vietnamese sandwich," though as it's gained recognition in the west, journalists have gone slightly beyond the exonym to call them "bánh mì sandwiches" (which, if you know Vietnamese, is a bit redundant because the phrase means "bread sandwiches" – the same reason people are ridiculed for saying "chai tea"). One particularly egregious offender is the exonym "East Indian," which was used by colonizing Europeans and still lingers today as a way to describe people from South Asia and to differentiate them from "American Indians," another exonym.

In many cases, you'll see that an exonym is just a word familiar to English readers with a nationality attached to it. Do you like tapas? Then you'll love dim sum, which is Chinese tapas! There is an episode of *The Office* in which the character Kelly Kapoor invites her white colleagues to celebrate Diwali for the first time. Her colleagues understand it to be an "Indian Halloween."[19] Aside from exonyms, similes are sometimes used to bring "foreign" people into a Western frame of reference. The CBC published an essay that called Jose Mari Chan the "Michael Bublé of Filipino Christmas."[20]

I've interviewed sources who, knowing that I serve an English-speaking audience, spoke to me using exonyms rather than endonyms, telling me specifically that they wouldn't use words from their own language because English speakers "wouldn't understand." For example, an Indian dairy manufacturer I once interviewed told me about making "Indian cheese" rather than "chhena."

However, endonyms like "sushi" and "kimchi" have ended up in stories because audiences in Canada have become familiar enough with them to avoid using "rice rolls" or "Korean pickled cabbage." But as people in the business of providing a public service by informing audiences about the world around them, journalists can play a role in introducing new words to their audiences, especially those used by ethnocultural groups in Canada.

That way, we can all avoid the clumsy – and in some cases ridiculous – exonyms that insist on putting everything within a Western frame of reference.

Learning new language is part of consuming media. Who cracks open a book and expects to know every word or concept within? The same applies to journalism, which is a form of communication that informs audiences about the world around them. If representative journalism is about telling stories about underrepresented groups from the inside out rather than the outside in, audiences should expect to learn some new words along the way.

The Explanatory Pause

How can journalists introduce a term in a news story that might be new to some members of the audience? Why, by taking a brief pause to explain it.

An "explanatory comma" is a punctuation mark in which you can almost hear the journalist behind a story clearing their throat before launching into an explanation of a term. "Today is Eid al-fitr (ahem), the holiday which marks the end of Ramadan." "Ramadan (ahem), the holy month for Muslims during which they fast." "Yasmin and her family are making ma'maoul (ahem), shortbread cookies with fillings like dates, walnuts, and pistachios."

The term "explanatory comma" was coined by an editor at the *Code Switch* podcast, who called it a "signpost" for audiences.[21] It is practical punctuation that punches above its weight, though the podcast goes on to explore two minds about its usage.

There's the question of whether an explanatory pause is "over-explaining for white people." It's as if the comma is a starting pistol for a journalist to go running over to their white audience members to share the explanation, which is brief and could minimize and understate the importance of the term at hand. To the same effect, I've inserted explanatory paragraphs, briefing an audience on famous people, historic events, and cultural practices. After such a pause, the journalist continues telling the story.

"How you decide whether to explain something or not tells you a lot about who a storyteller understands their audience to be," explained the podcast's editor. People from an ethnocultural group might be turned off when a journalist's explanation of something from their lives that they are intimately familiar with caters instead to outsiders. As in a sentence like, "The restaurant sells phở, a beef noodle soup enjoyed in Vietnam." I've put down such journalism because of how it so glaringly adopts the white gaze.

However, journalists also have to take into account that not everyone in their audience is going to be starting out with the same set of references. In response to *Code Switch's* discussion of the explanatory comma, the hosts were contacted by "angry" listeners who said it's the job of journalists to explain things. After all, there are going to be Canadians who might not know who BTS are or the details of the Iranian revolution. The explanatory comma's brevity can be a good thing too, offering a quick, nonintrusive primer.

Journalists could also try to integrate explanations into their stories more naturally. The CBC headline "International Students Celebrate Their First Diwali Away From Home – Together"[22] works great because the audience is told about a specific experience of a holiday in Canada. The journalist reports on international students in Waterloo getting together to celebrate the holiday, and along the way sprinkles in contextual information about Diwali from practices to decorations like rangoli. The journalist teaches a lot about the holiday without the aside of an explanatory pause, which places the characters at the centre of the story while ensuring that the audience isn't left behind.

So is the explanatory comma a mark of the white gaze? Or is it a helpful tool for accessibility? Journalists will have to decide whether their story begs for an explanation, how much of one, and how to avoid using othering language.

But if there are words that should have entered common usage, like phở or bhangra, I don't believe audiences deserve a pause. They can look it up!

Too Much Colour for People of Colour

While journalism is about reporting the truth, crafting creative headlines and leads to open a story is a welcome and regular part of our day-to-day work. These strong teasers and openings can be lively and attention-grabbing, but not, as the Canadian Press cautions, at the expense of accuracy and fairness. According to the CP stylebook, "Many readers stop at the headline; if it gives them a misleading impression of the story, they will take that with them."[23]

Lighthearted stories can also invite opportunities for a journalist to employ colourful language throughout. I don't think journalism students should be allowed to graduate without an education on puns. Though when it comes to stories about people of colour, there is a danger of using too much colour. Journalists might perpetuate racial and cultural stereotypes or treat serious topics without sensitivity when, say, talking about how a Black Canadian is marching to the beat of his own drum, or how an ethnically Indian politician is bringing the spice.

The *Globe and Mail* once published a rare story that interviewed wealthy Chinese immigrants to Vancouver about their experiences with the housing market during the years they were blamed for supercharging prices. The headline for the online edition of the story was "The Dragon in the Room."[24] Okay, it's playing off of the "elephant in the room," but dragons are not mentioned anywhere in the story. If the dragon is a stand-in for Chinese nationals, does the word choice conjure up images of an ancient and powerful beast, of an interloper, essentializing them to audiences before they have a chance to dive into the story?

Another *Globe* story interviewed the Taiwanese Canadian family who founded T&T, the country's largest East and Southeast Asian supermarket chain, when they sold it Loblaws in 2009.[25] The headline: "A Dynasty Built on Instinct." Hm, would the writer have chosen the word "dynasty" if it wasn't an East Asian family behind the chain? What does such a word communicate to the audience in a story about a racialized company on the rise?

I was introduced to this problem during my first year as a journalist, when one of my editors changed a headline I wrote for a story about aging buildings in Chinatown to include the words "rickety heritage." I worried whether such a description might conjure up orientalist images of rickshaws, junks, opium dens, and Fu Manchu caricatures.

In and beyond display copy like headlines, journalists should ask themselves how the race, ethnicity, and culture of sources shape how they are described. Journalists should also question how this language adds to the coverage and whether there is potential for othering or harm, such as relying on dated imagery and furthering stereotypes of underrepresented and misrepresented groups. A CBC story about Lunar New Year celebrations during the year of the rabbit – a return to pre-pandemic festivities for Newfoundland – ran the headline "Hopping Back into Action."[26] No orientalist imagery here: a fun informative pun with no harm done.

Aside from language that surfaces stereotypes of racialized people, journalists should avoid exoticizing language that emphasizes their other-ness. For example, a headline like "The Secret

Lives of Toronto's Chinese Bottle Ladies,"[27] published by the *Globe,* communicates to audiences that the story is going to be told from the perspective of normal people who just so happen to glimpse these Chinese bottle ladies scurrying around. Announcing that racialized people live "secret" lives, do "quirky" things, or have "hidden histories," for no reason other than that they're not white, frames them as the other.

This othering language might not be the fault of the reporter at all. Their editor or a non-journalist responsible for data entry working in another city and time zone could be the one making the final call on how a story is packaged – a common practice. But they should be more sensitive when writing display copy that concerns racialized and ethnocultural groups. Or, at the very least, check with the reporter who worked on the story.

The R-Word

In 2019, the Associated Press updated its stylebook[28] with new policies on race-related coverage. In it, they told journalists not to use euphemisms for racism, from "racially charged" to "racially tinged." The Canadian Press didn't use as much detail in its latest version, though it told journalists not to "shy away" from calling racism what it is. As a result, Harvard University's Nieman Foundation for Journalism proclaimed that it's time for journalists to use the "R word."[29]

"I don't see journalists struggle this way on any other issue," said the author of the Nieman article. "We are taught to use the right word, the precise word, not the almost right word – except when it comes to race." If journalists are clear in labelling sexism and homophobia in their work, why not racism? Especially if it is at the heart of a story?

American race and history scholar Khalil Gibran Muhammad
said that toning down the language of racism would be like toning
down the reality of climate change. "When the actual statements
and acts are clear, unmistakable and verified, they should be labeled
racist based on the context, the history and the academic literature
that has blossomed and exploded over the last 40 years to help us
understand what individual racism looks like as well as institutional racism," said Muhammad in an interview with *Journalist's
Resource*.[30] "There is no shortage of research to substantiate what
racism looks like, where it comes from, how it is understood in
historical context."

For journalists who fear libel, the Associated Press recommends
being specific about a person's racist words or actions, which, as
Muhammad says, can be proven. "The only question that should
guide concern about libel is a question of fact and attribution."[31]

In 2021 in London, Ontario, a Muslim family was killed in a truck
attack. Police said they were weighing possible terrorism charges
and believed the attack to be a hate crime.[32] Was it racially motivated? Specifically, was it anti-Muslim hate? Journalists did their
due diligence to include details of past anti-Muslim hate crimes
in Canada in their coverage, supplying audiences with the context
they needed without toning it town to a "racially-tinged incident."[33]

In Their Own Words

What to do when a source says something about race, ethnicity, or
culture that might go against the style guides on hand? Is it worth
including verbatim? Is it worth paraphrasing? Or is it better to ex-
clude it entirely?

If they're a politician or someone prominent with power, it's
important to have their exact words on the record. But let's say

someone is using dated language, talking about "Caucasians," "Orientals," "visible minorities" in their community, or misusing a word like calling racialized people inherently "diverse."

Quoting them verbatim, especially when journalists wouldn't use such language in the body of the story themselves, could imply to the audience that there is no problem with using such language. If a source is making an important point that deserves quoting in the story but uses dated and othering language, the journalist can paraphrase them. This isn't specific to terms related to race or culture. Journalists should be doing the same when sources use words that are derogatory and dated, for example "crackhead" or "prostitute." Their sources might even appreciate them doing this if they didn't realize their words would be perceived as problematic or would distract from the main point they were trying to express.

It can be tricky when sources make sweeping claims about racism. The *Vancouver Sun* once interviewed Stanley Kwok, a prominent architect and real estate developer, at age 96.[34] What to do when a source like Kwok says something like, "I don't believe Canada is a racist place"? "I really don't think there is a race issue," Kwok went on to say. "It's all about whether you can deliver. If you can deliver, race has nothing to do with it." In this case, the source's positionality is key: audiences deserve to know Kwok's privilege – he was educated at a prestigious school in Shanghai and arrived in Vancouver at a time when the local government welcomed overseas investment. Rather than leading audiences to believe that racism doesn't exist in Canada based on the words of an immigrant, a journalist could offer important context to audiences, showing them why someone of Kwok's standpoint might say such a thing.

There will also be sources who rely on stereotypes in their quotes, sometimes about groups they belong to. This can come from sources of all backgrounds, white or not. "I had typical

Korean parents that wanted me to become a doctor or lawyer." "Chinese people always sound like they're yelling." "Our Muslim families would flip out if we moved out at eighteen." "The best Vietnamese restaurants are rundown dives where the owners wear flip-flops." These are colourful quotes that contain telling details, but should they be included when journalists wouldn't be using such language themselves?

I remember interviewing a young woman who divided her time between Richmond, BC, and Hong Kong, where her family was born. The story was about how teenagers navigated issues of race and culture in a city like Richmond, which is mostly comprised of people with roots in Hong Kong, Taiwan, and mainland China. She told me that her Hong Kong relatives would tell her that she was "whitewashed" or "so white" for talking back to her parents. She also used the phrases to describe classmates of colour in Richmond who were not as familiar with their cultures of heritage. For example, she mentioned having Indian Canadian friends who were "whitewashed brown."

I was taken by the candid, colloquial, indelicate language she used. "It's not meant to be discriminatory," she told me. I used some of her quotes, as I felt as though they captured the organic feeling of teenagers trying to make sense one another's differences growing up in a multicultural city, and supplied a disclaimer detailing how this is the unfiltered language you would hear if you were to walk into a Richmond high school, where discussions of identity often bubble up.

Some questions for journalists to consider when they encounter quotes like these: Do the quotes offer insight to the story at hand? Are the quotes surrounded by context that offers more detail about their meaning? Does a source's expertise or experience back up a sweeping statement they are making about a group? Do the quotes and the story as a whole promote essentialist depictions?

Too often I come across stories that use such quotes purely for colour but without that needed context. Let's say a journalist wants to keep the quote above, about the "typical Korean parents that wanted me to become a doctor or lawyer." On its own, without context, it plays into stereotypes about tiger parenting and the model minority, but it could be made more complex. Depending on the angle of the story, the journalist could include a line about immigrant families wanting their children to climb out of poverty, or an acknowledgment of the stereotype and how it creates pressure for children who don't conform to it.

Journalists can examine the quotes they've collected that might be a little raw, to see if they can make a strong case for their inclusion.

The Language of Lack

What to do when a journalist and a source do not speak a common language fluently? It's going to be difficult for such a journalist to report on their source's experiences if they're not able to share fully, lacking the words to do so or by using unconventional syntax.

There are times when journalists quote such sources verbatim anyway, using their level of English as a means of showing their character. We get quotes like "I work hard fifty year, no complain," and "I vote this mayor, no tax, very good." They often show up in stories that follow the diversity Ds, spoken by some cute darling or damaged refugee. Think back to the story about the "angel of East Hastings" who was quoted saying, "I see people, no food, no money, sleep outside, they need money, I give them money."

While colourful, journalists should be aware that such quotes can be othering, possibly robbing the sources of their humanity or making them sound like childish adults. This is one reason why it's helpful to have journalists in a newsroom, or a translator, who speak multiple languages, so that sources can express themselves fully and accurately. There is a world of difference between a quote like "Everyone happy, I happy" and "It's been rewarding to see how thankful people are of our work."

Unlike print journalists who have more leeway when it comes to handling quotes, broadcast journalists are heavily reliant on sound bites like the above. But they can build language around those quotes to give dignity to sources who aren't able to express themselves as well in English.

Journalists should also avoid descriptions that emphasize their sources' lack of English in a way that makes them sound like incomplete individuals. Journalists use the words "doesn't speak English" to describe a source as if they don't speak at all. It's helpful to mention the language they do speak to chase away any misconceptions that a source is illiterate. Sometimes, journalists play up drama with a phrase like "not a word of English"[35] or "didn't speak a lick of English."[36] These embellishments are unnecessary and stigmatizing, as are descriptions of racialized people speaking "perfect English." Such words might be intended to compliment a character for their assimilation, but they also imply that anyone whose degree of English fluency falls outside of what is believed to be normative speaks imperfectly.

Floods of Migrants

There's a set of dramatic but unspecific words in journalese used to describe masses of people of colour coming to Canada. "Surge" is a common one. In 2023, migrants coming into Ontario from an American border crossing were described as such in a CBC headline.[37] "Flood" is another, as in a *National Post* story that talks about what happens when "Syrians flood in."[38] Sometimes it's accompanied by "wave," as in stories like a *Vancouver Magazine* survey of Chinese restaurants that opened in the 1990s, the region being "flooded with waves of Hong Kong immigrants."[39] Other stories talk about how newcomers are "overwhelming" the country, from social services to the government being unable to process their large number.[40] In 2021, the *Vancouver Sun* ran an incredible op-ed about climate refugees that takes home the Bingo prize for using them all in a single breath: "The thought of those millions *flowing* into Canada would constitute not just another *wave* of immigration, but a *human tsunami* that would *inundate* the idea of Canada itself."[41]

Journalists should avoid framing migration in terms of natural disasters because it tells audiences to understand them as such.[42]

Assimilating Italics

Why don't we italicize words like café or kimono even though they come from other languages? As they're increasingly used, they're incorporated into English. Or as the federal government's style guide puts it, they are "assimilated."[43]

Words uncommonly used in English are italicized in news reports. But if too many of them are used, style conventions make it so that a story starts to look like Tolkien's Elvish or a Latin taxonomy. It also feels imbalanced if some words in a sentence are italicized and others are not, as in, "The meal combo features chicken adobo and *halo-halo* for dessert," making adobo seem normal and halo-halo seem abnormal. At the *Tyee,* we italicize the first appearance – like how we use quotation marks for a technical term that we introducing – and leave it without italics upon subsequent mentions. But it's a rule that we've occasionally bent, especially for stories with lots of non-English words that would be otherwise marked up with italics.

Author Khairani Barokka published a strongly argued case against italicizing foreign words in an article in *Catapult* magazine.[44] Rather than describing non-italicized foreign words as assimilated, she calls them "dominated." It's a kind of linguistic gatekeeping, deciding what aspects of the other are acceptable enough to be incorporated into English. Why is shawarma no longer italicized? Because white people like eating it now.

Worth Mentioning Identity at All?

Is a marker of identity – race, religion, national identity, immigration status, and so on – relevant to the story at hand? We touched on this in Chapter 4, and it is advice supported by the Canadian Press: if a marker of identity is not relevant, journalists should not include it. And even if it is a telling detail that deserves mentioning, journalists should be careful about how they do so. Identity should not be sensationalized, as if being an other is somehow a smoking gun.

If a Japanese Canadian teenager wins a math competition, their ethnic background shouldn't be mentioned if the story of their participation has nothing to do with their background. If a migrant is accused of a crime, the history of their time in Canada might be relevant to the story; however, journalists should be careful about how they frame the story, to avoid racializing the alleged crime. In 2018, a man was charged with the first-degree murder of a thirteen-year-old girl in a Burnaby park. A number of local outlets called him just that in their headlines: a "man."[45] But right-wing American media that picked up the story honed in on the fact that he was a Syrian refugee, with the *New York Post*'s headline reading "Syrian Refugee Arrested For Murder of Canadian Teen," and Fox News' reading "Syrian Refugee Charged in 'Random' Murder of Girl, 13, in Canada."[46] The problem with these stories is not that his identity wasn't important; it's that in this coverage, audiences may interpret the story to mean that his identity as a refugee, specifically from Syria, is what was put on public trial.

Identity deserves space in stories about rights and discrimination, whether systemic or based on individual actions. It also deserves to be celebrated when a historically marginalized group achieves a milestone. But it shouldn't be given a place of prominence in a way that equates race with behaviour.

Back to the Source

Let's say you're a journalist who's just finished a story, but you have a few doubts. Are you spelling someone's name correctly; or for broadcasters, pronouncing it correctly? Not sure if you're describing a cultural practice accurately? Or whether a story topic is inappropriate?

We've already discussed that it's important to check with your source if you're unsure how to describe them. When identity and intersectionality matter in a story, journalists shouldn't be guessing. That goes for sources' specific cultural backgrounds, gender and pronouns, names in non-English languages, and beyond. Better to risk a bit of awkwardness than to get their identity wrong, whether by adding a dimension they don't identify with or don't wish to publicly share, or leaving out an important one. It never hurts to ask and give your sources the opportunity to let you know how they wish to present their true selves.

I once wrote a story about the gentrification and displacement of affordable places for people to eat in Vancouver's Downtown Eastside, a neighbourhood with one of the lowest median household incomes in Canada at around $23,000.[47] I tagged along with a resident to visit diners that still provided a nutritious bite for only a few bucks. I was just about to part ways with him when I realized that if I was writing a story that centred on low-income people, I should probably check whether he was okay with being called low-income. It was an awkward thing to ask, but crucial to confirm. "Oh yes, I'm definitely low-income!" he told me. "I'm as low-income as they come!"

Sometimes the fact checks can be more extensive. I know there is a segment of journalists out there who believe it's blasphemy to share anything concerning your story with a source. Maybe so if you're interviewing a wily politician. But if you're writing a story about a culture – especially one you don't belong to – that hinges on getting the details right, it's worth running sentences or snippets by them, especially if you have a nagging feeling in your gut.

If there's no one in your newsroom to help you, you could go to a trusted expert for a fact check or a sensitivity check. Many times over the years, I've shared sentences or story frames with experts who I've developed relationships with. I've had a wide range of queries: whether I'm describing a religious practice correctly, whether I'm choosing the right spelling for a dessert, whether it's offensive to make a generalization about character for an entire ethnocultural group. When writing a story that focused on the multigenerational households of ethnically South Asian families, I didn't want my audiences to come away with the conclusion that all South Asian people like to live in houses with a lot of their relatives. Experts took the time to explain the intersectionalities of this to me: that culture is a part of it, but it's also about immigrants sticking together for social and material support, especially in discriminatory and expensive places. I wove this important context into my story.

This kind of follow-up isn't specific to issues of race, ethnicity, and culture. The same goes for any story that requires a journalist to explain something that a mass audience might not know, whether it's about an economic theory or how viruses behave. This isn't giving special treatment to a source, like asking a politician if they really meant to say what they did; it's about striving for accuracy when there's a risk of misrepresentation.

Next time, when you've finished your story but are still iffy about a line, ask that extra question as part of your final check. You'll be glad you did.

Gazing Beyond

For all the challenges of being a journalist of colour in a white-dominated industry, there is one upside. At the sidelines of scrums and conferences where we're outnumbered, it's easy for us to find each other. Newsroom demographics haven't changed much since I started this job,[1] so I can't help but still be excited every time I come across the byline of a journalist who isn't white and is still in the game. In our conversations, it's never long before one of us mentions race. How did you end up with a job? What racial and racist hurdles did you have to clear? What do you have to put up with on the regular? What stories are you striving to report?

In recent years, more and more journalists of colour have been speaking out publicly about the challenges we face and what it's like to work in the industry. Some of the candour comes as they are leaving their outlets or exiting journalism entirely.

I've already mentioned Desmond Cole and his decision to leave the *Toronto Star*, which raised the question of whether racialized columnists are held to a stricter standard when it comes to engaging in activism. There's also Sunny Dhillon, who left the *Globe and Mail*, after not a single incident but what he called a "continuing pattern."[2] "When a story or column does not adequately, if at all, understand or consider the perspectives of the nonwhite people it involves, what do you say?" he wrote in an essay following his departure titled "Journalism While Brown and When to Walk Away." "When a story involving people of colour is assigned with a colour-blind lens and a false sense of objectivity, what do you do?" His concluding feeling: "What I brought to the newsroom did not matter." These prominent Canadian newspapers benefitted from the work these journalists did, and it was disappointing to see them step away.

Similar stories have come out of broadcasting. In 2020, the Canadian Association of Black Journalists wrote an open letter to Corus Entertainment, the parent company of Global News, about "microaggressions, overt racism and a lack of representation at the company," ranging from the downplaying of racism in Black Lives Matter coverage to racist comments in the newsroom. The company's president and CEO promised some changes in response.[3] At the CBC, a *Review of Journalism* investigation into the experiences of the public broadcaster's temporary workers revealed how racialized journalists were particularly affected. "It felt like I could only report on diverse stories, and those were the only stories that they wanted because they have to fill this diversity quota," shared a journalist who was the only person of colour on her team. One union leader said that racialized temps felt like they had to keep their "mouths shut" in fear of losing opportunities in what was already a precarious system of employment, not to mention worrying that if they spoke up for identities they belonged to they would be "perceived as being biased."[4]

Does a newsroom's purported values make it any easier on journalists of colour? Matthew DiMera, who was the first Black editor-in-chief of the left-leaning online publication rabble.ca before he resigned, believes that progressive publications aren't immune to such problems. In 2020, staff of the publication wrote a letter to the publisher saying that rabble.ca "has long prioritized the perspectives of white progressives at the expense of BIPOC voices."[5] rabble.ca's board subsequently apologized and made commitments toward anti-racism.[6] DiMera resigned a few months later. "When you suggest to white progressives that they might be racist or that they're complicit in racist structures, immediately their backs go up," he said in an interview with *Briarpatch* magazine. "And the typical response becomes 'I am a good person, how dare you impugn that I'm not?' instead of 'I wasn't aware of this; how can we deal with it?'"

Then there's the abuse that journalists of colour face due to their public-facing work. Aaron Hemens, who is of Filipino and European ancestry, told *J-Source* what it was like being a visible person of colour in the dominantly white small town of Creston, BC.[7] He received "nasty looks" from people in public and racist harassment in the comments on his stories. After covering an anti-mask protest, Hemens received a phone call from a speaker who threatened to "metaphorically lynch" him. "I don't think I would have gotten a lynching comment if I was a white reporter," he said. "I stuck out like a sore thumb." Hemens was later followed by a car for ten minutes, with the driver shouting his name. Eight months after he took the job, he left for his health and safety. No wonder racialized journalists have a hard time outside of more racially and ethnoculturally diverse cities.

Women journalists of colour in particular have spoken up about the intensification of racist and sexually violent death threats they've received. In an interview with the Canadian Anti-Hate Network in 2022, journalist Erica Ifill, who writes for the *Hill Times* and is among those who have been targeted, said: "This is about us using our platforms to speak and attempts to silence us."[8]

It's a lot to worry about when we are just trying to do our jobs.

We battle the white gaze in our stories, but we are also subjects of the white gaze in our own industry. It sucks to be excluded, but it also sucks to be included by newsrooms as a racialized tool meant to satisfy or legitimize their diversity goals. The fight for representation in the news and in newsrooms can be tiring, lonely, hurtful, and demoralizing, and it is taking place against the backdrop of a tumultuous industry where layoffs, newsroom closures, and mass disruptions have all become commonplace, all while executives pocket bonuses.[9] Bad news about the news keeps on coming, impacting legacy media and start-ups alike.[10] I've watched reporters with a deep conviction for reporting untold stories get worn down, leaving journalism behind when the bigotry, toxicity, and sluggish pace of change becomes too much.

We're not alone in this fight. There are white journalists who are aware of their positionality and the lack of all kinds of diversity in the industry. But some of the things they've said to me and other journalists of colour have left us feeling confused and conflicted rather than complimented. "You are the future," I've often been told, but it's hard to think about the future when organizational culls come every few months. "Nobody wants to hear from old white guys anymore," veterans like to tell me, but it's hard to believe this when surveys show that's exactly who's at the top.[11] Such resignations also leave out what white journalists with power and experience can be doing to help meet diversity goals, from advocacy and mentorship to learning how to combat the white gaze in their own work and in their outlets.

At the newsroom level, the Canadian Journalists of Colour and the Canadian Association of Black Journalists published a list of seven "Calls to Action," which I believe lay good groundwork for the pursuit of racial and ethnocultural representation.[12]

The organizations stress that data is crucial. Without it, we don't have a clear picture of the composition of newsrooms and how journalists of colour are left behind. The first recommendation calls for the regular self-reporting of newsroom demographics, and to make that data publicly available. Canadian broadcasters are federally mandated to do so, but not newspapers and digital outlets.[13] Thankfully, we now have the Canadian Association of Journalists' annual newsroom diversity surveys, which launched in 2021. No similar survey had been conducted since 2004,[14] though a 2019 study on two decades of newspaper columnists found that as the proportion of white people in Canada's population has declined, the representation of white columnists has increased.[15]

In 2023, the country's largest outlets – among them the CBC and Radio-Canada, Global News, the *Globe and Mail,* the *Toronto Star,* and various Postmedia newspapers – participated in the third Canadian Association of Journalists newsroom diversity survey; however, many newsrooms were not part of this public industry-wide accounting. Of the 790 newsrooms invited, 273 newsrooms sent in their responses, 20 refused to participate, and the remaining 505 – which make up over 64 percent of contacted newsrooms – did not respond to repeated outreach. I wonder how many managers ignored the request because they considered the demographic makeup of their newsrooms a private matter, or disagreed with the premise that the identity of their journalists has any bearing on their work. The response to the 2004 survey, conducted by a Toronto Metropolitan University professor, revealed such resistance when a few respondents returned the survey empty. One scribbled across the page, "I find these questions insulting."[16]

Surveys like these are but one quantitative metric; however, in the words of Zane Schwartz, the chair of the Canadian Association of Journalists who led the effort to conduct the surveys, "You can't change what you can't measure."[17] *Nieman Reports,* a magazine promoting journalism leadership, has even suggested that newsrooms keep track of the diversity of their sources.[18]

Are aspiring journalists of colour being helped into the industry? The calls to action also recommend the creation of scholarships and mentorship opportunities that target underrepresented groups. It's thanks to the data from the newsroom diversity surveys that we know that journalists of colour experience more job precarity compared to their white counterparts and are overrepresented among part-time and internship roles.[19]

Full-time hires are great, no one is going to dispute that. But what happens after? Journalists of colour need to be mentored, supported, trusted, and eventually brought into positions with decision-making power and given a seat at tables that are still dominated by their white counterparts. Imagine someone with lived racial and ethnocultural experiences being given the ability to greenlight stories deemed newsworthy and to filter out those that cater to the white gaze. From the quality of current coverage on people of colour, we know that the current status quo of white-dominated leadership isn't working.

I once attended a journalism conference where the cheery manager of one of the country's largest newsrooms shared details about the diversification already underway. She cited her own experience as a journalist of colour breaking into a position of power. The diversification of the industry, she said, is something that will come with time as more people from diaspora groups pursue journalism. I was surprised to hear that sitting on one's hands could be considered a strategy. This reasoning gives newsroom leaders and veterans alike an excuse to recuse themselves of responsibility, citing the times, while they wait for journalists of colour to knock on the door.

Aside from who's in the newsroom, there's also work that newsroom leaders and veterans can be doing in the community. The calls to action encourage outlets to consult with racialized and ethnocultural groups they are covering. One suggestion from the report is to work with community advisory boards, so that newsrooms can hear how they are doing directly from their audience members.

As for the white gaze itself, journalists and newsrooms need to accept that it's not going anywhere for now. That's why this book is titled *Under the White Gaze* rather than *Ignoring the White Gaze* or *Smashing the White Gaze to Bits*. Accepting that the white gaze has the power to distort everything that gets aired and published, journalist can heed, but not heel to, its influence. That means investigating and not ignoring how the white gaze can twist a story at every stage of its life, from which pitches are deemed interesting or what context is included for an imagined audience, to the sources chosen and how the reporting is packaged. Only by being conscious of the white gaze can journalists seek to challenge it.

Part of that shift in consciousness is to avoid a binary view of the world: white normalcy and racialized otherness. A journalist should not be at their desk thinking, "Hm, I haven't reported a diversity story in a while. Let me do one today." Diversity is not a side dish. It's something that should be considered for all news coverage. It makes a story richer, whether the beat is politics, business, culture, education, environment, health, labour, or whatever else. The same goes for journalism education. Diversity is not some optional elective. It should be incorporated into journalism's very foundations, from ethics to editing, research to reporting. If the Canadian Press describes the mission of journalists as explaining "all of Canada to all Canadians,"[20] then diversity has to be part of the main course.

We've covered a lot of ground in this book: the power of gazes and how they can shape journalism; stereotypes and how to move beyond them; intersectionality and how to understand privilege and oppression; places and how to see them as social constellations; shutdown commands and how to combat them; and how to use specific language that doesn't other.

The fact that so much work is still needed is a testament to how poorly Canadian journalism has been representing racial and ethno-cultural groups. It's hard for journalists and audiences to cast off the white gaze because of how normalized it is. And journalists who learn to see the previously invisible frames and tropes of the white gaze will only find that their work becomes more challenging.

I'm as anxious as ever about how audiences might perceive race, ethnicity, and culture in my stories. The more popular the story, the more I worry that they might be reading it the wrong way. The worst thing would be for a story intended to offer representation backfiring. I once wrote about Vancouver's beloved Baklava Man, a former parliamentarian in Syria who came to Canada as a refugee and began selling the treats on the street. Did I do enough to communicate why marginalized people might turn to survival vending? Or did my audience read this as a yummy story of migrant achievement in utopian Canada? I wrote about "astronaut families," children raised by one full-time parent in Canada while the other works overseas. Did I do enough to explain the socio-economic benefits and familial strains behind such arrangements? Or did my audience read this as a story about racialized invaders with foreign bank accounts? I wrote about two young sisters, born in Canada, who began volunteering with the local chapter of their family's village society to connect with their roots. But what if my audience thinks that all Canadian-borns of colour are required to be "ethnic" and embrace their heritage at some point in their lives? How do you suggest that exploring identity is different for everyone? It's not easy knowing when to hold an audience's hand and when to trust them to read a story without coming to some othering conclusion.

Throughout this book, I've pointed out a vast minefield of potential blunders that can trip up any well-intentioned journalist, white or racialized. Sometimes I caution against using too much colour; at other times, I ask for more detail. Journalists, please don't walk away from this book worried that making a mistake on an issue of race, ethnicity, and culture means you're going to get cancelled! I still make mistakes myself, especially when reporting on groups I'm unfamiliar with. Mistakes happen. But don't let the fear of making a blunder stop you from reporting on an important story. Acknowledge it, talk about it, listen to what others have to say about it, learn from it, and do better next time. Good thing news comes out every day, right?

Currently, there is such a drought of representation that when a story offers even a glimpse of the racial and ethnocultural realities that audiences live in, it can go viral. It could be a story about a compelling character, a haunt that newcomers frequent, or an issue known to only people within a specific diaspora. Every time a story about Chinese Canadians hits the air, my family and friends will send around the same link, asking excitedly, "Have you seen this yet?" It doesn't matter if the story is cheesy or imperfectly reported; audiences are enthralled at the sight of something from their world being recognized in the white-dominated world of Canadian journalism. How can audiences learn to ask for more? How can journalists learn to listen?

We need news outlets to be serious about serving *all* of the people in their communities. Representation allows audiences to learn about people who are different from them – how they are navigating life and how they're shaping the places in which we live. I'm always on the lookout for journalism to teach me about racialized and ethnocultural groups in my community that I don't know well: migration stories, their successes and struggles, the systems they navigate, expressions of identity and how they are evolving. As I learn about these different ethnocultural groups, I'm learning more about our society. It's also important for there to be stories where the identities of people of colour are commonplace but not central to the story. There's a joy in seeing streeters with a diversity of people, where that diversity is just a fact of life. For people who are used to being underrepresented in media, authentic coverage offers both relatability and revelation: to gaze at themselves, to see how they fit into society at large, to participate in the public conversation, and to imagine new ways of being.

Explicitly racist stories might no longer be as common in mainstream media, but journalists need to learn how to do more than just stick people of colour in the news when the holiday calendar says so. We have a long way to go before newsrooms are representative of the populations they serve and are able to report on them without othering them. For now, every time I look at coverage and see race, ethnicity, and culture covered with careful nuance, refreshing portrayals, and challenging truths, I count it as a step forward.

Whether your daily news diet consists of the morning newspaper, an evening broadcast, a newsletter in your email inbox, or snappy summaries on your TikTok feed, I hope this book has shown you how to consume and produce journalism more consciously. Maybe you're already spotting stories where representation falls short, where people of colour are conspicuously missing, or where the same tired narratives are told about them again and again.

Build up and monitor your media diet. Get to know which news outlets are available where you live. Find out who owns them, what their funding model is, and what stories and opinions they prioritize. Subscribe and financially support the outlets that are doing good work and representing the diversity of people in your community. Follow the journalists who produce that good work. Don't be shy – reach out to editors, leave a comment, or chime in on social media when you feel that reporting has fallen short of representation or when it does it well. Considering the overwhelming amount of racist replies out there, your constructive criticism will be valuable. Share good journalism with people you know, whether a friend or a curmudgeonly uncle.

As time passes, I have no doubt that my four Ds will be swapped out for new clichés. Different groups will be celebrated and vilified for their race and cultures. People intent on avoiding discussions of racial privilege and discrimination will find fresh excuses to shut them down. The language we use to talk about diversity will evolve.

But to prevent people of colour from being othered, and to ensure that portrayals are reflective, journalists and audiences should always ask those fundamental questions about how the news of the day is constructed. Who are stories about? What stories are told about them? How are those stories shaped for the intended audience? And who decides which stories are worth telling?

There is admittedly a lot of doom and gloom right now as the journalism industry contracts and expands in the face of evolving tech, business models, and audience habits. If I were to walk into a press conference today, there would be fewer journalists present than when I started in the industry ten years ago.[21] And guess what? I'd still be the odd one out in the room. However, the conversation about representation of all kinds is moving forward. Waubgeshig Rice's "Letter to a Young Indigenous Journalist," written in 2020, will resonate with other racialized journalists who've experienced marginalization and the weight of the white gaze:

> The gatekeepers are finally listening and appear willing to make meaningful structural and cultural change. But it is a shrinking industry overall, and deadlines and the next day's coverage always take precedence. Those constant pressures could very well relegate these initiatives to fringe discussions and files, where so many other diversity and inclusion endeavours have gone to die. The inertia of white-centred journalism could easily continue to favour the status quo. So speak your truth.

I've seen the pursuit of diversity come and go, as the heat from social movements cools and special newsroom projects that uplift marginalized voices wrap up and are forgotten, leaving goals of racial and ethnocultural representation relegated once again to the margins. Canadian journalism needs to change, and journalists and audiences alike can help keep the pressure on the industry to do so.

Without representation, the news is a distortion of reality through a narrow gaze. But with representation, journalism can help us see our world more clearly.

Acknowledgments

In the middle of the COVID-19 pandemic, Melody Ma suggested that I enter the Friends of Canadian Broadcasting's Dalton Camp essay competition on media and democracy. I submitted "Blind Spots," a rant of sorts about the lack of representation in Canadian journalism, which ended up taking the award. Thanks to the team at Friends for this encouragement to take a closer look at how the industry is doing when it comes to the work of diversity.

From there came "Under the White Gaze." The *Tyee* has been the supportive home where I've spent the majority of my journalism career. They've given me room to do special projects like the original series this book is based on. Jacob Boon, Robyn Smith, and Tara Campbell helped get each essay off the ground, with editing support from David Beers, our editor-in-chief, and Olamide Olaniyan, Paul Willcocks, and Paula Carlson. We launched it as a newsletter, which would not have been possible without publisher Jeanette Ageson, who believed in email delivery before it was cool, and webmaster Bryan Carney. Stella Zheng supplied the perfect illustrations, and Erika Rathje and Alicia Carvalho lent their design talents to tie it all together. We livestreamed events during the pandemic, with the support of andrea bennett, Em Cooper, Sarah Krichel, and Simran Singh. This book is a lot of talking about journalism, so I have to thank my day-to-day editor Jackie Wong and our diversity committee for being there to ensure that my actual journalism work stays close to the lofty ideals I'm preaching here.

As the original *Tyee* series on the white gaze was rolling out, I ran into a friend at the grocery store who was a long-time reporter at a Vancouver newspaper. A person of colour, she too was reading the series. "I was scared you would find one of my old stories on sushi!" she said. In this book, yes, I quote from many examples of real journalism to illustrate my points, and that means I've inevitably singled out the real journalists who reported them. In fact, a number of you are my friends, and I want you to know that their inclusion is not to condemn you, but to show how we've all (me included) formed a habit, intentionally or not, of producing work under the white gaze. Yesterday's reporting on people of colour is going to fall short when compared to that of today's, and I hope it will be pale in comparison with what we see tomorrow.

Thanks to all the readers who tagged along with the series, especially Tiffany, Henrietta, and Nadine Pedersen at Purich Books, who believed that it could become the book that you are holding today.

After months of writing, I was nervous about showing the manuscript to anyone, but Theresa Wong and the two anonymous external readers engaged by UBC Press provided encouragement and invaluable suggestions. Thanks to Ann Macklem and her production team for their keen eyes.

How can I write about journalists of colour without mentioning the journalists of colour who were there for me along the way? Every single one of you knew what it was like to stick out in the industry and offered me support and inspiration about what more representative journalism could look like. Wanyee Li was there my first day on the job.

On the flip side, many of the white journalists I have encountered since the beginning of my career were keenly aware that newsrooms and news media needed to diversify. In the midst of a homogenous industry, they tried to their best to pursue untold stories and mentor young journalists of colour.

Not everyone makes it in this industry, and my earliest editors, Barry Link and Michael Kissinger of the *Vancouver Courier,* had my back. Kathryn Gretsinger at the University of British Columbia j-school still cheers me on today.

I'm indebted to a number of people who pointed me to scholarship that made my work richer: John Paul Catungal, Andy Yan, Zachary Hyde, and Minelle Mahtani. *Reckoning* by Candis Callison and Mary Lynn Young was by the side of my desk, as was *Decolonizing Journalism* by Duncan McCue, who was kind enough to take my call to chat about all things that start with D. Kaitlyn Fung and Josie Wu hustled the PDFs.

Speaking of my desk, writing this book was a lonely endeavour, most of it done in my home office, which now has a ragged computer chair. But I also had many productive sprints at the welcoming bubble tea shops of Burnaby, which provided tea, wheel cakes, air conditioning in the summer, and heating in the winter.

Thank you to my family for supporting me through the ups and downs of this career.

And finally, a thank you to you for reading this book. Whether you report or consume the news, I hope it's challenged you to see things differently.

Notes

Gazing Behind

1 Statistics Canada, "Census Profile."
2 Canadian Association of Journalists, *2023 Canadian Newsroom Diversity Survey,* 10.
3 Lounsberry, "Introduction," xii.
4 C.T. Lee, "Improvising 'Nonexistent Rights,'" 79.
5 Robinson, "Vancouver Eyes."
6 Kent, "Vancouver's Urban Farms."
7 DiAngelo, *White Fragility,* 41.
8 F. Henry and Tator, *Colour of Democracy,* xxiv.
9 Wechsler, "Half of Canadian Newsrooms."
10 Canadian Association of Journalists, *2023 Canadian Newsroom Diversity Survey.*
11 Buchanan, "Pandemic Field Notes."
12 Newkirk II, "Diversity as a Second Job."
13 SmartRecruiters, "Editorial Writer."
14 Cyca, "Nostalgia about Newsrooms."
15 Chowdhury, "Forever Battle."
16 S. Roberts, "Great White Nope."
17 Paradkar, "Lack of Diversity."
18 Robertson, "Meta Begins Blocking News."

19 Tunney, "CBC/Radio-Canada to Cut 10 Per Cent."
20 Takagi, "CTV Cancelling."
21 Canadian Press, "Black Press Ltd."
22 Yang, "Vice Media."
23 Zeng, "Token Effort."
24 Anderson and Robertson, *Seeing Red*, 36.
25 "Must Bar Oriental Completely."
26 Mattar, "Objectivity Is a Privilege."
27 Lattimore, "Journalism Can Do More."
28 Fleras, *Media Gaze*, 67–69.
29 Statistics Canada, "Census Profile."
30 Diversity Institute in Management and Technology, *DiverseCity Counts 2*.
31 McCarten, ed., *Canadian Press Stylebook*.

Chapter 1: Of Gaps and Gazes

1 Cheung, "Meet East Vancouver's."
2 Connecticut Forum, "Toni Morrison On Writing."
3 Sartre, *Being and Nothingness*; Foucault, *Discipline and Punish*.
4 Fanon, *Black Skin, White Masks*, 92, 175.
5 Fanon, "Fact of Blackness," 257.
6 Thompson and Prinsloo, "Returning the Data Gaze," 153–65.
7 Foucault, *Discipline and Punish*.
8 Urry, *Tourist Gaze*.
9 Mulvey, "Visual Pleasure."
10 Pulver, "Scarlett Johansson Criticises 'Hypersexualisation.'"
11 Rice, "Letter to a Young Indigenous Journalist."
12 Miao, "'Fairview' and Tackling."
13 Fleras, *Media Gaze*, 45.
14 Maras, *Objectivity in Journalism*, 57.
15 "Journalistic Standards and Practices (JSP)."
16 Rosen, "View from Nowhere."
17 Nagel, *View from Nowhere*, 5.
18 Callison and Young, *Reckoning*, 29.
19 Schudson, *Origins of the Ideal*.
20 Durham, "On the Relevance," 125.
21 Tuchman, "Objectivity as Strategic Ritual," 660–79.
22 Jones, *Losing the News*, 83.

23 Kovach and Rosenstiel, *Elements of Journalism.*

24 Wallace, *View from Somewhere.*

25 Global Reporting Centre, *Empowerment Journalism Guide.*

26 Alcoff, "The Problem of Speaking," 9.

27 Cole, "I Choose Activism."

28 J. Miller, "Desmond Cole's Decision."

29 Lowery, "Reckoning Over Objectivity."

30 Coburn, Williams, and Stroud, "Newsroom Objectivity."

31 Harriot, "War on Wokeness."

32 Musk, Twitter post.

33 Bernier, Twitter post.

34 Poilievre, Twitter post.

35 Lowman, "Journalism Schools Are Failing."

36 Burrows, "Indigenous Media Producers' Perspectives."

37 Pasqual, "'I Had to Break the Rules.'"

38 Demby, Twitter post.

39 Andrews et al., *COVID-19*; Blackwell, "Why People of Colour."

40 Scott, "How French Canadians," 59–83.

41 Reynolds, *Canada and Colonialism.*

42 McIntosh, "White Privilege and Male Privilege."

43 Canadian Press, "Multiculturalism Profiles."

44 Diversity Institute in Management and Technology, *DiverseCity Counts 2.*

45 McIntosh, "White Privilege: Unpacking," 10–12.

46 Sherwin, *Bridging Two Peoples*, 105.

47 "About," APTN.

48 Callison and Young, *Reckoning*, 141.

49 Fleras, *Media Gaze*, 231–42.

50 Canadian Radio-television and Telecommunications Commission, "Public Notice CRTC 1999–177."

51 Murray, Yu, and Ahadi, *Cultural Diversity.*

52 Fleras, *Media Gaze*, 249.

53 "About Darpan," Darpan.

54 "New Canadian Media."

55 Fleras, *Media Gaze*, 242.

56 S.S. Yu, *Diasporic Media*, 19.

57 S.S. Yu, "Instrumentalization of Ethnic Media," 349.

58 Greenfield-Sanders, *Toni Morrison.*

59 Alonge, "Writing Past the White Gaze."

60 Wu, "Racialized Early-Career Journalists," 33.
61 Du Bois, "Strivings of the Negro People."
62 Minh-ha, *Woman, Native, Other,* 65, 67.
63 Hoby, "Toni Morrison."

Chapter 2: Of Darlings and Deviants

1 Loayza, "Slaves, Nannies and Maids."
2 Godfrey, "'I Felt Seriously Cheated.'"
3 Fleras, *Media Gaze,* 75–76.
4 Fleras, *Media Gaze,* 45.
5 Roberts and Mahtani, "Neoliberalizing Race, Racing Neoliberalism."
6 Siddiqui, "Media and Race."
7 Anderson and Robertson, *Seeing Red.*
8 Cram, "Duncan McCue."
9 McCue, *Decolonizing Journalism.*
10 *Delgamuukw v. British Columbia.*
11 Wells, "A Warrior, a Soldier."
12 Rossi, "Master Chef Serves Up."
13 Brand, "New Whiz Kids."
14 "Surrey, B.C., Girl."
15 Seitz, "Offensive Movie Cliche."
16 Peng, "Eight Years."
17 G. Lawrence, "Meet the 'Angel of East Hastings.'"
18 Pettersen, "Success Story."
19 S.J. Lee, Wong, and Alvarez, "Stereotypes of Asian Americans," 70.
20 Chow, "Racial Wedge."
21 Arvin, Tuck, Morrill, "Decolonizing Feminism," 10.
22 Chen, "Stories of Immigration to Ottawa."
23 CBC Communications, "Meet Metro Vancouver."
24 Cheung, "On Bottle Binning."
25 Goode and Ben-Yehuda, *Moral Panics,* 35.
26 Goode and Ben-Yehuda, *Moral Panics,* 90.
27 Fleras, *Media Gaze,* 29.
28 Dennis, "Exploring the Model Minority," 40.
29 Jiwani, *Discourses of Denial,* 105.
30 Tomky, "Richmond, British Columbia."
31 Ansari, "'Everybody Fits In.'"

32 P.E. Roy, *White Man's Province*.

33 Pilkington, "What Is 'Great Replacement' Theory?"

34 Ericson, Baranek, and Chan, *Representing Order*, 115.

35 Donohue, Tichenor, and Olien, "A Guard Dog Perspective," 115–32.

36 Pabla, "Legacies of Bindy Johal," 228.

37 P. Sullivan, "Keep Your Head Down."

38 F. Henry and Tator, *Colour of Democracy*, 165.

39 A. Lawrence, "How the 'Natural Talent' Myth Is Used."

40 Wortley, "Misrepresentation or Reality?" 55–82.

41 Abusalim, "Study: 'NYT.'"

42 J. Miller and Sack, "Toronto-18 Terror Case," 281.

43 Kanji, "Framing Muslims," 274.

44 Wingrove, "Ottawa Shooter."

45 "Radicalization and Homegrown Terrorism."

46 Perry and Scrivens, *Right-Wing Extremism in Canada*, 393–413.

47 Indra, "South Asian Stereotypes," 174.

48 Buffam, "Cultural Confessions," 153–69.

49 C. Smith, "Culture Clash Over Kid Peeing."

50 *CBC News*, "Boy Peeing in B.C. Mall."

51 Young, "Picture of Boy Urinating."

52 Jiwani, *Discourses of Denial*, 105.

53 Hopper, "Richmond, B.C., Considers."

54 Ferreras and Hua, "There's Hardly a Word."

55 Hopper, "Richmond, B.C., Considers."

56 That, "Chinese-Only Sign."

57 Nolan, "Considering the So-Called."

58 McElroy, "Richmond City Council."

59 Ranger, "Environment Canada Issues."

60 Canadian Press, "If the Air Appears."

61 Omstead, "Environment Canada Removes Reference."

62 Andrew, Twitter post.

63 Hui, "Richmond Chinese Medicine Store."

64 Dished Staff, "Hon's Wun-Tun House."

65 Chan, "Fraser Health Issues Warning."

66 Griffin, "Ferris Wheel."

67 Fayerman, "Nothing Illegal."

68 Wood and Xiong, "Richmond Hospital."

69 Burns-Pieper and Mayor, "'All about the Money.'"

70 *CBC News*, "UBC's Vantage College."
71 Rana, "'Different Factors' Fuel Housing Crisis."
72 P. Roberts, "Is Your City Being Sold Off."
73 N. Roy, "News Outlets Criticized."
74 English, "Star Apologizes."
75 N. Roy, "News Outlets Criticized."
76 Jheeta, "Media Should Tell Real Stories."
77 Colley, "100,000 in Vaisakhi Parade."
78 Urback, "Feminism Is Standing Up."
79 "Islamophobia in Canada."
80 "Police-Reported Hate Crime, 2021."
81 Elghawaby, "Canadian Media Sucks."
82 Bronskill, "Islamic Schools."
83 Mastracci, "That Study About Extremist Mosques."
84 Mastracci, "That Study About Extremist Mosques."
85 Elghawaby, "News Media's Rush."
86 Siddiqui, "Muslims and the Media."

Chapter 3: Of Deliciousness and Damage

1 Said, *Orientalism*, 40.
2 hooks, *Black Looks*, 21.
3 Alibhai-Brown, *After Multiculturalism*.
4 CBC Kids Team, "Let's Celebrate Vaisakhi."
5 *CBC News*, "Ramadan."
6 Bonnyman, "Diwali 101."
7 Kwong, "He Wanted to Make."
8 Boothby, "Richmond Night Market Opens."
9 Robin, "Ottawa's Seven New Food Carts."
10 Associated Press, "Congee."
11 hooks, *Black Looks*, 21.
12 Narayan, *Dislocating Cultures*, 181.
13 Lim, "Definitive List."
14 Vors, "Walia's Ethiopian Dining."
15 "Unexplored Territory."
16 Johnston and Baumann, *Foodies*, 102.
17 "Noodles Featured in Oscar-Winning Film."

18 Waverman, "Smashed Cucumber."
19 Sax, "Toronto Suddenly."
20 Kleinplatz, "On The End Of Latab."
21 Stainsby, "Aleph Eatery Heals World."
22 Stainsby, "Heartfelt Servings."
23 Mendoza, "Hoping for Prosperity."
24 Abozaid, "Winnipeg Family."
25 Tran, "How This Lunar New Year."
26 "B.C. Muslims Celebrate."
27 Pearson, "This Is the Anti-Asian Hate Crime Capital."
28 Wanyee Li, "'A Disgusting Act.'"
29 Subramaniam, "Foreign Students."
30 Thanthong-Knight, "Foreign Students Accuse Canada."
31 Raza, "Jamaican Migrant Workers."
32 Wildes, "Even a Year's Worth."
33 Brayne, ed., *Trauma & Journalism.*
34 Cochrane and Laventure, "Syrian Family Celebrates."
35 Jabakhanji, "5 Afghan Siblings Arrive."
36 Dayal, "Saskatoon Woman Celebrating."
37 Boudjikanian, "Pakistan Warns Paperless Migrants."
38 Alkamli, "Fatma, a Syrian Refugee."
39 Dayal, "Saskatoon Woman Celebrating."
40 Bernhardt and Allen, "'Today Is a Fantastic Day.'"
41 "Refugees in Ottawa."
42 Keung, "Here's How Syrian Refugees."
43 Bernhardt and Allen, "'Today Is a Fantastic Day.'"
44 Bernhardt and Allen, "'Today Is a Fantastic Day.'"
45 Cochrane and Laventure, "Syrian Family Celebrates."
46 Andrew-Gee, "How Immigrants from Benin."
47 Buffam, "Cultural Confessions," 153–69.
48 Judd, "Police Warn Public."
49 Dart, "Gurdeep Pandher."
50 Nesbit, "'I Helped So Many Canadians.'"
51 Chang, *Disoriented.*
52 J. Roberts, "Ontario MP Visits Manitoba."
53 Rillorta, "OFW: Ang Bagong Bayani."
54 Wong and Attewell, "Donut Time Refugee Place-Making."

55 Mitchell, Stocking, and Matsa, *Long-Form Reading*.
56 Sensoy et al., "Moving beyond Dance," 4.
57 Butler, *Frames of War*, 12.
58 Public Broadcasting Service, "Constance Wu."

Chapter 4: Of Intersections and Identity

1   City of Vancouver, Social Policy and Projects, *Oakridge*.
2   Fung Bros, "Things Asian Parents Do."
3   Kwai, "How 'Subtle Asian Traits.'"
4   Mendoza, "These B.C. Podcasters."
5   Todd, "Ethnic Chinese Groups Protest."
6   Chung, "How My Chinese Parents."
7   Choe, "Many Cooks, One Mortgage."
8   "Fraser Health Targets."
9   Mohamed, "How Intersectionalism Betrays."
10 Coaston, "Intersectionality Wars."
11 Coaston, "Intersectionality Wars."
12 B. Cooper, "Intersectionality."
13 Crenshaw, "Demarginalizing the Intersection."
14 Crenshaw, "Why Intersectionality Can't Wait."
15 *DeGraffenreid v. General Motors Assembly Div.*
16 Grady, "Waves of Feminism."
17 Terrazano, "Crenshaw Delivers Thought-Provoking Lecture."
18 H. Miller, "Kimberlé Crenshaw Explains."
19 Logan, "Refugee Group Partners."
20 Peterson, "Why the Western Emphasis."
21 "Intersectionality Feminism."
22 Steinmetz, "She Coined the Term 'Intersectionality.'"
23 Tsai, "How Should Educators," E201–11.
24 Findlay and Köhler, "Too Asian."
25 *Richmond Hill Liberal*, "Richmond Hill 'Too Asian.'"
26 T. Wong, "Unbearable Lightness."
27 J. Miller, "Shame on Maclean's."
28 Canadian Coalition of Community Partners to Eliminate Anti-Asian Racism, *Open Letter*.
29 "Merit: The Best and Only Way."
30 H. Yu, "Macleans Offers a Nonapology"; J. Miller, "Shame on Maclean's."

31 Huynh, "Decade-Old Article."
32 B. Henry, "As We Venture Out"; Porter, "Top Doctor."
33 Staples, "Dr. Hinshaw on Cargill Outbreak."
34 A. Nguyen, "'Underpaid and Undervalued.'"
35 Babych, "Filipino Workers Face Backlash."
36 Donato, "Filipino Front-Line Workers."
37 Solnit, "Coronavirus Does Discriminate."
38 Young, "China Virus?"
39 Yeung, "Early Efforts."
40 Young, "China Virus?"
41 Yeung, "Early Efforts."
42 Cheung, "From Gurdwaras to Truckers."
43 Luk, "COVID-19 Rates."
44 Shen, "Vancouver's Chinatown."
45 Basu, "'They Don't Represent Me.'"
46 Sterritt, Twitter post.
47 Paik, "Why Sandra Oh's Speech."
48 Hong, "'Too Asian?' Debate."
49 Callison, "Climate Change Communication."
50 Cheung, "'Hope, Pray and Keep Clean.'"
51 Calabrese et al., "Proms from Coast to Coast."

Chapter 5: Of Maps and Monsters

1 Gross, "Asian Cuisine as Diverse."
2 Cheung, "Fraser Street's Affordability."
3 Johnson, "How Fraserhood Became."
4 "Fraser Street."
5 Cheung, "What's in a Neighbourhood Name?"
6 Said, Orientalism, 94.
7 Social Science Bites, "Doreen Massey On Space."
8 Massey, Space, Place and Gender.
9 Gilmor, "Scarborough Curse."
10 Aziz, "Scarborough Made Me."
11 Gold, "Highest Bidder."
12 Macdonald, "Ian Young."
13 Bula, "Astronaut Wives"; Pawson, "Vancouver Still Shaped"; Bilefsky, "'Astronaut' Families Stressed."

14 Wei Li, *Ethnoburb.*

15 Shen, "Vehicle Smashes."

16 Cheung, "Overrun with Buns."

17 "Live Chat on Ethnic Enclaves."

18 Proudfoot, "Ethnic Enclaves Weak Link."

19 Hopper, "Our Chinalands."

20 Hou and Picot, *Visible Minority Neighbourhoods.*

21 Duffy, "Needs Are Vast."

22 Todd, "Are Growing Ethnic Enclaves a Threat."

23 Putnam, *"E Pluribus Unum,"* 149.

24 Lloyd, "Study Paints Bleak Picture of Ethnic Diversity."

25 Abascal and Baldassarri, "Love Thy Neighbor?" 722–82.

26 Canada, *Minutes of the Proceedings,* 9.

27 Todd, "Ethnic Enclaves Hurt Canadian 'Belonging.'"

28 S. Cooper, "What Happens."

29 Duffy, "Needs Are Vast."

30 Todd, "Ethnic Enclaves Hurt Canadian 'Belonging.'"

31 "Should Chinese-Only Crest Toothpaste Ad Concern Richmond Residents?"

32 Jimenez, "Do Ethnic Enclaves Impede Integration?"

33 Todd, "Ethnic Enclaves Hurt Canadian 'Belonging.'"

34 Todd, "Ethnic Mapping 5."

35 Ahmed-Ullah, "Brampton, aka. Browntown," 242–54.

36 Caddell, "Studio Brewing."

37 S. Sullivan, *Revealing Whiteness,* 154.

38 Heller, "Curry, Sambal, Jerk, and Salsa."

39 Stainsby, "Following the Dumpling Trail."

40 Tsui, "Panaderia Latina."

41 Doss, "Afghan Restaurant."

42 Stainsby, "It May Not Be Fancy."

43 Merriam-Webster.com Dictionary, s.v. "hole-in-the-wall."

44 hooks, *Black Looks,* 26.

45 Gill, "Unassuming Hole-in-the-Wall."

46 Gill, "Smitten by a Humble South Indian Diner."

47 Sax, "Sriracha Argument for Immigration."

48 C. Smith, "Cheap Eats."

49 Faulder, "Out of the Way."

50 Steacy, "Vancouver Family-Run Diner."

51 Liu, "'Plazas Are Gold.'"
52 Liu, "One of Toronto's Best Food Courts."
53 Liu, "Aoyama Sushi Restaurant."
54 Wright, "Kim's Mart."
55 Wright, "Northern Cafe and Grill."
56 Syed, "End of the Line."
57 Thuncher, "About That 'Squampton' Saying."
58 Gangdev, "From Indigenous Trail."
59 "1868 – Victoria Is Named the Capital City."
60 Gangdev, "From Indigenous Trail."

Chapter 6: Of Silence and Shutdowns

1 DiAngelo, *White Fragility*, 23.
2 DiAngelo, *White Fragility*, 2.
3 F. Henry and Tator, *The Colour of Democracy*, 10–11.
4 CBC Audience Services, "Why Aren't Most Indigenous-Related Stories."
5 *Global News Commenting Policy*.
6 Krug, "Reactions Now Available Globally."
7 *Taking Care*.
8 King Jr., "I Have a Dream."
9 Tyee Staff, "What Was Said."
10 Dhillon, "Journalism While Brown."
11 Yi et al., "Ignoring Race," 258–75.
12 Zarathus-Cook, "Opera in Canada."
13 Goldberg, "Why 'Black Lives Matter.'"
14 Neville, Gallardo, and Sue, "Introduction," 10.
15 Boyd and Hadley-Burke, *Sacrifice Zones*.
16 Murphy, "Canada Is Not a Racist Country."
17 DiAngelo, *White Fragility*, 12.
18 Haki, "When Writing About Race."

Chapter 7: Of Words and Worry

1 Rawlinson, "AP Apologises."
2 McArdle, Twitter post.
3 Demby, "Why We Have So Many Terms."
4 "What Racial Terms Make You Cringe."

5 *Elimin8Hate Style Guide.*

6 McCarten, *Canadian Press Stylebook*, 26.

7 Xu, "Cultures Clash."

8 McGarvey, "South Asian Painter."

9 Wright Allen, "Nelly Shin."

10 Juric, "Number of Hate Motivated Crimes."

11 Kerr, "Korean Community Stays United."

12 Canadian Press, "Toronto's Korean Community."

13 "Diwali Celebrated Across B.C."

14 *Employment Equity Act.*

15 Hopper, "Richmond, B.C., Considers."

16 Peoples and Bailey, *Humanity,* 367.

17 Chaarani, "Some Wollwich Candidates."

18 Kapitan, "Should I Use the Adjective 'Diverse'?"

19 Arteta, *The Office,* "Diwali."

20 Agapito, "I Feel Like a Grinch."

21 "Sometimes Explain, Always Complain."

22 Shetty, "International Students Celebrate."

23 McCarten, *Canadian Press Stylebook*, 91.

24 Gold, "Highest Bidder."

25 Strauss, "Loblaw Buys Asian Grocery Chain."

26 Ping, "Hopping Back into Action."

27 Gee, "Secret Lives."

28 Froke et al., eds., *Associated Press Stylebook*, 318.

29 Bailey, "It's Time for Journalists."

30 Ordway, "Calling Racism What It Is."

31 Ordway, "Calling Racism What It Is."

32 "Muslim Family."

33 Gilmore, "'Racist City.'"

34 Todd, "Upzone Everything."

35 Peng, "Eight Years."

36 Clarke, "Children of Today."

37 Serebrin, "'Surge' in Demand."

38 Dharssi, "As Syrians Flood In."

39 "Vancouver's New Asian Restaurant Scene."

40 "Canada Debates How to Address"; "Canada Wants to Welcome."

41 McMartin, "Historic Human Tsunami" (emphasis added).

42 Dempsey and McDowell, "Disaster Depictions," 153–60.
43 "Italics."
44 Barokka, "Case Against Italicizing 'Foreign' Words."
45 McSheffrey, "Trial Postponed Again."
46 Lam, "Syrian Refugee Charged."
47 Cheung, "'We Don't Do Eggo Waffles.'"

Gazing Beyond

1 Canadian Association of Journalists, *2023 Canadian Newsroom Diversity Survey.*
2 Dhillon, "Journalism While Brown."
3 *Open Letter to Corus Entertainment.*
4 A. Wong, "Forever Temporary."
5 Krishnan, "Editor of Progressive News Site."
6 rabble.ca Board of Directors, "Recognition of Shortcoming."
7 Buchanan, "Pandemic Field Notes."
8 P. Smith, "Women and Racialized Journalists."
9 "Postmedia Execs Pocketed $1M."
10 Vescera, "Bold Experiment."
11 Canadian Association of Journalists, *2023 Canadian Newsroom Diversity Survey.*
12 Canadian Journalists of Colour and Canadian Association of Black Journalists, "Canadian Media Diversity."
13 Malik and Fatah, "Newsrooms Not Keeping Up."
14 J. Miller, "Who's Telling the News?"
15 Malik and Fatah, "Newsrooms Not Keeping Up."
16 Zeng, "Token Effort."
17 Schwartz, email.
18 Brandel and Kho, "Want to Make Real Progress."
19 Canadian Association of Journalists, *2023 Canadian Newsroom Diversity Survey,* 4.
20 McCarten, *Canadian Press Stylebook,* 26.
21 Cheung, "We're Losing Journalists."

Bibliography

Abascal, Maria, and Delia Baldassarri. "Love Thy Neighbor? Ethnoracial Diversity and Trust." *American Journal of Sociology* 121, 3 (November 2015): 722–82. https://doi.org/10.1086/683144.

Abdullah, Hammad. "Surjeet Kalsey on Domestic Violence in the South Asian Community and the Need for Men to Dismantle the Patriarchy." *5X Press,* February 23, 2023. https://www.5xfest.com/5xpress/surjeet-kalsey-domestic-violence-patriarchy.

"About." APTN, accessed November 5, 2023, https://www.aptn.ca/about.

"About Darpan." Darpan, accessed on November 5, 2023, https://www.darpanmagazine.com/about.

Abozaid, Lamia. "Winnipeg Family Tries to Keep Eid Rituals Alive far from Their Former Home in Bangladesh." *CBC News,* July 9, 2022. https://www.cbc.ca/news/canada/manitoba/eid-al-adha-winnipeg-2022-culture-1.6515676.

Abraham, George. "The Future of Immigrant Journalism in Canada." *J-Source,* August 18, 2014. https://web.archive.org/web/20140819175754/https://j-source.ca/article/future-immigrant-journalism-canada, archived at www.archive.org.

Abusalim, Dorgham. "Study: 'NYT' Portrays Islam More Negatively Than Alcohol, Cancer, and Cocaine." *Mondoweiss,* March 5, 2016. https://

mondoweiss.net/2016/03/study-nyt-portrays-islam-more-negatively-than-alcohol-cancer-and-cocaine.

Agapito, Jim. "I Feel Like a Grinch When My Fellow Filipinos Start Celebrating Christmas in September." *CBC Radio,* December 26, 2022. https://www.cbc.ca/radio/recovering-filipino-christmas-season-1.6691204.

Ahmed-Ullah, Noreen. "Brampton, aka. Browntown." In *Subdivided: City-Building in an Age of Hyper-Diversity,* edited by Jay Pitter and John Lorinc, 242–54. Toronto: Coach House Books, 2016.

Alcoff, Linda Martin. "The Problem of Speaking for Others." *Cultural Critique* 20 (Winter, 1991–92): 5–32.

Alibhai-Brown, Yasmin. *After Multiculturalism.* London: Foreign Policy Centre, 2000.

Alkamli, Teyama. "Fatma, a Syrian Refugee Finds Freedom and New Family in Canada." *CBC Docs Pov,* February 28, 2020. https://www.cbc.ca/cbcdocspov/features/fatma-a-syrian-refugee-finds-freedom-and-new-family-in-canada.

Alonge, LJ. "Writing Past the White Gaze as a Black Author." National Public Radio, March 4, 2017. https://www.npr.org/sections/codeswitch/2017/03/04/515790514/writing-past-the-white-gaze-as-a-black-author.

Anderson, Mark Cronlund, and Carmen L. Robertson. *Seeing Red: A History of Natives in Canadian Newspapers.* Winnipeg: University of Manitoba Press, 2011.

Andrew. Twitter post, October 24, 2022, 4:14 a.m. https://twitter.com/billsmachine/status/1584503633374109699.

Andrew-Gee, Eric. "How Immigrants from Benin Saved a Quebec Town's Storied Poutinerie." *Globe and Mail,* December 27, 2022. https://www.theglobeandmail.com/canada/article-quebec-rouyn-noranda-poutine.

Andrews, Gavin J., Valorie A. Crooks, Jamie R. Pearce, and Jane P. Messina, eds. *COVID-19 and Similar Futures: Pandemic Geographies.* Cham: Springer, 2021.

Ansari, Sadiya. "'Everybody Fits In': Inside the Canadian Cities Where Minorities Are the Majority." *Guardian,* September 4, 2018. https://www.theguardian.com/cities/2018/sep/04/canadian-cities-where-minorities-are-the-majority-markham-brampton.

Arteta, Miguel, dir. *The Office.* Season 3, episode 6, "Diwali." Aired November 2, 2006, on NBC.

Arvin, Maile, Eve Tuck, and Angie Morrill. "Decolonizing Feminism: Challenging Connections between Settler Colonialism and Heteropatriarchy."

Feminist Formations 25, 1 (Spring 2013): 8–34. https://doi.org/10.1353/ff.2013.0006.

Associated Press. "Congee: A Fresh, Flavourful Way to Eat Rice Any Time of Day." *National Post*, January 15, 2016. https://nationalpost.com/life/food/congee-a-fresh-flavourful-way-to-eat-rice-any-time-of-day.

Aziz, Omer. "Scarborough Made Me Who I Am Today. I Love It. Why Don't You?" *Globe and Mail*, April 1, 2023. https://www.theglobeandmail.com/opinion/article-scarborough-made-me-who-i-am-today-i-love-it-why-dont-you.

Babych, Stephanie. "Filipino Workers Face Backlash in Towns Over COVID-19 Outbreaks at Packing Plants." *Calgary Herald*, April 28, 2020. https://calgaryherald.com/news/filipino-employees-not-to-blame-for-meat-packing-plant-outbreaks-that-have-surpassed-1000-cases.

Bailey, Issac J. "It's Time for Journalists to Use the 'R' Word: Racism." *Nieman Reports*, January 31, 2019. https://niemanreports.org/articles/its-time-for-journalists-to-use-the-r-word-racism.

Barokka, Khairani. "The Case against Italicizing 'Foreign' Words." *Catapult Magazine*, February 11, 2020. https://catapult.co/stories/column-the-case-against-italicizing-foreign-words-khairani-barokka.

Basu, Brishti. "'They Don't Represent Me': LGBTQ Muslims, Allies Speak Out after 'Parental Rights' Protests." *CBC News*, October 5, 2023. https://www.cbc.ca/news/canada/lgbtq-muslims-speak-out-1.6985792.

"B.C. Muslims Celebrate First In-Person Eid in Two Years with Large Get-Togethers." *CBC News*, May 2, 2022. https://www.cbc.ca/news/canada/british-columbia/eid-al-fitr-bc-2022-1.6438878.

Beauvais, Edana, and Dietlind Stolle. "The Politics of White Identity and Settlers' Indigenous Resentment in Canada." *Canadian Journal of Political Science/Revue canadienne de science politique* 55, 1 (March 2022): 59–83. https://doi.org/10.1017/S0008423921000986.

Bernhardt, Darren, and Jenn Allen. "'Today Is a Fantastic Day': Manitoba Welcomes More Than 320 Afghan Refugees." *CBC News*, August 26, 2022. https://www.cbc.ca/news/canada/manitoba/manitoba-afghan-refugees-august-2022-1.6562867.

Bernier, Maxime. Twitter post. April 3, 2023, 3:51 p.m. https://twitter.com/MaximeBernier/status/1643023481615835137.

Bilefsky, Dan. "'Astronaut' Families Stressed by Straddling 2 Worlds: China and Canada." *New York Times*, March 21, 2020. https://www.nytimes.com/2020/03/21/world/canada/vancouver-chinese-immigrants.html.

Blackwell, Kelsey. "Why People of Color Need Spaces without White People." *Arrow*, August 9, 2018. https://arrow-journal.org/why-people-of-color-need-spaces-without-white-people.

Bonnyman, Clare. "Diwali 101: How to Celebrate the Festival of Lights." *CBC News*, October 24, 2022. https://www.cbc.ca/news/canada/edmonton/diwali-101-how-to-celebrate-the-festival-of-lights-1.6625468.

Boothby, Lauren. "Richmond Night Market Opens Friday Night." CityNews, May 10, 2019. https://vancouver.citynews.ca/2019/05/10/richmond-night-market-opens-friday-night.

Boudjikanian, Raffy. "Pakistan Warns Paperless Migrants about Jail Time, Alarming Afghans Waiting to Come to Canada." *CBC News*, November 13, 2022. https://www.cbc.ca/news/politics/afghan-migrant-refugee-canada-pakistan-1.6645091.

Boyd, David R., and McKenna Hadley-Burke. *Sacrifice Zones: 50 of the Most Polluted Places on Earth*. Office of the United Nations High Commissioner for Human Rights, accessed October 30, 2023. https://www.ohchr.org/sites/default/files/2022-03/SacrificeZones-userfriendlyversion.pdf.

Brand, David. "The New Whiz Kids." *Time*, August 31, 1987. https://content.time.com/time/subscriber/article/0,33009,965326,00.html.

Brandel, Jennifer, and Jennifer Kho. "Want to Make Real Progress in Newsroom DEI? Audience Engagement Is Essential." *Nieman Reports*, February 2, 2022. https://niemanreports.org/articles/audience-engagement-newsrooms-diversity-dei.

Brayne, Mark, ed. *Trauma & Journalism: A Guide for Journalists, Editors & Managers*. Dart Centre for Journalism and Trauma, 2007. https://dartcenter.org/sites/default/files/DCE_JournoTraumaHandbook.pdf.

Bronskill, Jim. "Islamic Schools, Mosques in Canada Are Filled with Extremist Literature: Study." *Canadian Press*, August 22, 2016. https://www.thestar.com/news/canada/islamic-schools-mosques-in-canada-are-filled-with-extremist-literature-study/article_d546dce7-3368-5986-8ca4-b1a700f33e1f.html.

Buchanan, Emma. "Pandemic Field Notes from Small Market Media." *J-Source*, December 21, 2022. https://j-source.ca/pandemic-field-notes-from-small-market-media.

Buffam, Bonar. "Cultural Confessions: Law and the Racial Scrutiny of the Indo-Canadian Home in Metro Vancouver." *Crime, Media, Culture* 14, 2 (November 16, 2016): 153–69. https://doi.org/10.1177/1741659016676864.

Bula, Frances. "Astronaut Wives: Chinese Spouses Looking for Belonging in Vancouver." *Vancouver Magazine,* November 8, 2016. https://www. vanmag.com/city/people/astronaut-wives-chinese-spouses-looking-belonging-vancouver.

Burns-Pieper, Annie, and Lisa Mayor. "'All about the Money': How Women Travelling to Canada to Give Birth Could Strain the Health-Care System." *CBC News,* January 4, 2020. https://www.cbc.ca/news/canada/birth-tourism-strain.

Burrows, Elizabeth. "Indigenous Media Producers' Perspectives on Objectivity, Balancing Community Responsibilities and Journalistic Obligations." *Media Culture & Society* 40, 8 (November 2018): 1117–34. https://journals.sagepub.com/doi/10.1177/0163443718764807.

Butler, Judith. *Frames of War: When Is Life Grievable?* London: Verso, 2009.

Caddell, Nathan. "Studio Brewing Just Gave You a Great Reason to Go to South Burnaby." *Vancouver Magazine,* March 10, 2021. https://www. vanmag.com/drink/beer/studio-brewing-just-gave-you-a-great-reason-to-go-to-south-burnaby.

Calabrese, Darren, Melissa Tait, Todd Korol, and Jackie Dives. "Proms from Coast to Coast." *Globe and Mail,* June 27, 2018. https://www. theglobeandmail.com/canada/article-proms-from-coast-to-coast-five-canadian-coming-of-age-celebrations.

Callison, Candis. "Climate Change Communication and Indigenous Publics." *Oxford Research Encyclopedia of Climate Science,* September 26, 2017. https://doi.org/10.1093/acrefore/9780190228620.013.411.

Callison, Candis, and Mary Lynn Young. *Reckoning: Journalism's Limits and Possibilities.* New York: Oxford University Press, 2020.

Canada. Parliament. House of Commons. Standing Committee on Citizenship and Immigration. *Minutes of the Proceedings and Evidence.* 2d sess., 40th Parliament, 2009. https://www.ourcommons.ca/Content/Committee/402/CIMM/Evidence/EV3660274/CIMMEV02-E.PDF.

"Canada Debates How to Address Asylum Seekers Entering from US." *Al Jazeera,* February 2, 2023. https://www.aljazeera.com/news/2023/2/22/rising-number-of-asylum-seekers-at-us-canada-border-causes-row.

"Canada Wants to Welcome 500,000 Immigrants a Year by 2025. Can Our Country Keep Up?" *Globe and Mail,* November 26, 2022. https://www.theglobeandmail.com/business/article-canada-immigration-population-boom.

Canadian Association of Journalists. *2022 Canadian Newsroom Diversity Survey*. https://caj.ca/wp-content/uploads/Canadian-Newsroom-Diversity-Survey-2022.pdf.

–. *2023 Canadian Newsroom Diversity Survey*. https://caj.ca/wp-content/uploads/Diversity_Survey_Report_2023_EN.pdf.

Canadian Coalition of Community Partners to Eliminate Anti-Asian Racism. *Open Letter – A Call to Eliminate Anti-Asian Racism*. AsianCanadianStudies.ca, November 23, 2010. https://web.archive.org/web/20120425231224/http://asiancanadianstudies.ca/node/31, archived at www.archive.org.

Canadian Journalists of Colour and Canadian Association of Black Journalists. "Canadian Media Diversity: Calls to Action." News release, January 28, 2020. https://www.cabj.news/calls-to-action.

Canadian Multiculturalism Act. Revised Statutes of Canada 1985, c.24. https://laws-lois.justice.gc.ca/eng/acts/c-18.7.

Canadian Press. "Black Press Ltd. Files for Creditor Protection, Announces Sale." CBC News, January 15, 2024. https://www.cbc.ca/news/canada/british-columbia/black-press-announces-sale-1.7084562.

–. "If the Air Appears Smoky Over Toronto Tonight, It's Not the Weather, It's Diwali Fireworks." *National Post*, October, 24, 2022. https://nationalpost.com/news/if-the-air-appears-smoky-over-toronto-tonight-its-not-the-weather-its-diwali-fireworks.

–. "Multiculturalism Profiles: Uganda – Mike Mehta." *National Post*, June 27, 2017. https://nationalpost.com/pmn/news-pmn/canada-news-pmn/multiculturalism-profiles-uganda-mike-mehta.

–. "Toronto's Korean Community Excited after Blue Jays Sign Star Pitcher Hyun-Jin Ryu." CityNews, December 27, 2019. https://toronto.citynews.ca/2019/12/27/torontos-korean-community-excited-after-blue-jays-sign-star-pitcher-hyun-jin-ryu.

Canadian Radio-television and Telecommunications Commission. "Public Notice CRTC 1999-177." Government of Canada, 1999. https://crtc.gc.ca/eng/archive/1999/PB99-117.HTM.

CBC Audience Services. "Why Aren't Most Indigenous-Related Stories Open to Comments." Canadian Broadcasting Corporation, September 25, 2019. https://cbchelp.cbc.ca/hc/en-ca/articles/360035784114-Why-aren-t-most-Indigenous-related-stories-open-to-comments-.

CBC Communications. "Meet Metro Vancouver's Inspiring Asian-Canadians." *CBC News,* May 10, 2022. https://www.cbc.ca/news/canada/british-columbia/community/asian-heritage-month-1.6441116.

CBC Kids Team. "Let's Celebrate Vaisakhi." *CBC Kids,* April 13, 2022. https://www.cbc.ca/kids/articles/whats-the-story-vaisakhi.

CBC News. "Asylum Seekers Flocking to Toronto Overwhelm City's Resources." Canadian Broadcasting Corporation, June 27, 2018. https://www.cbc.ca/player/play/1264781891722.

–. "Boy Peeing in B.C. Mall Trash Bin Photo Sparks Online Debate." Canadian Broadcasting Corporation, August 30, 2013. https://www.cbc.ca/news/canada/british-columbia/boy-peeing-in-b-c-mall-trash-bin-photo-sparks-online-debate-1.1337883.

–. "Ramadan: What's It All About?" Video, 2:19. Posted July 10, 2014. https://www.cbc.ca/player/play/2472557568.

–. "UBC's Vantage College: Canadians Need Not Apply." Canadian Broadcasting Corporation, November 7, 2014. https://www.cbc.ca/news/canada/british-columbia/ubc-s-vantage-college-canadians-need-not-apply-1.2826142.

Chaarani, James. "Some Wollwich Candidates Have a Diverse Vision for the Township's Future." *CBC News,* September 21, 2022. https://www.cbc.ca/news/canada/kitchener-waterloo/woolwich-candidates-township-s-future-1.6588119.

Chan, Cheryl. "Fraser Health Issues Warning about Potentially Poisonous Sand Ginger Powder." *Vancouver Sun,* March 9, 2022. https://vancouversun.com/news/local-news/fraser-health-warning-poisonous-sand-ginger-powder.

Chang, Robert. *Disoriented: Asian Americans, Law, and the Nation-State.* New York: NYU Press, 2000.

Chen, Jennifer. "Hard Work, Surprises, Tough Choices: Stories of Immigration to Ottawa." *CBC News,* July 26, 2021. https://www.cbc.ca/news/canada/ottawa/immigrant-stories-ottawa-1.6079193.

Cheung, Christopher. "Fraser Street's Affordability Draws New Businesses." *Vancouver Courier,* July 10, 2014. https://www.vancouverisawesome.com/courier-archive/community/fraser-streets-affordability-draws-new-businesses-2981585.

–. "From Gurdwaras to Truckers, How to Protect a Diverse, Working Suburb." *Tyee,* December 11, 2020. https://thetyee.ca/News/2020/12/11/Gurdwaras-Truckers-Diverse-Working-Suburb.

—. "'Hope, Pray and Keep Clean': Driving Taxis in a Pandemic." *Tyee,* December 1, 2020. https://thetyee.ca/News/2020/12/01/Driving-Taxis-Pandemic.

—. "Meet East Vancouver's Original Urban Farmers." *Vancouver Courier,* August 10, 2016. Canadian Newsstream.

—. "On Bottle Binning in Chinatown." *Tyee,* May 18, 2013. https://thetyee.ca/News/2023/05/18/Bottle-Binning-Chinatown/.

—. "Overrun with Buns." *Tyee,* January 27, 2023. https://thetyee.ca/News/2023/01/27/Overrun-With-Buns.

—. "Putting Down Roots in Vancouver's Backyard Gardens." *Tyee,* September 21, 2023. https://thetyee.ca/News/2021/09/21/Putting-Down-Roots-Vancouver-Backyard-Gardens/.

—. "'We Don't Do Eggo Waffles': Dining Out in the Downtown Eastside." *Tyee,* September 6, 2018. https://thetyee.ca/Culture/2018/09/06/Dining-Out-DTES-Style.

—. "We're Losing Journalists. And PR Jobs Are Rising." *Tyee,* December 16, 2022. https://thetyee.ca/News/2022/12/16/Losing-Journalists-PR-Jobs-Rising.

—. "What's in a Neighbourhood Name? How Vancouver's Mountainview Became Fraserhood." *Metro News,* December 15, 2017. https://web.archive.org/web/20180119112838/http://www.metronews.ca/news/vancouver/2017/12/15/history-of-fraserhood-reveals-vancouver-s-evolution.html, archived at www.archive.org.

Chiang, Chuck. "Bridging the Asian Cannabis Cultural Divide in B.C." *Business in Vancouver,* November 13, 2018. https://biv.com/article/2018/11/bridging-asian-cannabis-cultural-divide-bc.

—. "Cultivating Cannabis Attitudes in Conservative Asian Communities." *Richmond News,* April 16, 2019. https://www.richmond-news.com/local-business/cultivating-cannabis-attitudes-in-conservative-asian-communities-3097769.

Choe, Ellis. "Many Cooks, One Mortgage. Multigenerational Homes Are Taking Off in Calgary." *CBC News,* November 3, 2022. https://www.cbc.ca/news/canada/calgary/multi-generational-calgary-homes-1.6633826.

Chow, Kat. "'Model Minority' Myth Again Used as a Racial Wedge Between Asians and Blacks." *National Public Radio,* April 19, 2017. https://www.npr.org/sections/codeswitch/2017/04/19/524571669/model-minority-myth-again-used-as-a-racial-wedge-between-asians-and-blacks.

Chowdhury, Radiyah. "The Forever Battle of a Journalist of Colour." *Toronto Star,* July 11, 2020. https://www.thestar.com/opinion/contributors/the-forever-battle-of-a-journalist-of-colour-dalton-camp-award-winning-essay/article_d2cc0426-dd37-5528-85ed-2135935d56cf.html.

Chung, Amy. "How My Chinese Parents Reluctantly Embraced and Perfected Their Christmas Turkey." *CBC News,* December 20, 2021. https://www.cbc.ca/news/canada/first-person-christmas-turkey-1.6290377.

City of Vancouver. General Manager of Planning, Urban Design and Sustainability. *Report - Downtown Eastside Plan Implementation and Strategic Grant Allocation – 2022.* May 24, 2022. https://council.vancouver.ca/20220608ag/documents/cfsc3.pdf.

City of Vancouver. Social Policy and Projects. *Oakridge: Neighbourhood Social Indicators Profile 2020.* October 4, 2020. https://vancouver.ca/files/cov/social-indicators-profile-oakridge.pdf.

Clarke, Tyler. "Children of Today in 102-Year-Old's Thoughts Recently." *Brandon Sun,* May 3, 2021. https://www.brandonsun.com/coronavirus/2021/05/03/children-of-today-in-102-year-olds-thoughts-recently.

Coaston, Jane. "The Intersectionality Wars." *Vox,* May 18, 2019. https://www.vox.com/the-highlight/2019/5/20/18542843/intersectionality-conservatism-law-race-gender-discrimination.

Coburn, Claire, Kat Williams, and Scott R. Stroud. "Newsroom Objectivity in the Age of Black Lives Matter." Center for Media Engagement, January 20, 2021. https://mediaengagement.org/research/newsroom-objectivity-in-the-age-of-black-lives-matter.

Cochrane, David, and Lisa Laventure. "Syrian Family Celebrates 1st Canada Day away from Scars of War." *CBC News,* July 1, 2016. https://www.cbc.ca/news/politics/canada-day-syrian-refugees-1.3661635.

Cole, Desmond. "I Choose Activism for Black Liberation." *Cole's Notes* (blog), May 5, 2017. https://thatsatruestory.wordpress.com/2017/05/04/i-choose-activism-for-black-liberation/.

Colley, Ted. "100,000 in Vaisakhi Parade; Watts Wades Into the Crowd," *Surrey Now,* April 15, 2008. Canadian Newsstream.

Connecticut Forum. "Toni Morrison on Writing for Black Readers under the White Gaze." YouTube video, 3:47. Posted December 9, 2020. https://www.youtube.com/watch?v=oP_-m7V58_I.

Cooper, Brittney. "Intersectionality." In *The Oxford Handbook of Feminist Theory,* edited by Lisa Disch and Mary Hawkesworth, 385–406. New

York: Oxford University Press, 2016. https://academic.oup.com/edited-volume/34617/chapter-abstract/294775093.

Cooper, Sam. "What Happens When the Minority Becomes the Majority?" *Province,* October 10, 2013. https://theprovince.com/news/racism/what-happens-when-the-minority-becomes-the-majority.

Cram, Stephanie. "Duncan McCue on How to Report in Indigenous Communities." *CBC Radio,* November 18, 2019. https://www.cbc.ca/radio/unreserved/challenging-media-stereotypes-of-indigenous-people-1.5358798/duncan-mccue-on-how-to-report-in-indigenous-communities-1.5361175.

Crenshaw, Kimberlé. "Demarginalizing the Intersection of Race and Sex: A Black Feminist Critique of Antidiscrimination Doctrine, Feminist Theory and Antiracist Politics." *University of Chicago Legal Forum* 1 (1989). https://chicagounbound.uchicago.edu/cgi/viewcontent.cgi?article=1052&context=uclf.

—. "Why Intersectionality Can't Wait." *Washington Post,* September 24, 2015. https://www.washingtonpost.com/news/in-theory/wp/2015/09/24/why-intersectionality-cant-wait.

Cyca, Michelle. "Nostalgia about Newsrooms Ignores How Much They Need to Change." *Walrus,* May 31, 2023. https://thewalrus.ca/nostalgia-about-newsrooms-ignores-how-much-they-need-to-change.

Dart, Chris. "Gurdeep Pandher Is Canada's Favourite Bhangra Dancer and All-Purpose Good Vibes Ambassador." *CBC Arts,* 2022. https://www.cbc.ca/artsprojects/22artists/gurdeep-pandher.

Dayal, Pratyush. "Saskatoon Woman Celebrating 1st Christmas with Daughter and Granddaughter 18 Years after Family Was Separated." *CBC News,* December 2, 2022. https://www.cbc.ca/news/canada/saskatoon/sasaktoon-woman-reunited-with-her-daughter-and-granddaughter-1.6670940.

DeGraffenreid v. General Motors Assembly Div., etc. 413 F. Supp. 142 (E.D. Mo. 1976).

Delgamuukw v. British Columbia. 1991 CanLII 2372 (BCSC).

Delva, John. "The Canadian Association of Black Journalists Is Relaunching." *J-Source,* April 18, 2018. https://j-source.ca/the-canadian-association-of-black-journalists-is-relaunching.

Demby, Gene. "Why We Have So Many Terms For 'People of Color.'" National Public Radio, November 7, 2014. https://www.npr.org/sections/codeswitch/2014/11/07/362273449/why-we-have-so-many-terms-for-people-of-color.

–. Twitter post. March 12, 2018, 11:32 a.m. https://twitter.com/GeeDee215/ status/973265484547350533.

Dempsey, Kara E., and Sara McDowell. "Disaster Depictions and Geopolitical Representations in Europe's Migration 'Crisis.'" *Geoforum* 98 (2009): 153–60. http://appstate.edu/~perrylb/Courses/5000/Readings/ Faculty/Dempsey&McDowell_2019.pdf.

Dennis, Elisabeth. "Exploring the Model Minority: Deconstructing Whiteness Through the Asian American Example." *Cartographies of Race and Social Difference,* edited by George J. Sefa Dei and Shukri Hilowle, 33–48. Cham, CH: Springer Nature, 2018.

Dharssi, Ali. "As Syrians Flood In, a Bolivian Refugee Family Has Been in Limbo for Four Years." *National Post,* March 21, 2016. https:// nationalpost.com/news/canada/legacy-refugee-claimants-wait-years-to-find-out-if-they-can-stay-in-canada.

Dhillon, Sunny. "Journalism While Brown and When to Walk Away." *LEVEL,* October 29, 2018. https://level.medium.com/journalism-while-brown-and-when-to-walk-away-9333ef61de9a.

DiAngelo, Robin. *White Fragility: Why It's So Hard for White People to Talk about Racism.* Boston: Beacon Press, 2018.

DiMera, Matthew, and Nora Loreto. "Independent Media's Bad Labour Problem." *Briarpatch,* January 3, 2023. https://briarpatchmagazine.com/ articles/view/independent-medias-bad-labour-problem.

Dished Staff. "Hon's Wun-Tun House in Coquitlam Ordered to Close by Fraser Health." *Daily Hive,* March 17, 2023. https://dailyhive.com/ vancouver/hons-wun-tun-house-health-inspection-closure.

The Diversity Institute in Management and Technology. *DiverseCity Counts 2: A Snapshot of Diverse Leadership in the GTA.* Toronto: Ryerson University, 2010. https://www.torontomu.ca/content/dam/diversity/ reports/diversitycounts_report_2010_lowres.pdf.

"Diwali Celebrated Across B.C. with Message of Light over Darkness, Good over Evil, Knowledge over Ignorance." *CBC News,* October 24, 2022. https://www.cbc.ca/news/canada/british-columbia/diwali-bc-2022-1.6626957.

Donato, Al. "Filipino Front-Line Workers Risk Their Lives to Keep Canada Running." *Huffington Post,* May 21, 2020. https://www. huffpost.com/archive/ca/entry/filipino-workers-canada-frontlines_ ca_5ec3eb66c5b63e39157bef51.

Donohue, George A., Phillip J. Tichenor, and Clarice N. Olien. "A Guard Dog Perspective on the Role of Media." *Journal of Communication* 45, 2 (1995): 115–32. https://doi.org/10.1111/j.1460-2466.1995.tb00732.x.

Doss, Suresh. "Afghan Restaurant Serves Up a Spicy Taste of 'Back Home.'" *Toronto Star*, August 10, 2022. https://www.thestar.com/news/gta/2022/08/10/afghan-restaurant-serves-up-a-spicy-taste-of-back-home.html.

Du Bois, W.E.B. "Strivings of the Negro People." *Atlantic*, August 1897. https://www.theatlantic.com/magazine/archive/1897/08/strivings-of-the-negro-people/305446/.

Duffy, Andrew. "Needs Are Vast in Ethnic Enclaves." *Toronto Star*, September 27, 2004. Canadian Newsstream.

Durham, Meenakshi Gigi. "On the Relevance of Standpoint Epistemology to the Practice of Journalism: The Case for 'Strong Objectivity.'" *Communication Theory* 8, 2 (May 1998): 117–40. https://doi.org/10.1111/j.1468-2885.1998.tb00213.x.

"1868 – Victoria Is Named the Capital City." Legislative Assembly of British Columbia, accessed August 7, 2023. https://www.leg.bc.ca/dyl/Pages/1868-Victoria-Named-Capital-City.aspx.

Elghawaby, Amira. "Canadian Media Sucks at Representing Muslims in Canada." *This Magazine,* December 13, 2016. https://this.org/2016/12/13/canadian-media-sucks-at-representing-muslims-in-canada.

–. "News Media's Rush to Be First Can Have Real Consequences." *Hill Times,* September 6, 2016. https://www.hilltimes.com/2016/09/05/new-medias-rush-to-be-first-can-have-real-consequences/79184.

Elimin8Hate Style Guide: Reporting on Asian Canadian Communities. Elimin8Hate, June 2021. https://www.elimin8hate.org/style-guide.

Employment Equity Act, Statutes of Canada 1995, c. 44. https://laws-lois.justice.gc.ca/eng/acts/e-5.401/FullText.html.

English, Kathy. "Star Apologizes to Toronto-Area Mosque for Publishing Wrong and Misleading Photo." *Toronto Star*, August 26, 2016. https://www.thestar.com/opinion/public-editor/star-apologizes-to-toronto-area-mosque-for-publishing-wrong-and-misleading-photo/article_84d6e119-441c-50f3-861d-b1808bf6017a.html.

Ericson, Richard V., Patricia M. Baranek, and Janet B.L. Chan. *Representing Order: Crime, Law, and Justice in the News Media.* Toronto: University of Toronto Press, 1991.

"Ethnic and Racial Minorities & Socioeconomic Status." American
  Psychological Association, accessed September 1, 2023. https://
  www.apa.org/pi/ses/resources/publications/minorities.
Fanon, Frantz. *Black Skin, White Masks*. Translated by Richard Philcox.
  New York: Grove Press, 2007.
–. "The Fact of Blackness." In *Theories of Race and Racism: A Reader*, edited by
  Les Back and John Solomos, 257–65. London and New York: Routledge,
  2000.
Faulder, Liane. "Out of the Way and Out of This World." *Edmonton Journal*,
  November 3, 2010. Canadian Newsstream.
Fayerman, Pamela. "Nothing Illegal about Birth Tourism at B.C. Hospitals."
  Vancouver Sun, August 6, 2016. https://vancouversun.com/news/
  local-news/nothing-illegal-about-birth-tourism-at-b-c-hospitals.
Ferreras, Jesse, and John Hua. "There's Hardly a Word of English on This
  TransLink Bus Ad." *Global News*, January 18, 2018. https://globalnews.ca/
  news/3974662/translink-bus-ad-chinese.
Findlay, Stephanie, and Nicholas Köhler. "Too Asian: Some Frosh Don't
  Want to Study at an Asian University." *Maclean's*, November 10, 2010.
  https://macleans.ca/news/canada/too-asian.
Fleras, Augie. *The Media Gaze: Representations of Diversities in Canada*.
  Vancouver: UBC Press, 2011.
Fong, Petti. "Much Ado About Chinese-Only Signs in Richmond, B.C."
  Toronto Star, March 23, 2013. https://www.thestar.com/news/canada/
  2013/03/23/much_ado_about_chineseonly_signs_in_richmond_
  bc.html.
Foucault, Michel. *Discipline and Punish: The Birth of the Prison*. Translated by
  Reg Keeland. New York: Vintage Books, 1977.
"Fraser Health Targets South Asian Diet to Improve Health, Diabetes."
  CBC News, December 18, 2016. https://www.cbc.ca/news/canada/british-
  columbia/fraser-health-targets-south-asian-diet-to-improve-heart-health-
  diabetes-1.3902726.
"Fraser Street." *Vancouver City Guide 2017*, July 7, 2017, 58.
Froke, Paula, Anna Jo Bratton, Jeff McMillan, Pia Sarkar, Jerry Schwartz,
  and Raghuram Vadarevu, eds. *The Associated Press Stylebook*, 55th edition.
  New York: Basic Books, 2020.
Fung Bros. "Things Asian Parents Do." YouTube video, 3:32. Posted March
  27, 2013. https://www.youtube.com/watch?v=eqeiHIl3XY8.

Gangdev, Srushti. "From Indigenous Trail to Wagon Road: Kingsway before the Kings." *Burnaby Beacon*, September 29, 2021. https://burnabybeacon. com/p/from-indigenous-trail-to-wagon-road-kingsway-before-the-kings.

Gee, Marcus. "The Secret Lives of Toronto's Chinese Bottle Ladies." *Globe and Mail*, December 23, 2016. https://www.theglobeandmail.com/news/ toronto/the-secret-lives-of-torontos-chinese-bottleladies/article33425364.

Gill, Alexandra. "Smitten by a Humble South Indian Diner." *Globe and Mail*, October 3, 2014. Canadian Newsstream.

–. "An Unassuming Hole-in-the-Wall for Adventurous Eaters." *Globe and Mail*, November 2, 2012. https://www.theglobeandmail.com/life/ food-and-wine/restaurant-reviews/an-unassuming-hole-in-the-wall-for-adventurous-eaters/article4900839.

Gilmor, Don. "The Scarborough Curse." *Toronto Life*, December 1, 2007. https://torontolife.com/city/the-scarborough-curse.

Gilmore, Rachel. "'A Racist City That Pretends It Isn't': London, Ont. Attack Didn't Happen in Vacuum, Residents Say." *Global News*, June 8, 2021. https://globalnews.ca/news/7931553/islamophobia-muslim-london-hate-crime-white-supremacy.

Global News Commenting Policy. Global News, accessed on September 3, 2023. https://globalnews.ca/pages/global-news-commenting-policy.

Global Reporting Centre. *Empowerment Journalism Guide*. Vancouver: Global Reporting Centre, 2023. https://globalreportingcentre.org/ empowerment-guide/guide.pdf.

Godfrey, Chris. "'I Felt Seriously Cheated': Djimon Hounsou on the Oscars, Poor Pay Days, Stardom and Struggle." *Guardian*, March 16, 2023. https:// www.theguardian.com/film/2023/mar/16/i-felt-seriously-cheated-djimon-hounsou-on-the-oscars-poor-pay-days-stardom-and-struggle.

Gold, Kerry. "The Highest Bidder: How Foreign Investors Are Squeezing Out Vancouver's Middle Class." *Walrus*, March 30, 2016. https:// thewalrus.ca/the-highest-bidder.

Goldberg, David Theo. "Why 'Black Lives Matter' Because All Lives Don't Matter in America." *Huffington Post*, September 25, 2015. https:// www.huffpost.com/entry/why-black-lives-matter_b_8191424.

Goldsbie, Jonathan. "'Degrading and Aggressive': Star Newsroom Rises Up against Rosie DiManno." *Canadaland*, August 26, 2020. https://www. canadaland.com/toronto-star-newsroom-rises-up-against-rosie-dimanno.

Goode, Erich, and Nachman Ben-Yehuda. *Moral Panics: The Social Construction of Deviance,* 2nd ed. West Sussex: Blackwell Publishing, 2009.

Grady, Constance. "The Waves of Feminism, and Why People Keep Fighting over Them, Explained." *Vox,* July 20, 2018. https://www.vox.com/2018/3/20/16955588/feminism-waves-explained-first-second-third-fourth.

Greenfield-Sanders, Timothy, director. *Toni Morrison: The Pieces I Am.* Magnolia Pictures, 2019. 120 minutes.

Griffin, Kevin. "Ferris Wheel at Surrey Wedding Reception Helps Send Neighbours into Orbit." *Vancouver Sun,* October 21, 2021. https://vancouversun.com/news/ferris-wheel-at-surrey-wedding-reception-helps-send-neighbours-into-orbit.

Gross, Matt. "Asian Cuisine as Diverse as Vancouver." *New York Times,* September 23, 2009. https://archive.nytimes.com/frugaltraveler.blogs.nytimes.com/2009/09/23/asian-cuisine-as-diverse-as-vancouver.

Haki, Gary. "When Writing about Race, Abuse Follows. Especially for Journalists of Color and Women." *Poynter,* March 12, 2021. https://www.poynter.org/ethics-trust/2021/when-writing-about-race-abuse-follows-especially-for-journalists-of-color-and-women.

Harriot, Michael. "War on Wokeness: The Year the Right Rallied around a Made-Up Menace." *Guardian,* December 21, 2022. https://www.theguardian.com/us-news/2022/dec/20/anti-woke-race-america-history.

Heller, Carolyn B. "Curry, Sambal, Jerk, and Salsa Mark the Way along Surrey's Diverse Spice Trail." *Montecristo Magazine,* June 23, 2021. https://montecristomagazine.com/food-and-drink/curry-sambal-jerk-salsa-mark-way-along-surreys-diverse-spice-trail.

Henry, Bonnie. "As We Venture Out into the World Again, Let's Do So Steadily but Cautiously." *Vancouver Sun,* April 5, 2022. https://vancouversun.com/opinion/op-ed/dr-bonnie-henry-as-we-venture-out-into-the-world-again-lets-do-so-steadily-but-cautiously.

Henry, Frances, and Carol Tator. *The Colour of Democracy: Racism in Canadian Society,* 4th ed. Toronto: Nelson Education, 2010.

Hoby, Hermione. "Toni Morrison: 'I'm Writing for Black People ... I Don't Have to Apologise.'" *Guardian,* April 25, 2015. https://www.theguardian.com/books/2015/apr/25/toni-morrison-books-interview-god-help-the-child.

Hong, Beth. "The 'Too Asian?' Debate: Why I Don't Support *Maclean's* or TooAsian.ca." *Schema Magazine*, December 8, 2010. http://schemamag.ca/2010/12/08/the_too_asian_debate.

hooks, bell. *Black Looks: Race and Representation*. New York: Routledge, 2015.

–. "Representing Whiteness in the Black Imagination." In *Cultural Studies*, edited by Lawrence Grossberg, Cary Nelson, and Paula Treichler, 338–42. New York: Routledge, 1992.

Hopper, Tristin. "Our Chinalands: As Immigration Booms, Ethnic Enclaves Swell and Segregate Coast to Coast." *National Post*, February 11, 2012. Canadian Newsstream.

–. "Richmond, B.C., Considers Banning Chinese-Only Signs amid Uproar Over City's 'Un-Canadian' Advertisements." *National Post*, October 19, 2014. https://nationalpost.com/news/politics/richmond-b-c-considers-banning-chinese-only-signs-amid-uproar-over-citys-un-canadian-advertisements.

Hou, Feng, and Garnett Picot. *Visible Minority Neighbourhoods in Toronto, Montréal, and Vancouver. Canadian Social Trends*, Spring 2004, Statistics Canada, 1–13. https://www150.statcan.gc.ca/n1/en/pub/11-008-x/2003004/article/6803-eng.pdf?st=Ajivmp94.

Hui, Vikki. "Richmond Chinese Medicine Store Closed for Rodent Infestation." *Richmond News*, August 22, 2023. https://www.richmond-news.com/local-business/richmond-chinese-medicine-store-closed-for-rodent-infestation-7440407.

Huynh, Mandy. "Decade-Old Article on Universities Being 'Too Asian' Sparks Panel Conversation on Anti-Asian Racism at UBC." *Ubyssey*, November 23, 2020. https://www.ubyssey.ca/news/too-asian-panel.

Indra, Doreen M. "South Asian Stereotypes in the Vancouver Press." *Ethnic and Racial Studies* 2, 2 (September 13, 2010): 166–89.

"Intersectionality Feminism: What It Means and Why It Matters Right Now." *UN Women*, July 1, 2020. https://www.unwomen.org/en/news/stories/2020/6/explainer-intersectional-feminism-what-it-means-and-why-it-matters.

"Islamophobia in Canada: Four Mindsets Indicate Negativity Is Nationwide, Most Intense in Quebec." *Angus Reid Institute*, March 13, 2023. https://angusreid.org/islamophobia-canada-quebec.

"Italics." *Canadian Style*, last modified October 15, 2015. https://www.btb.termiumplus.gc.ca/tcdnstyl-chap?lang=eng&lettr=chapsect6&info0=6.

Jabakhanji, Sara. "5 Afghan Siblings Arrive in Toronto More Than a Year after Being Stuck in Limbo in UAE Refugee Camp." *CBC News,* December 5, 2022. https://www.cbc.ca/news/canada/toronto/afghan-siblings-arrive-toronto-1.6674106.

Jheeta, Hardeep Kaur. "Media Should Tell Real Stories behind Vaisakhi." *Surrey Now,* April 18, 2008. Canadian Newsstream.

Jimenez, Marina. "Do Ethnic Enclaves Impede Integration?" *Globe and Mail,* February 8, 2007. Canadian Newsstream.

Jiwani, Yasmin. *Discourses of Denial: Mediations of Race, Gender, and Violence.* Vancouver: UBC Press, 2006.

Johnson, Gail. "How Fraserhood Became a Vancouver Foodie Hub." *Georgia Straight,* October 11, 2016. https://www.straight.com/food/804931/how-fraserhood-became-vancouver-foodie-hub.

Johnston, Josée, and Shyon Baumann. *Foodies: Democracy and Distinction in the Gourmet Foodscape.* New York and London: Routledge, 2010.

Jones, Alex. *Losing the News: The Future of the News That Feeds Democracy.* New York: Oxford University Press, 2009.

"Journalistic Standards and Practices (JSP)." CBC/Radio-Canada. Accessed August 5, 2023. https://cbc.radio-canada.ca/en/vision/governance/journalistic-standards-and-practices.

Judd, Amy. "Police Warn Public to Stay away from 2 Surrey Men with Gang Connections." *Global News,* December 30, 2022. https://globalnews.ca/news/9379146/public-warning-surrey-men-gang-connections.

Juric, Sam. "The Number of Hate Motivated Crimes Reported to Sudbury Police Is Climbing. So What Does That Tell Us?" *CBC News,* March 25, 2022. https://www.cbc.ca/news/canada/sudbury/sudbury-hate-crimes-climbing-1.6396617.

Kanji, Azeezah. "Framing Muslims in the 'War on Terror': Representations of Ideological Violence by Muslim versus Non-Muslim Perpetrators in Canadian National News Media." *Religions* 9, 9 (2018): 274. https://www.mdpi.com/2077-1444/9/9/274.

Kapitan, Alex. "Should I Use the Adjective 'Diverse'?" *Radical Copy Editor,* October 2, 2017. https://radicalcopyeditor.com/2017/10/02/should-i-use-the-adjective-diverse/.

Kent, Joie Alvaro. "Vancouver's Urban Farms: A Growing Reality." *Montecristo Magazine,* September 24, 2012. https://montecristomagazine.com/magazine/autumn-2012/vancouvers-urban-farms.

Kerr, Jaren. "Korean Community Stays United in the Aftermath of Yonge St. Van Rampage." *Toronto Star*, April 26, 2018. https://www.thestar.com/news/gta/2018/04/25/korean-community-stays-united-in-the-aftermath-of-yonge-st-van-rampage.html.

Keung, Nicholas. "Here's How Syrian Refugees Who Came to Canada Say They're Doing – Seven Years Later." *Toronto Star*, December 17, 2022. https://www.thestar.com/news/canada/2022/12/17/heres-how-syrian-refugees-who-came-to-canada-say-theyre-doing-seven-years-later.html.

King, Martin Luther, Jr. "I Have a Dream." August 28, 1963, Lincoln Memorial, Washington DC, transcript. National Public Radio. https://www.npr.org/2010/01/18/122701268/i-have-a-dream-speech-in-its-entirety.

Kleinplatz, Talia. "On the End of Latab and the Delicious Things That Refugees Bring." *Scout*, February 14, 2017. https://scoutmagazine.ca/2017/02/14/intelligence-briefs-on-the-end-of-latab-and-the-delicious-things-that-refugees-bring.

Kovach, Bill, and Tom Rosenstiel. *The Elements of Journalism: What Newspeople Should Know and the Public Should Expect,* 3rd ed. New York: Three Rivers Press, 2014.

Krishnan, Manisha. "Editor of Progressive News Site Quits over Systemic Racism, Labour Practices." *Vice News*, January 6, 2021. https://www.vice.com/en/article/5dpwjq/editor-of-rabble-progressive-news-site-quits-over-systemic-racism-labour-practices.

Krug, Sammi. "Reactions Now Available Globally." Meta, February, 24, 2016. https://about.fb.com/news/2016/02/reactions-now-available-globally.

Kwai, Isabella. "How 'Subtle Asian Traits' Became a Global Hit." *New York Times*, December 11, 2018. https://www.nytimes.com/2018/12/11/world/australia/subtle-asian-traits-facebook-group.html.

Kwong, Evelyn. "He Wanted to Make Lunar New Year Snacks Connecting His Hong Kong Roots to Canada. 17 Years Later, Wai Tack Kee Is Still Going Strong." *Toronto Star*, January 27, 2022. https://www.thestar.com/life/food_wine/2022/01/27/he-wanted-to-make-lunar-new-year-snacks-connecting-his-hong-kong-roots-to-canada-17-years-later-wai-tack-kee-is-still-going-strong.html.

Lam, Katherine. "Syrian Refugee Charged in 'Random' Murder of Girl, 13, in Canada." *Fox News*, September 13, 2018. https://www.foxnews.com/world/syrian-refugee-charged-in-random-murder-of-girl-13-in-canada.

Lattimore, Ashton. "Journalism Can Do More Than Report on Racial Injustice. It Can Also Help Solve It." *Poynter*. October 20, 2020. https://

www.poynter.org/commentary/2020/opinion-journalism-can-do-more-than-report-on-racial-injustice-it-can-also-help-solve-it.

"Lavish, Loud Ferris-Wheel Wedding of Singer and Politician in Surrey Ticks off Neighbourhood." *CBC News,* October 20, 2021. https://www.cbc.ca/news/canada/british-columbia/surrey-ferris-wheel-wedding-1.6218708.

Lawrence, Andrew. "How the 'Natural Talent' Myth Is Used as a Weapon against Black Athletes." *Guardian,* October 2, 2018. https://www.theguardian.com/sport/2018/oct/02/athletes-racism-language-sports-cam-newton.

Lawrence, Grant. "Meet 'The Angel of East Hastings' Who Collects Empties for Those in Need." *Vancouver Courier,* December 17, 2018. https://www.vancouverisawesome.com/courier-archive/community/meet-the-angel-of-east-hastings-who-collects-empties-for-those-in-need-3090099.

Lee, Charles T. "Improvising 'Nonexistent Rights': Immigrants, Ethnic Restaurants, and Corporeal Citizenship in Suburban California." *Social Inclusion* 7, 4 (2019): 79–89. https://doi.org/10.17645/si.v7i4.2305.

Lee, Stacey J., Nga-Wing Anjela Wong, and Alvin N. Alvarez. "The Model Minority and the Perpetual Foreigner: Stereotypes of Asian Americans." In *Asian American Psychology: Current Perspectives,* edited by Nita Tewari and Alvin Alvarez, 69–84. New York and London: Psychology Press, 2009.

Li, Anita. "How Canadian Journalists of Colour Grew from a Grassroots Facebook Group into a Major Force for Change." *The Other Wave,* January 23, 2022. https://theotherwave.substack.com/p/canadian-journalists-of-colour-cjoc-history.

Li, Wanyee. "'A Disgusting Act': Vancouver Video Captures Another Attack against Victim of Asian Descent." *Toronto Star,* May 5, 2020. https://www.thestar.com/news/canada/2020/05/05/video-captures-another-attack-against-victim-of-asian-descent-in-vancouver.html.

Li, Wei. *Ethnoburb: The New Ethnic Community in Urban America.* Honolulu: University of Hawai'i Press, 2009.

Lim, Audrey. "A Definitive List of Dim Sum Dishes Ranked from Worst to Best." *Daily Hive,* August 26, 2021. https://dailyhive.com/vancouver/dim-sum-dishes-ranked-from-worst-to-best.

Liu, Karon. "Aoyama Sushi Restaurant Is a Hidden Gem in a Tiny Plaza on the Border of North York and Scarborough." *Toronto Star,* May 22, 2021. https://www.thestar.com/news/gta/2021/05/22/aoyama-sushi-restaurant-is-a-hidden-gem-in-a-tiny-plaza-on-the-border-of-north-york-and-scarborough.html.

—. "One of Toronto's Best Food Courts Is in the Back of a Giant Flea Market." *Toronto Star*, February 24, 2022. https://www.thestar.com/life/food-and-drink/one-of-toronto-s-best-food-courts-is-in-the-back-of-a-giant-flea/article_7dc7722a-c866-534b-af14-e27f7310dd47.html.

—. "'Plazas Are Gold.' Why the Neighbourhood Strip Mall Has All the Delicious Eats You Are Looking For." *Toronto Star*, November 22, 2020. https://www.thestar.com/news/gta/2020/11/22/plazas-are-gold-why-the-neighbourhood-strip-mall-has-all-delicious-eats-you-are-looking-for.html.

"Live Chat on Ethnic Enclaves in Metro Vancouver." *CBC News*, May 30, 2012. https://www.cbc.ca/news/canada/british-columbia/live-chat-on-ethnic-enclaves-in-metro-vancouver-1.1206006.

Lloyd, John. "Study Paints Bleak Picture of Ethnic Diversity." *Financial Times*, October 8, 2006. https://www.ft.com/content/c4ac4a74-570f-11db-9110-0000779e2340.

Loayza, Beatrice. "Slaves, Nannies, and Maids: Oscars Value Women of Colour – In Subservient Roles." *Guardian*, January 14, 2020. https://www.theguardian.com/film/2020/jan/14/slaves-nannies-and-maids-how-oscars-value-female-actors-of-colour.

Logan, Nick. "Refugee Group Partners with Ottawa to Bring Hundreds of LGBTQ Afghans to Canada." *CBC News*, December 22, 2022. https://www.cbc.ca/news/canada/canada-afghanistan-lgbtq-refugees-1.6694650.

Lounsberry, Barbara. "Introduction." In *The Gay Talese Reader: Portraits and Encounters*, by Gay Talese, vii–xv. New York: Walker Publishing Company, 2003.

Lowery, Wesley. "A Reckoning Over Objectivity, Led by Black Journalists." *New York Times*, June 23, 2020. https://www.nytimes.com/2020/06/23/opinion/objectivity-black-journalists-coronavirus.html.

Lowman, Harrison. "Journalism Schools Are Failing a Generation of Students." *Hub*, February 7, 2024. https://thehub.ca/2024-02-07/have-journalism-schools-failed-a-generation-of-students.

Luk, Vivian. "COVID-19 Rates in South Asian Communities Require Nuanced Understanding, Scholar Explains." *CBC News*, November 20, 2020. https://www.cbc.ca/news/canada/british-columbia/Covid-19-rates-in-south-asian-communities-require-nuanced-understanding-scholar-explains-1.5810591.

Macdonald, Nancy. "Ian Young on Vancouver's 'Freak Show' Housing Market." *Maclean's,* May 10, 2016. https://macleans.ca/economy/economicanalysis/ian-young-on-vancouvers-freak-show-housing-market.

Malik, Asmaa, and Sonya Fatah. "Newsrooms Not Keeping Up with Changing Demographics, Study Suggests." *The Conversation,* November 11, 2019. https://theconversation.com/newsrooms-not-keeping-up-with-changing-demographics-study-suggests-125368.

Maras, Steven. *Objectivity in Journalism.* Cambridge: Polity Press, 2013.

Massey, Doreen. *Space, Place and Gender.* Cambridge: Polity Press, 1994.

Mastracci, Davide. "That Study About Extremist Mosques in Canada Is Mostly Bullshit." *Vice,* August 23, 2016. https://www.vice.com/en/article/dpkjgy/that-study-about-extremist-mosques-in-canada-is-mostly-bullshit.

Mattar, Pacinthe. "Objectivity Is a Privilege Afforded to White Journalists." *Walrus,* August 21, 2020. https://thewalrus.ca/objectivity-is-a-privilege-afforded-to-white-journalists.

McArdle, Megan. Twitter post, January 26, 2023, 10:09 a.m.

McCarten, James, ed. *The Canadian Press Stylebook: A Guide for Writers and Editors,* 19th ed. Toronto: Canadian Press, 2021.

McCue, Duncan. *Decolonizing Journalism: A Guide to Reporting in Indigenous Communities.* Don Mills, ON: Oxford University Press, 2021.

McElroy, Justin. "Richmond City Council Passes Policy Encouraging 50% English on Commercial Signs." *CBC News,* September 11, 2017. https://www.cbc.ca/news/canada/british-columbia/richmond-commercial-signs-english-50-sept-11-1.4284713.

McGarvey, Dan. "South Asian Painter Hopes to Inspire Others to Express Themselves Through Art." *CBC News,* June 11, 2022. https://www.cbc.ca/news/canada/calgary/south-asian-art-calgary-india-1.6484648.

McIntosh, Peggy. "White Privilege: Unpacking the Invisible Knapsack." *Peace and Freedom Magazine,* July–August 1989, 10–12.

–. "White Privilege and Male Privilege: A Personal Account of Coming to See Correspondences through Work in Women's Studies." Working paper, no. 189. Center for Research on Women, Wellesley College, 1988.

McMartin, Pete. "Historic Human Tsunami Likely in Canada's Future." *Vancouver Sun,* August 20, 2021. https://vancouversun.com/opinion/pete-mcmartin-historic-human-tsunami-likely-in-canadas-future.

McSheffrey, Elizabeth. "Trial Postponed Again for Man Accused of Killing B.C. Teen Marrisa Shen." *Global News,* January 6, 2023. https://globalnews.ca/news/9392738/trial-postponed-murder-marissa-shen.

Mendoza, Gian-Paolo. "Hoping for Prosperity: How 3 Different Asian Cultures Celebrate the Lunar New Year." *CBC News,* February 10, 2021. https://newsinteractives.cbc.ca/longform/lunar-new-year-2021.

–. "These B.C. Podcasters Are Calling Out Toxic Attitudes in Filipino Culture." *CBC News,* June 1, 2021. https://www.cbc.ca/news/canada/british-columbia/filipino-fridays-vancouver-podcast-1.6025838.

"Merit: The Best and Only Way to Decide Who Gets into University." *Maclean's,* November 25, 2010. http://www.macleans.ca/general/who-gets-into-university.

Merriam-Webster.com Dictionary, s.v. "hole-in-the-wall," accessed September 3, 2023. https://www.merriam-webster.com/dictionary/hole-in-the-wall.

Miao, Hannah. "'Fairview' and Tackling the White Gaze." *Chronicle,* October 17, 2019. https://www.dukechronicle.com/article/2019/10/fairview-and-tackling-the-white-gaze-5da7b82701a0f.

Miller, Hayley. "Kimberlé Crenshaw Explains the Power of Intersectional Feminism in 1 Minute." *Huffington Post,* August 11, 2017. https://www.huffpost.com/entry/kimberle-crenshaw-intersectional-feminism_n_598de38de4b090964296a34d.

Miller, John. "Desmond Cole's Decision to Leave the *Toronto Star* Suggests a Double Standard on Activism." rabble.ca, May 4, 2017. https://rabble.ca/political-action/silenced-why-desmond-cole-leaving-toronto-star/.

–. "Shame on Maclean's." *Journalism Doctor,* blog, January 27, 2011. https://www.thejournalismdoctor.ca/Blog.php/archived/20110101/shame-on-maclean-s.

–. "Who's Telling the News? Racial Representation among News Gatherers in Canada's Daily Newsrooms." *International Journal of Diversity in Organizations, Communities, and Nations: Annual Review* 5, 4: 133–42. https://doi.org/10.18848/1447-9532/CGP/v05i04/39084.

Miller, John, and Cybele Sack. "The Toronto-18 Terror Case: Trial by Media? How Newspaper Opinion Framed Canada's Biggest Terrorism Case." *International Journal of Diversity in Organizations, Communities & Nations* 10, 1 (2010): 279–95. https://doi.org/10.18848/1447-9532/CGP/v10i01/39808.

Minh-ha, Trinh T. *Woman, Native, Other: Writing Postcoloniality and Feminism.* Bloomington: Indiana University Press, 1989.

Mitchell, Amy, Galen Stocking, and Katerina Eva Matsa. *Long-Form Reading Shows Signs of Life in Our Mobile News World.* Pew Research Center, May 5,

2016. https://www.pewresearch.org/journalism/2016/05/05/long-form-reading-shows-signs-of-life-in-our-mobile-news-world.

Mohamed, Omayma. "How Intersectionalism Betrays the World's Muslim Women." *Quillette*, April 28, 2019. https://quillette.com/2019/04/28/how-intersectionalism-betrays-the-worlds-muslim-women.

Monaghan, Jeffery, and Adam Molnar. "Radicalisation Theories, Policing Practices, and the 'Future of Terrorism?'" *Critical Studies on Terrorism* 9, 3 (2016): 393–413. https://doi.org/10.1177/1741659020966370.

Mulvey, Laura. "Visual Pleasure and Narrative Cinema." *Screen* 16, 3 (1973): 6–18. https://doi.org/10.1093/screen/16.3.6.

Murphy, Rex. "Canada Is Not a Racist Country, Despite What the Liberals Say." *National Post*, January 1, 2020. https://nationalpost.com/opinion/rex-murphy-canada-is-not-a-racist-country-despite-what-the-liberals-say.

Murray, Catherine, Sherry Yu, and Daniel Ahadi. *Cultural Diversity and Ethnic Media in British Columbia*. Centre for Policy Studies on Culture and Communication, Simon Fraser University, October 2007. http://www.bcethnicmedia.ca/Research/cultural-diversity-report-oct-07.pdf, archived at www.archive.org.

Musk, Elon. Twitter post. December 12, 2022, 4:25 a.m. https://twitter.com/elonmusk/status/1602278477234728960.

"Muslim Family in Canada Killed in 'Premeditated' Truck Attack." British Broadcasting Corporation, June 8, 2021. https://www.bbc.com/news/world-us-canada-57390398.

"Must Bar Oriental Completely to Save B.C. for White Race." *Victoria Daily Times*, November 11, 1922, A1.

Nagel, Thomas. *The View from Nowhere*. New York: Oxford University Press, 1986.

Narayan, Uma. *Dislocating Cultures: Identities, Traditions, and Third Wave Feminism*. New York: Routledge, 1997.

Nesbit, Ben. "'I Helped So Many Canadians': Former Afghan Interpreter Fears for Family's Safety, Pleads with Feds for Help." *CTV News*, December 11, 2022. https://bc.ctvnews.ca/i-helped-so-many-canadians-former-afghan-interpreter-fears-for-family-s-safety-pleads-with-feds-for-help-1.6190421.

Neville, Helen A., Miguel E. Gallardo, and Derald Wing Sue. "Introduction: Has the United States Really Moved beyond Race?" In *The Myth of Racial Color Blindness: Manifestations, Dynamics, and Impact*, edited by Helen A.

Neville, Miguel E. Gallardo, and Derald Wing Sue, 3–22. Washington, DC: American Psychological Association, 2016.

"New Canadian Media – The Pulse of Immigrant Canada." *New Canadian Media*, accessed on November 12, 2023. https://www.newcanadianmedia.ca.

Newkirk, Vann R., II. "Diversity as a Second Job." *Columbia Journalism Review*, November 13, 2018. https://www.cjr.org/special_report/journalist-of-color-second-job.php.

Nguyen, Alex. "'Underpaid and Undervalued': Filipino Communities Face Disproportionate Impact from COVID-19." *Ricochet*, May 9, 2020. https://ricochet.media/en/3099/underpaid-and-undervalued-filipino-communities-face-disproportionate-impact-from-Covid-19.

Nguyen, Truc. "What's in a Name? We Talk to Experts about Racial Bias in Hiring and How to Work to Change It." *CBC Life*, September 13, 2018. https://www.cbc.ca/life/culture/what-s-in-a-name-we-talk-to-experts-about-racial-bias-in-hiring-and-how-to-work-to-change-it-1.4822467.

Nolan, Elanna. "Considering the So-Called Richmond 'Signage Issue.'" The University of British Columbia, Department of Geography News, June 29, 2015. https://geog.ubc.ca/news/considering-the-so-called-richmond-signage-issue.

"Noodles Featured in Oscar-Winning Film *Parasite* a Hot Seller for B.C. Korean Supermarket." *CBC News*, February 23, 2020. https://www.cbc.ca/news/canada/british-columbia/parasite-noodles-h-mart-sales-1.5471380.

Omstead, Jordan. "Environment Canada Removes Reference to Diwali in GTA Air Quality Statement." *Canadian Press*, October 24, 2022. https://www.cbc.ca/news/canada/toronto/ont-diwali-air-quality-1.6627261.

An Open Letter to Corus Entertainment. Canadian Association of Black Journalists, June 29, 2020. https://www.cabj.news/news-and-updates/813bkdrjttabn54pr7cu3llxj12ryk.

Ordway, Denise-Marie. "Calling Racism What It Is." *Journalist's Resource*, April 15, 2019. https://journalistsresource.org/race-and-gender/covering-racism-khalil-gibran-muhammad.

Pabla, Manjit. "The Legacies of Bindy Johal: The Contemporary Folk Devil or Sympathetic Hero." *Religions* 11, 5 (2020): 228. https://doi.org/10.3390/rel11050228.

Paik, Diane. "Why Sandra Oh's Speech at the Golden Globes Meant So Much to Me." *Vice*, January 8, 2019. https://www.vice.com/en/article/xwjbw7/why-sandra-ohs-speech-at-the-golden-globes-meant-so-much-to-me.

Paradkar, Shree. "Lack of Diversity in Media a Form of Oppression: Overwhelming White Newsrooms Have Led to Tone-Deaf, Biased Coverage of News." *Toronto Star,* October 5, 2018. Canadian Newsstream.

Pasqual, Solana. "'I Had to Break the Rules.'" *Tyee,* June 1, 2023. https://thetyee.ca/Culture/2023/06/01/Angela-Sterritt-Interview.

Pawson, Chad. "Vancouver Still Shaped by Hong Kong Handover 2 Decades Later." *CBC News,* July 1, 2017. https://www.cbc.ca/news/canada/british-columbia/hong-kong-handover-20-year-anniversary-vancouver-1.4186864.

Pearson, Natalie Obiko. "This Is the Anti-Asian Hate Crime Capital of North America." *Bloomberg,* May 7, 2021. https://www.bloomberg.com/features/2021-vancouver-canada-asian-hate-crimes/?srnd=premium.

Peng, Jenny. "Eight Years and Not a Word of English, Neighbourhood Auntie Teaches Vancouver Millennials Life-Long Values." *Toronto Star,* June 3, 2019. https://www.thestar.com/vancouver/2019/06/03/after-eight-years-and-not-a-word-of-english-an-unlikely-friendship-blossoms.html.

Peoples, James, and Garrick Bailey. *Humanity: An Introduction to Cultural Anthropology,* 10th ed. Stamford: Cengage Learning, 2015.

Perry, Barbara, and Ryan Scrivens. *Right-Wing Extremism in Canada: An Environmental Scan.* Public Safety Canada, September 2016. https://www.publicsafety.gc.ca/cnt/ntnl-scrt/cntr-trrrsm/r-nd-flght-182/knshk/ctlg/dtls-en.aspx?i=116.

Peterson, Jordan. "Why the Western Emphasis on Individuals Is the Ultimate in Intersectionality." *National Post,* November 22, 2019. https://nationalpost.com/opinion/jordan-peterson-why-the-western-emphasis-on-individuals-is-the-ultimate-in-intersectionality.

Pettersen, William. "Success Story, Japanese-American Style." *New York Times,* January 9, 1966. https://www.nytimes.com/1966/01/09/archives/success-story-japaneseamerican-style-success-story-japaneseamerican.html.

Pilkington, Ed. "What Is 'Great Replacement' Theory and How Did Its Racist Lies Spread in the US?" *Guardian,* May 17, 2022. https://www.theguardian.com/us-news/2022/may/17/great-replacement-theory-explainer.

Ping, William. "Hopping Back into Action: Lunar New Year Celebrations Return to N.L. for the Year of the Rabbit." *CBC News,* January 22, 2023. https://www.cbc.ca/news/canada/newfoundland-labrador/lunar-new-year-nl-2023-1.6722046.

Poilievre, Pierre. Twitter post. August 12, 2022, 4:06 p.m. https://twitter.com/PierrePoilievre/status/1558228452519682049.

"Police-Reported Hate Crime, 2021." *The Daily, Statistics Canada*, March 22, 2023. https://www150.statcan.gc.ca/n1/daily-quotidien/230322/dq230322a-eng.htm.

Porter, Catherine. "The Top Doctor Who Aced the Coronavirus Test." *New York Times*, June 5, 2020. https://www.nytimes.com/2020/06/05/world/canada/bonnie-henry-british-columbia-coronavirus.html.

"Postmedia Execs Pocketed $1M in Bonuses as Company Slashed Jobs." *CBC News*, November 27, 2015. https://www.cbc.ca/news/business/postmedia-executive-bonuses-paul-godfrey-1.3339702.

Proudfoot, Shannon. "Ethnic Enclaves Weak Link, Study Finds." *National Post*, June 2, 2010. Canadian Newsstream.

Public Broadcasting Service. "Constance Wu." *Tell Me More with Kelly Corrigan*, video, 26:27, April 10, 2023. https://www.pbs.org/video/constance-wu-xwayjt/.

Pulver, Andrew. "Scarlett Johansson Criticises 'Hypersexualisation' of Black Widow in *Iron Man 2*." *Guardian*, June 17, 2021. https://www.theguardian.com/film/2021/jun/17/scarlett-johansson-criticises-hypersexualisation-black-widow-iron-man-2.

Putnam, Robert D. "*E Pluribus Unum*: Diversity and Community in the Twenty-First Century. The 2006 Johan Skytte Prize Lecture." *Scandinavian Political Studies* 30, 2 (2007): 137–74. https://onlinelibrary.wiley.com/doi/abs/10.1111/j.1467-9477.2007.00176.x.

rabble.ca Board of Directors. "A Recognition of Shortcoming, Harm and Need for Structural Change regarding Anti-Racist Action: An Apology from the Board of rabble.ca." rabble.ca, blog, September 4, 2010. https://rabble.ca/anti-racism/recognition-shortcoming-harm-and-need-structural-change.

"Radicalization and Homegrown Terrorism: Four-in-Ten Say Radicalized Individuals Live in Their Communities." Angus Reid Institute and Canadian Race Relations Foundation, July 12, 2018. http://angusreid.org/radicalization-homegrown-terrorism/.

Rana, Uday. "'Different Factors' Fuel Housing Crisis, Not International Students: Trudeau." *Global News*, August 23, 2023. https://globalnews.ca/news/9914141/justin-trudeau-housing-crisis-canada.

Ranger, Michael. "Environment Canada Issues Special Air Quality Statement for Toronto, Parts of GTA." CityNews, October 24, 2022. https://toronto.citynews.ca/2022/10/24/diwali-fireworks-air-quality/.

Rawlinson, Kevin. "AP Apologises and Deletes Widely Mocked Tweet about 'the French.'" *Guardian*, January 28, 2023. https://www.theguardian.com/media/2023/jan/28/ap-issues-clarification-over-its-advice-not-to-use-term-the-french.

Raza, Ali. "Jamaican Migrant Workers in Ontario Pen Open Letter Likening Conditions to 'Systematic Slavery.'" *CBC News*, August 20, 2022. https://www.cbc.ca/news/canada/toronto/jamaican-migrant-workers-open-letter-1.6557678.

"Refugees in Ottawa Offer Advice to Newcomers." *CBC News*, December 8, 2015. https://www.cbc.ca/news/canada/ottawa/refugees-in-ottawa-offer-advice-to-newcomers-1.3347029.

Reynolds, Jim. *Canada and Colonialism: An Unfinished History*. Vancouver: Purich Books, 2024.

Rice, Waubgeshig. "Letter to a Young Indigenous Journalist." *Walrus*, August 31, 2020. https://thewalrus.ca/terra-cognita-letter-to-a-young-indigenous-journalist/.

Richmond Hill Liberal. "Richmond Hill's 'Too Asian' Motion Praised." YorkRegion.com, February 17, 2011. https://www.yorkregion.com/news-story/1429193-richmond-hill-s-too-asian-motion-praised.

Rillorta, Patrick T. "OFW: Ang Bagong Bayani." Republic of the Philippines, Department of Labor and Employment, Regional Office CAR (Cordillera Administrative Region), August 7, 2023. https://car.dole.gov.ph/news/ofw-ang-bagong-bayani.

Roberts, David J., and Minelle Mahtani. "Neoliberalizing Race, Racing Neoliberalism: Placing 'Race' in Neoliberal Discourses." *Antipode* 42, 2 (February 2010): 248–57. https://doi.org/10.1111/j.1467-8330.2009.00747.x.

Roberts, Joanne. "Ontario MP Visits Manitoba to Hear from Local Filipino Community." *CBC News*, April 10, 2022. https://www.cbc.ca/news/canada/manitoba/filipino-mp-rechie-valdez-manitoba-1.6415072.

Roberts, Paul. "Is Your City Being Sold Off to Global Elites?" *Mother Jones*, May–June 2017. https://www.motherjones.com/politics/2017/05/hedge-city-vancouver-chinese-foreign-capital/.

Roberts, Soraya. "The Great White Nope." *Longreads*, December 11, 2019. https://longreads.com/2019/12/11/the-great-white-nope/.

Robertson, Katie. "Meta Begins Blocking News in Canada." *New York Times*, August 2, 2023. https://www.nytimes.com/2023/08/02/business/media/meta-news-in-canada.html.

Robin, Laura. "Ottawa's Seven New Food Carts Will Spice Up Our Streets." *Ottawa Citizen,* May 9, 2013. https://ottawacitizen.com/uncategorized/ottawas-seven-new-food-carts-will-spice-up-our-streets-2.

Robinson, Matthew. "Vancouver Eyes Urban Farming Renaissance." *Vancouver Sun,* February 17, 2016. https://web.archive.org/web/20160910003605/http://www.vancouversun.com/life/vancouver+eyes+urban+farming+renaissance/11726090/story.html, archived at www.archive.org.

Rosen, Jay. "The View from Nowhere: Questions and Answers." *PressThink.* November 10, 2010. https://pressthink.org/2010/11/the-view-from-nowhere-questions-and-answers/.

Rossi, Cheryl. "Master Chef Serves Up Cheap Food with a Side of Chinese Poetry." *Vancouver Courier,* August 1, 2013. https://www.vancouverisawesome.com/courier-archive/community/hastings-sunrise-master-chef-serves-up-cheap-food-with-side-of-chinese-poetry-2957140.

Roy, Natasha. "News Outlets Criticized for Using Chinatown Photos in Coronavirus Articles." *NBC News,* March 5, 2020. https://www.nbcnews.com/news/asian-america/news-outlets-criticized-using-chinatown-photos-coronavirus-articles-n1150626.

Roy, Patricia E. *A White Man's Province: British Columbia Politicians and Chinese and Japanese Immigrants, 1858–1914.* Vancouver: UBC Press, 2007.

Said, Edward W. *Orientalism.* Toronto: Random House of Canada, 1979.

Sartre, Jean-Paul. *Being and Nothingness.* Translated by Hazel Estella Barnes. Avenel, NJ: Random House, 1956.

Sax, David. "The Sriracha Argument for Immigration." *New Yorker,* March 27, 2017. https://www.newyorker.com/culture/culture-desk/the-sriracha-argument-for-immigration.

–. "Toronto Suddenly Has a New Craving: Syrian Food." *New York Times,* January 12, 2018. https://www.nytimes.com/2018/01/12/dining/toronto-syrian-food.html.

Schudson, Michael. *Origins of the Ideal of Objectivity in the Professions: Studies in the History of American Journalism and American Law, 1830–1940.* New York: Garland Publishing, 1990.

Schwartz, Zane. 2023. Email message to author, August 10.

Scott, Corrie. "How French Canadians Became White Folks, Or Doing Things with Race in Quebec." *Ethnic and Racial Studies* 39, 7 (November 2015): 1280–97. https://doi.org/10.1080/01419870.2015.1103880.

Seitz, Matt Zoller. "The Offensive Movie Cliche That Won't Die." *Salon,* September 14, 2010. https://www.salon.com/2010/09/14/magical_negro_trope.

Sensoy, Ozlem, Raj Sanghera, Geetu Parmar, Nisha Parhar, Lianne Nosyk, and Monica Anderson. "Moving beyond Dance, Dress, and Dining in Multicultural Canada." *International Journal of Multicultural Education* 12, 1 (2010): 1–15. https://files.eric.ed.gov/fulltext/EJ1104900.pdf.

Serebrin, Jacob. "'Surge' in Demand for Services as Quebec Migrants Transferred to Ontario." *Canadian Press,* February 17, 2023. https://www.cbc.ca/news/canada/montreal/roxham-road-migrants-resources-1.6751872.

Shen, Nono. "Vancouver's Chinatown in a Generational Divide over Ken Sim's Election as Mayor." *Canadian Press,* October 20, 2022. https://nationalpost.com/pmn/news-pmn/canada-news-pmn/vancouvers-chinatown-in-a-generational-divide-over-ken-sims-election-as-mayor.

–. "Vehicle Smashes in Front of Richmond Restaurant." *Richmond News,* July 25, 2020. https://www.richmond-news.com/local-news/vehicle-smashes-into-front-of-richmond-restaurant-3125524.

Sherwin, Allan. *Bridging Two Peoples: Chief Peter E. Jones, 1843–1909.* Waterloo: Wilfred Laurier University Press, 2012.

Shetty, Aastha. "International Students Celebrate Their First Diwali away from Home – Together." *CBC News,* October 24, 2022. https://www.cbc.ca/news/canada/kitchener-waterloo/diwali-family-international-students-1.6626784.

"Should Chinese-Only Crest Toothpaste Ad Concern Richmond Residents?" *CBC News,* April 23, 2014. https://www.cbc.ca/news/canada/british-columbia/should-chinese-only-crest-toothpaste-ad-concern-richmond-residents-1.2619295.

Siddiqui, Haroon. "Media and Race: Failing to Mix the Message." *Toronto Star,* April 24, 1993. Canadian Newsstream.

–. "Muslims and the Media." *Literary Review of Canada,* January/February 2022. https://reviewcanada.ca/magazine/2022/01/muslims-and-the-media.

SmartRecruiters. "Editorial Writer – Future Opportunities." Accessed August 5, 2023. https://jobs.smartrecruiters.com/Torstar/743999837970035-editorial-writer-future-opportunities?trid=804c6794-916b-4528-80f3-4885a377683f.

Smith, Charlie. "Cheap Eats: The Samosa House Delivers a Bang for a Buck." *Georgia Straight,* June 6, 2021. https://www.straight.com/food/cheap-eats-samosa-house-delivers-a-bang-for-a-buck.

–. "Culture Clash over Kid Peeing in a Garbage Can in a Richmond Shopping Mall." *Georgia Straight,* August 30, 2013. https://www.straight.com/news/417596/culture-clash-over-kid-peeing-garbage-can-richmond-shopping-mall.

Smith, Peter. "Women and Racialized Journalists in Canada Facing New Wave of Harassment and Threats." *Canadian Anti-Hate Network,* August 22, 2022. https://www.antihate.ca/women_racialized_journalists_canada_facing_new_wave_harassment_threats.

Social Science Bites. "Doreen Massey On Space." *Social Science Space,* February 1, 2013. https://www.socialsciencespace.com/2013/02/podcastdoreen-massey-on-space.

Solnit, Rebecca. "Coronavirus Does Discriminate, Because That's What Humans Do." *Guardian,* April 17, 2020. https://www.theguardian.com/commentisfree/2020/apr/17/coronavirus-discriminate-humans-racism-sexism-inequality.

"Sometimes Explain, Always Complain." *Code Switch,* National Public Radio, November 27, 2019. https://www.npr.org/transcripts/782331005.

St. Denis, Jen. "Jenny Kwan's Case for an Inquiry into China Election Interference Claims." *Tyee,* March 30, 2023. https://thetyee.ca/News/2023/03/30/Jenny-Kwan-Inquiry-China-Election-Interference.

Stainsby, Mia. "Aleph Eatery Heals World One Dish at a Time." *Province,* May 3, 2018. PressReader.com. https://www.pressreader.com/canada/the-province/20180503/281883003964341.

–. "Following the Dumpling Trail in Richmond." *Vancouver Sun,* September 15, 2016. https://vancouversun.com/life/food/following-the-dumpling-trail-in-richmond.

–. "Heartfelt Servings of Afghan Food at Zarak." *Vancouver Sun,* March 2, 2022. https://vancouversun.com/life/food/local-food-reviews/restaurant-review-zarak.

–. "It May Not Be Fancy, But the Food Is Good." *Vancouver Sun,* September 24, 2009. Canadian Newsstream.

Staples, David. "Dr. Hinshaw on Cargill Outbreak: 'I Take Every Case That Could Have Been Prevented as an Opportunity to Learn.'" *Edmonton Journal,* April 22, 2020. https://edmontonjournal.com/news/local-news/

david-staples-dr-hinshaw-on-cargill-outbreak-i-take-every-case-that-could-have-been-prevented-as-an-opportunity-to-learn.

Statistics Canada. "Census Profile." 2021 Census of Population, last modified June 8, 2023. https://www12.statcan.gc.ca/census-recensement/2021/dp-pd/prof/index.cfm?Lang=E.

Steacy, Lisa. "Vancouver Family-Run Diner No. 1 on Yelp's Top 100 Restaurants in Canada List." *CTV News,* January 25, 2023. https://bc.ctvnews.ca/yelp-says-this-vancouver-diner-is-the-no-1-restaurant-in-canada-here-s-why-1.6246875.

Steinmetz, Katy. "She Coined the Term 'Intersectionality' over 30 Years Ago. Here's What It Means to Her Today." *Time,* February 20, 2020. https://time.com/5786710/kimberle-crenshaw-intersectionality.

Sterritt, Angela. Twitter post, November 2, 2023, 2:26 p.m. https://twitter.com/AngelaSterritt/status/1720190736799518875.

Strauss, Marina. "Loblaw Buys Asian Grocery Chain." *Globe and Mail,* July 24, 2009. https://www.theglobeandmail.com/globe-investor/loblaw-buys-asian-grocery-chain/article4389458.

Subramaniam, Vanmala. "Dozens of Migrant Workers in Vancouver Victims of Immigration Scam, Lawsuit Alleges." *Globe and Mail,* December 7, 2022. https://www.theglobeandmail.com/business/article-dozens-of-migrant-workers-in-vancouver-victims-of-immigration-scam.

–. "Foreign Students Say Canada Is Exploiting Them for 'Cheap Labor.'" *Bloomberg,* November 1, 2022. https://www.bloomberg.com/news/articles/2022-11-01/foreign-students-say-canada-is-exploiting-them-for-cheap-labor.

Sullivan, Paul. "Keep Your Head Down in Vancouver These Days." *Globe and Mail,* June 26, 2002. https://www.theglobeandmail.com/opinion/keep-your-head-down-in-vancouver-these-days/article1336108/.

Sullivan, Shannon. *Revealing Whiteness: The Unconscious Habits of Racial Privilege.* Bloomington: Indiana University Press, 2006.

"Surrey, B.C., Girl Heads to National Spelling Bee after Arriving in Canada 2 Years Ago." *CBC News,* November 13, 2020. https://www.cbc.ca/news/canada/british-columbia/spelling-bee-bc-1.5801817.

Syed, Sakeina. "End of the Line." *Maisonneuve,* December 16, 2022. https://maisonneuve.org/article/2022/12/16/end-line.

Takagi, Andy. "CTV Cancelling Most Noon and Weekend Newscasts as Bell Cuts 4,800 Jobs. Here's What Shows Are Coming to an End." *Toronto Star,* February 8, 2024. https://www.thestar.com/business/

ctv-cancelling-most-noon-and-weekend-newscasts-as-bell-cuts-4-800-jobs-heres-what/article_abe5d964-c6ab-11ee-800a-0b227e178666.html.

Taking Care: A Report on Mental Health, Well-Being & Trauma Among Canadian Media Workers. Canadian Journalism Forum on Violence and Trauma, May 2022. https://static1.squarespace.com/static/60a28b563f87204622eb0cd6/t/6285561b128d0447d7c37 3b2/1652905501967/TakingCare_EN.pdf.

Terrazano, Sarah. "Crenshaw Delivers Thought-Provoking Lecture on Intersectionality." *Brandeis Hoot,* October 27, 2017. https://brandeishoot.com/2017/10/27/crenshaw-delivers-eye-opening-lecture-on-intersectionality.

Thanthong-Knight, Randy. "Foreign Students Accuse Canada of Exploiting Them for 'Cheap Labour.'" *Bloomberg News,* November 1, 2022. https://financialpost.com/fp-work/foreign-students-accuse-canada-exploiting-cheap-labour.

That, Corinne Ton. "Chinese-Only Sign Reignites Language Debate in Richmond, B.C." *CTV News,* April 23, 2014. https://www.ctvnews.ca/canada/chinese-only-sign-reignites-language-debate-in-richmond-b-c-1.1788427.

Thompson, Terrie Lynn, and Paul Prinsloo. "Returning the Data Gaze in Higher Education." *Learning, Media and Technology* 48, 1 (2023): 153–65. https://doi.org/10.1080/17439884.2022.2092130.

Thuncher, Jennifer. "About That 'Squampton' Saying." *Squamish Chief,* July 10, 2020. https://www.squamishchief.com/local-news/about-that-squampton-saying-3351589.

Todd, Douglas. "Are Growing Ethnic Enclaves a Threat to Canada?" *Vancouver Sun,* September 11, 2010. Canadian Newsstream.

–. "Ethnic Chinese Groups Protest LGBT Programs Again." *Vancouver Sun,* May 28, 2014. https://vancouversun.com/news/staff-blogs/ethnic-chinese-once-again-protest-lgbt-programs.

–. "Ethnic Enclaves Hurt Canadian 'Belonging.'" *Vancouver Sun,* September 11, 2010. https://vancouversun.com/news/staff-blogs/ethnic-enclaves-hurt-canadian-belonging.

–. "Ethnic Mapping 5: Find Metro's Dutch, Germans, Iranians and Italians." *Vancouver Sun,* October 19, 2011. https://vancouversun.com/news/staff-blogs/ethnic-mapping-5-find-metros-dutch-blacks-germans-and-iranians.

–. "Upzone Everything, Suggests Developer Who Changed Vancouver Forever." *Vancouver Sun,* October 17, 2023. https://vancouversun.

com/opinion/columnists/douglas-todd-upzone-everything-suggests-developer-who-changed-vancouver-forever.

Tomky, Naomi. "Richmond, British Columbia: North America's Most Chinese City." CNN, March 22, 2018. https://www.cnn.com/travel/article/richmond-british-columbia-chinese/index.html.

Tran, Cindy. "How This Lunar New Year Is Being Celebrated by Ottawans from Different Backgrounds." *CBC News*, January 31, 2022. https://www.cbc.ca/news/canada/ottawa/lunar-new-year-pandemic-four-cultures-1.6328341.

Tsai, Jennifer. "How Should Educators and Publishers Eliminate Racial Essentialism?" *American Medical Association Journal of Ethics* 24, 3 (March 2022), E201–11. https://doi.org/10.1001/amajethics.2022.201.

Tsui, Ken. "The Panaderia Latina Bakery's Magnificent Lunchtime Sugar High." *Scout*, March 3, 2014. https://scoutmagazine.ca/2014/03/03/never-heard-of-it-the-panaderia-latina-bakerys-magnificent-lunchtime-sugar-high.

Tuchman, Gaye. "Objectivity as Strategic Ritual." *American Journal of Sociology* 77, 4 (January 1972): 660–79. https://www.jstor.org/stable/2776752.

Tunney, Catharine. "CBC/Radio-Canada to Cut 10 Per Cent of Workforce, End Some Programming As It Faces $125M Budget Shortfall." *CBC News*, December 4, 2023. https://www.cbc.ca/news/politics/cbc-radio-canada-layoffs-budget-1.7048530.

Tyee Staff. "What Was Said, and What Wasn't, in BC's Election Debate." *Tyee*, October 14, 2020. https://thetyee.ca/News/2020/10/14/What-Said-BC-Election-Debate.

"Unexplored Territory." *Vancouver Magazine*, December 12, 2014. https://www.vanmag.com/city/general/unexplored-territory.

Urback, Robyn. "Feminism Is Standing Up for Women When It Is Uncomfortable. Trudeau Missed a Chance to Show That." *National Post*, September 15, 2016. https://nationalpost.com/opinion/robyn-urback-feminism-is-standing-up-for-women-when-it-is-uncomfortable-trudeau-missed-a-chance-to-show-that.

Urry, John. *The Tourist Gaze: Leisure and Travel in Contemporary Societies.* London: Sage Publications, 1990.

"Vancouver's New Asian Restaurant Scene." *Vancouver Magazine*, March 10, 2011. https://www.vanmag.com/taste/restaurants/vancouvers-new-asian-restaurant-scene.

Vescera, Zak. "A Bold Experiment in Local Journalism Hits the Rocks." *Tyee*, February 3, 2023. https://thetyee.ca/News/2023/02/03/Bold-Experiment-Local-Journalism-Hits-Rocks.

Vors, Liv. "Walia's Ethiopian Dining Is an Experience Best Shared." *Globe and Mail*, December 16, 2016. https://www.theglobeandmail.com/life/food-and-wine/walias-ethiopian-dining-is-an-experience-best-shared/article33357597.

Wallace, Lewis Raven. *The View from Somewhere*. Chicago: University of Chicago Press, 2019.

Waverman, Lucy. "Smashed Cucumber Is All the Rage – But the Technique Isn't New." *Globe and Mail*, August 25, 2021. https://www.theglobeandmail.com/life/food-and-wine/article-smashed-cucumber-is-all-the-rage-but-the-technique-isnt-new.

Wechsler, Steph. "Half of Canadian Newsrooms Entirely White, Says First CAJ Survey of Race in Media." *J-Source*, December 10, 2021. https://j-source.ca/half-of-canadas-newsrooms-entirely-white-says-first-caj-survey-of-race-in-media.

Wei, Clariss. "How Boba Became an Integral Part of Asian-American Culture in Los Angeles." *LA Weekly*, January 16, 2017. https://www.laweekly.com/how-boba-became-an-integral-part-of-asian-american-culture-in-los-angeles.

Wells, Jennifer. "A Warrior, a Soldier and a Photographer – Remembering the Oka Crisis." *Toronto Star*, August 22, 2015. https://www.thestar.com/news/insight/a-warrior-a-soldier-and-a-photographer-remembering-the-oka-crisis/article_23702ad7-767e-5a81-8a68-c81ea96b1f91.html.

"What Racial Terms Make You Cringe." *New York Times*, March 26, 2017. https://www.nytimes.com/2017/03/26/us/cringeworthyraceterms.html.

Wildes, Andrew. "Even a Year's Worth of Rent Can't Get Recent Immigrants into Decent Housing in Winnipeg, They Say." *CBC News*, August 2, 2022. https://www.cbc.ca/news/canada/manitoba/new-canadians-housing-1.6534760.

Wingrove, Josh. "Ottawa Shooter Referred to Allah in Video, RCMP Says." *Globe and Mail*, October 27, 2014. https://www.theglobeandmail.com/news/national/ottawa-shooter-praised-allah-in-video-rcmp-says/article21327760.

Wong, Aloysius. "Forever Temporary." *Review of Journalism*, April 25, 2023, https://reviewofjournalism.ca/cbc-forever-temporary.

Wong, Danielle, and Wesley Attewell. "Donut Time Refugee Place-Making in 24/7 Afterwar." *Canadian Literature,* no. 246, 2021. Canadian Newsstream.

Wong, Tony. "The Unbearable Lightness of Being Too Asian." *Georgia Straight,* December 9, 2010. https://www.straight.com/article-363918/vancouver/tony-wong-unbearable-lightness-being-too-asian.

Wood, Graeme, and Daisy Xiong. "Richmond Hospital Becomes Passport Mill." *Richmond News,* October 13, 2017. https://www.richmond-news.com/weekly-feature-archive/feature-richmond-hospital-becomes-passport-mill-3060263.

Wortley, Scott. "Misrepresentation or Reality? The Depiction of Race and Crime in the Toronto Print Media." In *Marginality and Condemnation: An Introduction to Critical Criminology,* edited by Bernard Schissel and Carolyn Brooks, 55–82. Halifax: Fernwood Press, 2002.

Wright, Daryn. "Kim's Mart: A Community Market for Produce and Korean Goods." *Daily Hive,* May 25, 2022. https://dailyhive.com/vancouver/kims-mart-vancouver-hidden-gem.

–. "Northern Cafe and Grill: The Hidden Spot Everyone Is Talking About." *Daily Hive,* February 1, 2023. https://dailyhive.com/vancouver/northern-cafe-and-grill-inside.

Wright Allen, Samantha. "Nelly Shin Becomes Canada's First-Ever Korean-Born MP After 'Nail-Biter' Race." *Hill Times,* November 20, 2019. https://www.hilltimes.com/story/2019/11/20/nelly-shin-survives-nail-biter-race-to-become-canadas-first-korean-born-mp/280096.

Wu, Jiaxuan. "Racialized Early-Career Journalists in Canada and Alternative Journalistic Approaches." Master's thesis, University of British Columbia, 2023.

Wyton, Moira. "Report Finds 'Widespread and Insidious' Racism against Indigenous People in Health Care." *Tyee,* November 30, 2020. https://thetyee.ca/News/2020/11/30/Anti-Indigenous-Racism-Health-Care-Report.

Xu, Xiao. "Cultures Clash over Wearing Masks amid Virus." *Globe and Mail,* March 29, 2020. https://www.theglobeandmail.com/canada/british-columbia/article-cultures-clash-over-wearing-masks-amid-virus.

Yang, Maya, "Vice Media to Lay Off Hundreds of Workers and Stop Publishing On Its Site." *Guardian,* February 22, 2024. https://www.theguardian.com/media/2024/feb/22/vice-media-layoffs-cease-publishing.

Yeung, Lien. "Early Efforts by Chinese Community to Curb COVID-19 Should Be 'Applauded,' Says B.C. Doctor." *CBC News,* June 8, 2020. https://www.cbc.ca/news/canada/british-columbia/early-efforts-by-chinese-community-to-curb-Covid-19-should-be-applauded-says-b-c-doctor-1.5600943.

Yi, Jacqueline, Helen A. Neville, Nathan R. Todd, and Yara Mekawi. "Ignoring Race and Denying Racism: A Meta-Analysis of the Associations between Colorblind Racial Ideology, Anti-Blackness, and Other Variables Antithetical to Racial Justice." *Journal of Counseling Psychology* 70, 3 (2023): 258–75. https://www.apa.org/pubs/journals/releases/cou-cou0000618.pdf.

Young, Ian. "China Virus? North America's Most Chinese City Is One of the Most Coronavirus-Free Places on the Continent." *South China Morning Post,* September 18, 2020. https://www.scmp.com/comment/blogs/article/3102174/china-virus-north-americas-most-chinese-city-one-most-coronavirus.

–. "Picture of Boy Urinating in Vancouver Bin Sparks Anti-China Vitriol." *South China Morning Post,* August 30, 2013. https://www.scmp.com/news/world/article/1300582/photos-boy-urinating-canadian-mall-spark-strong-online-reaction.

Yu, Henry. "Macleans Offers a Nonapology for Writing a Nonstory Called 'Too Asian?'" *Georgia Straight,* November 27, 2010. https://www.straight.com/article-361680/vancouver/henry-yu-macleans-offers-nonapology-writing-nonstory-called-too-asian.

Yu, Sherry S. *Diasporic Media beyond the Diaspora: Korean Media in Vancouver and Los Angeles.* Vancouver: UBC Press, 2018.

–. "Instrumentalization of Ethnic Media." *Canadian Journal of Communication* 41 (2016): 343–51. https://cjc.utpjournals.press/doi/10.22230/cjc.2016v41n2a3019.

Zarathus-Cook, Michael. "Opera in Canada Is Putting Black Creatives Centre Stage." *Globe and Mail,* March 25, 2023. https://www.theglobeandmail.com/arts/theatre-and-performance/article-opera-in-canada-is-putting-black-creatives-center-stage.

Zeng, Anda. "Token Effort." *Review of Journalism,* April 6, 2016. https://rrj.ca/token-effort.

Index

Bailey, Issac J., 74
Bains, Deljit, 106
Bains, Satwinder, 118
Baklava Man, Vancouver, 204
Barokka, Khairani, 193
Baumann, Shyon, 86
behaviour, racialized, 37, 61–63, 75, 77–78, 193–94
Ben-Yehuda, Nachman, 59
Berger, John, 24
Bernier, Maxime, 31–32
birth tourism, 70–71
Black Canadian journalists: abuse of, 154–55, 166–67, 199; calls to action on representation, 200–3; double standard for objectivity, 30–31, 197
Black Canadians: authentic stories, 158–59; Black Lives Matter, 10, 30–31, 90, 198; Black people, as term, 174; double consciousness, 43–44; intersectional contexts, 108–9, 164; magical minorities, 52–54; stereotypes, 41–42, 45–46, 52, 62; the white gaze, 17–18, 22–24, 41, 43–44; women, 108–9, 164; words and phrases, 174
Blacktop (series), 41–42
Brampton (ON), 133, 137–38
broadcast journalism, 35, 37–38, 191, 194, 198, 201
Burdin, Peter, 93
Burnaby (BC), 139–40, 193, 211
Burnaby Beacon, 148
Butler, Judith, 101

calendar journalism, 81–82. *See also* holidays and celebrations
Calgary Herald, 115
Callison, Candis, 38, 120

calls to action on representation, 200–3
Cambodia, 99–100
Canadaland, 38
Canadian Association of Black Journalists, 200–1
Canadian Association of Journalists, 9, 43, 201
Canadian Journalism Forum on Violence and Trauma report (2022), 155
Canadian Journalists of Colour, 200–1
Canadian Press: on headlines, 184; homogeneity frames, 119; journalists' standards, 19, 203; on racism, 186; style guides, 169–71, 186, 193
Canadian Radio-television and Telecommunications Commission (CRTC), 39
cannabis legalization, 119
Cantonese, 1–2, 5, 6, 21
Cargill meatpackers, High River (AB), 113–16
Catapult, 193
CBC: challenges to white gaze, 119; diversity surveys, 201; explanatory commas, 183; intersectional contexts, 117; journalistic neutrality, 27; online comments, 154–55; racialized journalists, 198
CBC stories: on damaged people, 94; on darlings, 56; on deliciousness, 89, 97; on deviants, 63, 64–65, 69, 70–71; on ethnic enclaves, 134; on identity, 105; on migrants, 191

Crenshaw, Kimberlé, 107–10, 115
criminals, 41–42, 59–63, 75. *See also* deviants
Crooks, Valorie, 118
cucumbers, smashed, 87
cuisines. *See* food
cultures, non-Western: about, 79–81, 205–8; assimilation, 55–56, 65, 179; authenticity in portrayals, 19, 44, 206; calendar journalism, 81–82; commodity culture, 80, 84; contextual information, 89–90, 106–7; cultural pathologies, 64–65; diaspora, as term, 173–74; diversity Ds overview, 49, 99; endonyms and exonyms, 180–82; essentialism overview, 110–13; exoticizing language, 83–86, 89–90, 185–86; how to report on, 69, 75, 82–83, 86, 89–91, 121–24; multiculturalism, 2, 55, 136–37, 153, 162; non-white people, as term, 176–77; normalizing of, 122; orientalism, 80, 128, 141; representative journalism, 19, 44, 205–8; white gaze, 90–91, 137; words and phrases, 176–78. *See also* diversity Ds; people of colour; places of colour; stereotypes; white gaze; words and phrases

Ds. *See* diversity Ds
Daily Hive, 84, 144, 146
damaged people: about, 49, 91–99; agency of, 92–93, 95; contextual information, 92–93, 95–96; diversity Ds overview, 49, 99; dystopias and utopias, 94–95; how to report on, 92–93, 95–96, 100–2; key questions, 101; language of lack, 190–91; overrepresentation of groups, 92; power dynamics, 93; sources for stories, 72–73, 98–99; white gaze, 92. *See also* diversity Ds
darlings: about, 49–59, 96–102; assimilation stories, 55–56, 96–97; contextual information, 57–58; diversity Ds overview, 49, 99–100; how to report on, 56–59, 99–102; key questions, 56–59, 101; magical minorities, 52–54; magical negro, 52; model minorities, 50–51, 55, 58–59, 99–100; romanticized hardships, 50, 55–58; sacrificial survivors, 50–51, 57–58, 204; sources for stories, 57, 72–73, 98–99; trailblazing firsts, 51–52; whiz kids, 51–52. *See also* diversity Ds
Darpan, 40
Dart Center for Journalism and Trauma, 93
Decolonizing Journalism (McCue), 18, 48–49, 98, 100–1
deliciousness: about, 49, 79–91, 96–102; commodity culture, 80, 84; distance as value, 85–86, 141–43; diversity Ds overview, 49, 99–100; hidden gem restaurants, 17, 141–46; how to report on, 86, 88, 90–91, 99–102; key questions, 101; orientalism, 80, 128; romanticization, 85, 89; sources for stories, 72–73, 98–99; white gaze, 79. *See also* diversity Ds
Demby, Gene, 34
democratic racism, 154, 156, 158
descriptors, specific, 17, 172–76

137–38, 178; histories of places, 125–27, 138–39, 146, 148–49; how to report on, 129–30, 132–33, 138, 140, 145–50; invasion narrative, 60–61, 70–73, 131–32, 135–36; key questions, 129–30, 132, 138, 147, 149; multiple identities in, 133–34, 148; names of places, 125–27, 139, 147; orientalism, 80, 128, 141; racialized places, 133–34; as social constellations, 130–33, 148–50; sources for, 140, 148–50; stereotypes, 80, 128, 130–31, 137–38, 141, 172; white accessibility, 140–41, 142, 147; white gaze, 128–30, 140–41, 147; white invasion narrative, 138–41. *See also* ethnic enclaves; restaurants

Poilievre, Pierre, 32

point of view. *See* "the gaze" theory; white gaze

politics: far-right violence, 63; trail-blazing firsts, 51–52; wokeness accusations, 31–32, 34, 161, 171

power dynamics: damaged people, 93; invisible knapsack of white privilege, 36–37, 153; journalists of colour, 202–3; methods for objectivity, 28–29; news media industry, 9, 11–13, 40–41; presence vs power, 163; theory of "the gaze," 23–26; whiteness as social process, 8. *See also* white gaze; white privilege

Poynter, 17, 166

privilege. *See* white privilege

problem people. *See* deviants

Province, 88, 136

puns, 184–85

Putnam, Robert, 135

Qingming, 82–83

quotes from sources. *See* sources

rabble.ca, 198–99

race: about, 34, 151–68; colour-blind lens, 8, 158–60, 198; community, as term, 118–20, 124, 172–74, 176; democratic racism, 154, 156, 158; diversity Ds overview, 49, 99; essentialism, 110–13, 116; homogeneity frames, 118–20, 124; how to report on, 34, 176–78, 193–94; intersectional contexts, 16, 108–10, 161; as monoliths, 172–74, 176; racialized behaviour, 37, 193–94; reasoned vs bigoted views, 153–54; as social construct, 34; specific descriptors of, 17, 172–76; words and phrases, 167–68, 176–78. *See also* diversity Ds; people of colour; places of colour; racism; stereotypes

race and racism, resistance to reporting on: about, 17, 151–68; "All Lives Matter" ideology, 159; how to respond to silence, 166–68; key questions, 157; logical fallacies, 156, 157, 160, 161, 163, 165; "my experience as different," 165–66; online comments, 154–56, 159–61, 165, 199; "race as irrelevant," 163–64; reasoned vs bigoted views, 153–54; "report on bigger issues instead," 161–62; "reporting as divisive," 157; "reporting as false," 162–63; "reporting as racist," 15–16, 152, 156–57; "reporting as worsening racism," 33–34, 160; "reporting not needed as all part of